PRESCRIPTION
for a
HEALTHY NATION

PRESCRIPTION
for a
HEALTHY NATION

*A New Approach to Improving Our Lives
by Fixing Our Everyday World*

TOM FARLEY *and* DEBORAH A. COHEN

BEACON PRESS
BOSTON

Beacon Press
25 Beacon Street
Boston, Massachusetts 02108-2892
www.beacon.org

Beacon Press books
are published under the auspices of
the Unitarian Universalist Association of Congregations.

08 07 06 05 8 7 6 5 4 3 2 1

This book is printed on acid-free paper that meets the uncoated paper ANSI/NISO
specifications for permanence as revised in 1992.

Text design by Robert Kosturko
Composition by Wilsted & Taylor Publishing Services

Library of Congress Cataloging-in-Publication Data

Farley, Tom (Tom Alexander).
Prescription for a healthy nation : a new approach to improving our lives
by fixing our everyday world / Tom Farley and Deborah A. Cohen.
p. cm.
Includes bibliographical references and index.
ISBN 0-8070-2116-4 (cloth : alk. paper)
1. Public health—United States. 2. Medical care—United States.
3. Medicine, Preventive—United States. I. Cohen, Deborah (Deborah Ann). II. Title.

RA445.F27 2005
362.1'0973—dc22   2004024188

To the memory of our fathers,
John Farley and Barnett Cohen.

We shape our buildings, and thereafter they shape us.
—Winston Churchill

Contents

In America we spend more than twice as much for health care as any other nation. So why are we among the sickest people in the industrialized world?

We have built a medical complex capable of stunning feats. Doctors can repair our hearts by remote control through pencil-thin catheters, put us in an anesthetic trance and swap out our organs, and train viruses to plug DNA fragments into our genes. We are so awed by this system that we pay the 1.4 *trillion* dollar annual cost—about one-seventh of our gargantuan economy—with little complaint. The only problem with our health care system, many Americans seem to believe, is that there is not enough of it to go around. To many, the benefits of being able to go to a doctor are so great that lack of access to the medical care system is one of the great social injustices of our time.

But Americans don't seem to be obsessed only with being able to visit doctors and hospitals after we get sick. Americans have learned—in principle, at least—that it makes a lot more sense to prevent sickness than to treat it after it happens. In the last quarter century the United States has seen an explosion of health clubs, health food stores, articles on nutrition, health and fitness magazines, and health segments on television. Some of the television segments show the latest high-tech surgical procedures or research on rare and tragic genetic diseases, but many explain the health advantages of fish oil or oat bran or aerobic dancing. We just can't seem to hear enough about what makes our bodies tick and what we ought to do to keep them ticking longer.

Our nation also has a vast—if often unrecognized—system of public health agencies dedicated to keeping us healthy. Every state has a health department claiming a broad mission to maintain health and prevent illness in all of its citizens. Behind all of them is a phalanx of acronymic federal agencies (CDC, HRSA, AHRQ, SAMHSA, NIH) with equally ambitious goals of health for the entire nation. And they have local equivalents—health departments in cities and counties and even private non-profit groups—with broad agendas for health.

What do we have to show for all this? We are an economic colossus, the wealthiest country in the history of the world, but our national vital signs are barely better than some Third-World countries. According to statistics compiled by the World Bank, the United States ranks twenty-fourth among nations for age-adjusted mortality rate in men and thirty-first for women, below Slovenia and Costa Rica. Our infant mortality rate is twenty-sixth, more than twice that of Singapore and tied with Croatia and Cuba. We have more births to teens than over half of the world's nations. Our health statistics in America are gradually getting better, but that is hardly an accomplishment when other countries do so much better with so much less. The question will not go away: If we spend so lavishly on medical care and we care so much about our health, why are we so unhealthy?

Something is wrong about the way we are approaching health in the United States. We don't need another health care reform plan. We need a new way to think about health.

This book is our attempt to introduce that new way of thinking. The basic concept is simple: just as poor sanitation caused infectious diseases in the nineteenth century, an unhealthy physical and social environment is causing major killers like heart disease, cancer, and AIDS today. And just as the solution to the outbreaks of cholera 150 years ago meant redesigning the industrial revolution's urban infrastructure, the solution to epidemics of disease today will mean reshaping our everyday world.

The book is organized in three parts. In the first part we explain how and why we took a wrong turn in health in the United States and point to our everyday world as the key source of disease or health. In the second we show exactly how four features of our world—what we call "curve shifters"—exert their effect on us. In the third part we take up each of the leading killers of our time and discuss specific ideas on fixing our everyday world to tame them. These ideas don't form a complete list. Other people will surely come up with more ideas and will fill in the details of how to make these ideas real. But by laying out some ideas, we hope to show that this way of thinking about health is very practical.

This is not a book on politics, but if we want to fix our everyday world we will need to act politically. In the last chapter we discuss some of the politics of health in this country, and for readers who are skeptical that we really can change our everyday world, we show that it is possible.

There is nothing wrong with our obsession with health in America. Our perspective on the sources of disease and the way we spend money to prevent illness are what is wrong. Although we Americans are the ones who are becoming sick, the fundamental source of disease is not inside us. Disease arises from the world around us. We can use our everyday world to prevent our modern society's epidemics. But to do that, we must start by rethinking our assumptions about what causes disease and health.

PART I

The
LEADING CAUSES
of HEALTH

CHAPTER I

THE WRONG REMEDY

As we have all been told, health care in the United States is in crisis. Insurance premiums are up and covered services are down. Employers are sinking under the weight of benefit costs. HMOs are denying people referrals to specialists. The number of uninsured has sailed well past 40 million, and public hospitals are closing. Medicare is insolvent and Medicaid is devouring state finances. The cost of prescription drugs is skyrocketing. While the total costs of medical care grow relentlessly, people feel they are getting less and less of it. Every politician seems to have a plan for fixing the system, but it seems no two can agree on anything, leaving more and more of us to fend for ourselves, defenseless against the ravages of disease.

The dire warnings of what the collapse of the system is doing to us are everywhere. Pick up any paper and look for articles on health or disease. You might find a "personal health" article somewhere near *Dear Abby* giving you tips on exercise or your diet. You might find a piece in the science section on a newly identified gene that increases people's risk for, say, stomach cancer. But if you find a "hard news" article in the front section it is certain to be about the tragedy of desperate people cut off from life-saving medical care:

  • *U.S. News and World Report* describes Francisco Garcia, a part-time janitor married to a part-time housekeeper, making all of $340 a week, with no health insurance. "I am afraid for my family," he says. "What if I have to go one day to the emergency room? God help us, what would we do? Would we be left to die?"[1]

  • The *Daily News* of Los Angeles reports that Mary Munoz's prescription drug costs were so high that she didn't refill her diabetes medication in order to pay her other bills. "She could have died," the article says. The lack of access to prescription drugs is a "crisis" that "will only grow with each passing year." An expert adds, "I'm shuddering, just thinking about the impact this is going to have."[2]

• Just in case readers might ignore this crisis because it only affects the poor, the *New York Times* tells us that as the economy slumps "the health care crisis is spreading up the income ladder and deep into the ranks of those with full-time jobs," illustrating the story with a tale of a contractor making $60,000 who couldn't afford medicines for his family because they were uninsured.[3]

An apparent island of calm in the middle of this growing national calamity is a woman named Gwen Longworth. Gwen is fifty-eight. She's large, solid, and matronly, dressing colorfully but not elegantly. She speaks rapidly and intensely, with relentless confidence about her children, her life, and her work, which is as a part-time psychotherapist and, it seems, full-time community activist. Her activism is Californian and eclectic, ranging from aiding Latino immigrants and serving as a district governor for the Rotary Club to lying down in front of bulldozers to block commercial development of a wildlife area outside her town. Her family follows the same pattern: she has raised seven children, including two adopted Mexican immigrants and one foster child, and she estimates that she's housed about five hundred exchange students over the last twenty-five years.

Gwen has withstood the health care crisis because her husband is a research analyst at a county college, a civil service job that brings with it the coverage that others can only dream of: as she explains it, 100 percent coverage of hospitalizations, 100 percent coverage of office visits for the whole family, and prescription drugs covered except for a $10 copay every three months. Which means that Gwen never has to wonder about where the money will come from for her doctor visits or the drugs she takes.

And drugs are what the medical system offers. Every day Gwen takes two medicines (glyburide and Glucophage) for her diabetes, and one (Accupril) for her high blood pressure. For the arthritis in her knees she takes ibuprofen (an anti-inflammatory drug) and glucosamine/chondroitin (an arthritis remedy sold as a nutritional supplement). She has a regular doctor whom she likes and visits every three months. Because of their insurance, Gwen doesn't worry about draining her life savings if her husband has chest pain or she finds a lump in her breast. If advocates of health care reform were to win every battle they fought, everyone would have Gwen's coverage—and the peace of mind that goes along with it.

But is this the victory we want? Ever since she was a teenager, Gwen's been gaining weight. She passed 150 with her first pregnancy, kept gaining during and between her others, and is growing heavier still. Gwen is too confident and upbeat to lament her weight, but she has tried to stop gaining more—tried "everything . . . all the 'great diets' like Atkins and Pritikin"—and failed. More precisely, they all work, temporarily.

At five feet nine inches and carrying 236 pounds, Gwen has a body mass index (BMI) of 36, enough to earn her the designation of Class II "morbid obesity" by the National Institutes of Health. As such, she has a high risk of dying from colon cancer or breast cancer. She's got a good chance of needing to have gallstones removed. She'll have diabetes for the rest of her life, even if she takes a mountain of glyburide, and even if she starts injecting herself with hypodermics of insulin every day. Over time, her diabetes will likely cause problems with her eyesight (from cataracts to blindness from retinal hemorrhages), raw sores on her feet that refuse to heal (perhaps requiring amputation of a toe, a foot, or a leg), and a distinct possibility that failing kidneys will require her to finish her days tethered to a dialysis machine three days a week. All the health insurance coverage in the world and years of Accupril will not cure her high blood pressure. The combination of hypertension and diabetes means that before she even reaches retirement age she has about one chance in twenty of having a stroke and one chance in three of fatal or near-fatal heart disease. The arthritis in Gwen's knees prevents her from walking on the trails near her house, a loss of pleasure in life which she says makes her want to cry.

Gwen has wonderful health insurance and an abundance of health care. What Gwen does not have is health. And there is nothing our health care system can do to give it to her.

Even if the needed trillions of dollars fell from the sky to give every player in the health care scramble what he wants, the future we Americans would inherit is Gwen's present: addicted to doctors and drugs, and distinctly and inexorably unhealthy.

As our politicians wage guerrilla war over health care reform, the battle cry is always *health*: it is health that is at stake. But in fact the struggle has always been over *health care*. Or to be more exact, *medical care*. Medical care, our politicians and newspapers are telling us, *is* health. It is a matter of life and death. To liberals, that makes it unjust to deny any American a visit to a doctor whenever he wants it. Access to medical care is a fundamental right, about on par with the rights of free speech, free assembly, and a presumption of innocence until proven guilty.

The truth is that medical care is what people get after they are sick. And as Gwen Longworth's story shows, medical care is not health. The entire terms of the national debate are wrong. They reflect not just sloppy use of language, but a misconception of what disease and health are all about. And this misconception is preventing us from being healthier, as a society and individually.

The trillions we spend on medical care mean we care deeply about health in America. But if we *really* care about our health, individually and as a society, we ought to stop blindly paying for medical care and start asking what actually causes our poor health and what we can do about it.

America's modern epidemics

Each era and each society throughout history has its own killer diseases. Gwen Longworth is on the fast track to get many of ours, particularly heart disease, stroke, and kidney failure. In America today the leading causes of years of lost life fall almost entirely in two categories: chronic diseases and injuries. The big chronic disease killers are heart disease, lung and breast cancer, stroke, chronic lung disease, diabetes, and chronic liver disease. The injuries include both the unintentional ones (what most people call accidents) and the intentional ones (suicides and homicides). In the 1850s, infectious diseases would have dominated this list, but the only infectious disease on it today is HIV/AIDS. This short list of diseases and injuries is responsible for more than half of the lost years of life in America.[4]

Chronic diseases emerge from cumulative damage to the body over decades, such as cholesterol in the blood clogging the arteries, leading to heart attacks and stroke, or tobacco smoke irritating the airways, ending in chronic lung disease. Cancer also develops over years or decades, often stemming from the same exposures that cause other chronic lung disease (such as tobacco smoke). Injuries are often forgotten when people think of health, but suicide, homicide, and unintentional injuries rank higher than most medical causes.

These diseases and injuries are not only what we die from, but also what we live with. That is, even when they don't kill us, diseases such as diabetes and the consequences of stroke, heart attacks, and injuries are major causes of pain and disability.

The limits of medicine

For all of its inspiring, high-tech cures, medicine just is not very effective at curing our era's major killers.

Take injuries. The fact is, most car crashes, gunshot wounds, falls, and other major types of injuries either kill you instantly or never. It isn't often that the ambulances, EMTs, and valiant emergency room doctors have the time or the opportunity to save lives. When researchers have reviewed accident reports and autopsy records of persons dying in injuries, even the most optimistic classify only about 15 percent of deaths as "preventable" by medical care in a perfect world; the others are killed immediately on the scene or die rapidly and inevitably afterwards.[5] And when state-of-the-art ambulance systems and specialized trauma emergency rooms are put in place to get patients high-tech medical care as quickly as possible, the number of injury deaths drops by only 8 percent, meaning that the best medical care in the world can't help the other 92 percent of persons with potentially fatal injuries.[6]

Medicine doesn't do much better with chronic diseases. First, by the time most chronic diseases cause symptoms, the damage to the body is permanent. Modern drugs can't fix the weakened heart, burst blood vessels, and stiff lungs. The heart muscle tissue and brain cells that are dead are permanently dead. They cannot be repaired and they do not regrow. What is counted as success in cardiac care or stroke units is limiting further damage. Mortality rates from heart disease and stroke have fallen in recent decades, but most of this decline is probably due to the lower rates of smoking and saturated fat consumption, not medical care.[7] Doctors can't fix chronic liver disease and chronic lung disease either, unless you count organ transplants, which will never help most of the hundreds of thousands of people with these health problems.

Medicine's progress in curing cancer is also somewhat disappointing when you consider the billions we have invested in it. The newspapers trumpet the uplifting victories—such as Lance Armstrong's beating testicular cancer before dominating the Tour de France—but muffle the losses in small obituaries. In the last twenty-five years, the five-year survival rate for cancer has improved from about 50 percent to a little over 60 percent.[8] Most of the boost has been for cancers that can be spotted early and cut out by surgeons, such as cancer of the colon and breast. For cancers that hide well or spread quickly, most notably lung cancer, medical care is nearly useless; "breakthroughs" in treatment are usually measured in a few extra months or even extra weeks of survival. Overall, cancer mortality in the United States is unchanged in the last twenty-five years and higher now than it was in 1950 (even after taking into account the aging population) because a rise in the number of people developing cancer has swamped any improvements in treatment.[9] As recently as the mid 1990s, an expert trying to measure the benefits of medical care ignored cancer because he considered the effects of treatment negligible.[10]

If chronic diseases are only the body's announcement that a long, slow process has finally culminated in permanent damage, it makes logical sense to catch these processes early to prevent the diseases and the damage. But doctors can't do much to solve the underlying problems when they are spotted early, either. Of the hundreds of potential preventive screenings and medicines given a tough review by a task force assembled by the Public Health Service, only a handful were found to make any difference in the long run, and the differences they made were not large. For example, the group refused to recommend screening for lung cancer or diabetes.[11] Even if people with these chronic conditions go to doctors for their problems early, most will continue to deteriorate.

Gwen Longworth faithfully takes drugs to lower her high blood sugar from diabetes. But there have been two major studies comparing this treatment to no treatment except advice on diet—one in the United States involving one thousand diabetics in the 1960s and one in Britain involving several thousand that ran from 1977 to 1991. In both studies, the diabetics taking either pills or insulin injections were not any less likely to die from heart disease or stroke than diabetics who didn't take any medicine.[12] In fact, in the U.S. study diabetics taking one particular diabetes drug (tolbutamide) had a *higher* mortality rate than patients taking nothing.[13] So not only do Gwen's diabetes drugs not cure her, they may not be doing her any good at all.

The Public Health Service strongly endorsed screening and treatment for hypertension.[14] And the research does show that if Gwen takes her medicine religiously, she will cut the likelihood that she will die from a heart attack or a stroke by about 20 percent.[15] But no one claims that people taking medicines for hypertension are nearly as healthy as people without hypertension, and there is no such thing as a cure.

Real life is not a research study, though. Following doctor's orders for hypertension means taking one or more pills every single day, forever. That's a tough thing for people to do when they feel fine and when the drugs are expensive and have unpleasant side effects, especially since people have to shell out today's money to pay for a possible benefit years in the future. Saying people should be educated about balancing the risks and benefits is dodging the issue: the fact is that these very practical problems with long-term treatment render medical care many times less effective in the real world than in any scientific study. As many as 20 percent of people who get prescriptions don't even get them filled, and about 50 percent of people on routine medicines take them inconsistently.[16] After a major national push on hypertension, fewer than 60 percent of people with this condition are under treatment and fewer than 60 percent of those under treatment have the condition "controlled."[17] It is hard to be enthusiastic about the benefits of any wonder drug, available now or to be developed in the future, when the starting point is that less than a third of the people who need it will even take it regularly.

When the most common killers of our era are mostly incurable and our preventive treatments pretty feeble, you have to wonder about medical care as a whole. A small group of researchers scattered around the United States and Europe have spent years studying that fundamental question: Exactly what does our entire system of medical care do for us? One way they have tried to answer this is to comb through all the different causes of death and pull out those for which medical care *could* make a difference in a world where the medical system was functioning at its theoretical best—causes such as asthma, bacterial infections, and appendicitis. Typically, these "amenable" diseases cause about 5 percent to 15 percent of deaths in industrialized countries.[18] This may sound like a small fraction, but even it is optimistic. For example, the entire category of heart disease is on some lists as "amenable" to medical care, even though heart disease is mostly incurable.[19]

There was a time when these researchers thought they could use this list of causes of death that are "amenable" to medical care as a measuring stick for the quality of care; where medical care is better, you would expect the death rates from them to be lower. But then researchers testing this idea in eight different studies using different data sources bumped into the same unsettling problem: countries or areas within countries that have more medical care don't have lower rates of "amenable" causes of death at all.[20] And some studies found that the more doctors and hospitals an area has, the *higher* the death rates from such causes.[21] Whether they measured medical care by quantity or quality, in these studies medical care as a whole didn't seem to help.

Reading the heart-rending stories of miracle cures in newspapers, it is easy to believe that medical care is what makes our lives so much better than the short and disease-ridden lives of our ancestors, but experts in this area are much more likely to conclude that the effects of medical care are negligible. Researcher John Bunker started out a paper in the *Journal of the Royal College of Physicians of London* by stating, "There is a widely held view that medical care contributes little to health."[22] And John Bunker is a *defender* of medicine. He titled his paper "Medicine Matters After All" and based his counterattack on his own loose estimates (he acknowledges they are "guesses") about how many of the years of increased life expectancy that occurred between 1890 and 1990 could be attributed to medical care. From what we know about the effectiveness of treatment and the faithfulness with which people follow doctors' prescriptions, Bunker's estimates seem very optimistic indeed. For example, the biggest contribution to increased life expectancy, in his estimation, comes from the treatment of diabetes with insulin, but he arrived at this figure by applying the life-saving benefit of insulin in people with the relatively rare type 1 diabetes to the 6 million Americans with type 2 diabetes, even though insulin may not help people with type 2. But even if we accept his optimistic estimates, his calculations end up like this: of the thirty years of increased life expectancy achieved between the 1890s and the 1990s, only five years (or 16 percent) could be attributed to medical care.

The price we pay

Maybe the one thing that every politician will agree on is that medical care is costly. But when we buy medical care, as individuals or as a society, how smart are we as consumers? Are we buying what we ought to buy?

A group of researchers at Dartmouth attempted to answer this. First, they sorted the different procedures that doctors and hospitals charge for into three categories: "effective care," "preference-sensitive care," and "supply-sensitive care." Effective care treatments are those for which there is strong scientific evidence that they save lives or prevent disability, such as vaccination against pneumonia and the use of certain drugs in people with a heart attack to limit the damage. Preference-sensitive care treatments are those that patients often want but for which the scientific evidence is shaky, such as surgery for early prostate cancer. Supply-sensitive care treatments are ones that doctors and hospitals (rather than patients) choose but for which there is even less scientific evidence, like the use of intensive care units or office visits with specialists.

Then the Dartmouth researchers carved up the United States into 306 medical care regions and studied what happened to patients in the Medicare system. What they found is frightening. The range in spending was big, with Medicare spending about 60 percent more per capita in some regions than in others, even after taking into account the age of the people enrolled and the local cost of living.[23] Overall only about half of all patients received procedures classified as "effective care."[24] And in the regions where medical spending was higher, the percentage of patients getting "effective care" was generally *lower*. What was higher in the big-spending areas was "supply-sensitive care." So when we spend more on medical care we are just buying more expensive care, not higher quality care and certainly not health.

The Dartmouth studies also seemed to show that in regions where there was more medical care, people were *more* likely to die following such common events as hip fracture, colon cancer, and heart attacks.[25] It's hard to understand at first why, if medical care is mostly ineffective, it might *increase* our chances of dying, until you realize just how dangerous medicines and surgical procedures are. In 1999 we woke up to a report by the Institute of Medicine that mistakes made by doctors and hospitals were killing a stunning number of people—between 44,000 and 98,000 people a year.[26] Even the lower figure represents more deaths than due to car crashes, breast cancer, or AIDS.

That alone might make you think twice about visiting your doctor, but it gets worse: mistakes account for only a minor fraction of the total deaths caused by modern medicine. There are many more "iatrogenic deaths"— people killed by doctors—because many more die from medicines or procedures even when medical care is standard practice and the doctors perform flawlessly. How can people die from "correct" medical care? Some have a fatal allergic reaction to a medicine or an anesthetic. Others develop blood clots or pneumonia after surgery or have a fatal heart rhythm during a catheterization. Others acquire drug-resistant infections after being treated for another disease. Things can go wrong even when the doctors are doing everything right. An expert at Johns Hopkins estimates that these iatrogenic deaths total about 225,000 a year (the Institute of Medicine estimated even more), which, if it were classified that way, would make medical care the third largest killer in America.[27]

There must be some in that 225,000 who would have died anyway because they were under treatment for something fatal, so it is probably not fair to lay all these deaths at the feet of medicine. Still, some people die getting treatment for injuries or ailments that wouldn't have killed them. One of the more heavily publicized studies on this followed a doctors' strike in 1976. Over five weeks, in a dispute about malpractice insurance, about half of the doctors in Los Angeles County cut back on services, and because anesthesiologists were the most militant, hospitals cancelled most elective surgery. For those five weeks no surgeons were doing non-emergency hysterectomies, tubal ligations, knee repairs, or face-lifts. As much as the strike must have caused panic in people who could not see their doctors, researchers afterward found that it actually prevented more deaths than it caused.[28] The canceling of elective surgery by itself saved the lives of roughly a hundred people. These people weren't spared for long, though, because after the strike ended and the surgical machinery worked overtime to catch up, a study showed that the following year deaths after elective surgery increased by ninety.[29]

A brighter future?

It is easy to criticize medical care in the past. But isn't it getting better all the time? Aren't we, after all, on the cusp of the genomic revolution? We've deciphered the human genome and DNA technology is revolutionizing everything from agriculture to law enforcement. In the near future, won't doctors catalog all of our genes through a simple blood test and pop the results in a handheld computer, which will then prescribe molecular fine-tuning of the products of our unique DNA sequence—medicines that will be safer and more effective precisely because they are designed uniquely for us?

Given the complexity of the biologic system called the human body, it's hard to be very optimistic. We don't have one cell needing fixing, we have some 100 trillion cells, organized as thousands of cell types doing highly specialized tasks to help dozens of organs function, sending probably thousands of molecular messages back and forth through the blood and across neural networks. Giving a human body a splash of chemical to hypercharge one fragment of underproductive DNA (or to interfere with an overproductive one) is like dropping a massive dose of a heart-repair drug in New York City's water supply. Sure, it might help a few people with weak hearts, but it's a fair bet that it will also kill many more of the millions who don't need it and who are allergic to it. Our experience with obesity drugs like fen-phen that are initially hyped only to be yanked from the market because they kill people illuminates this larger underlying problem: it's exceedingly difficult to design drugs that can fix one broken piece of our complex biologic systems without damaging many others. Mapping the human genome will not solve this fundamental problem. The human DNA map is like a massive database that includes the occupation, hobbies, and medical records of every one of New York City's residents. As fascinating as that database is, and as much as that will tell us about New Yorkers, will it really make it any easier to find a heart-repair drug to drop into the water supply that is safe for everyone?

But what about gene therapy? Aren't most diseases genetic, and aren't we on the verge of techniques to just repair the broken genes? The hope for this technique is dizzying. A quick search on gene therapy in medical research databases turns up thoughtful articles on how we might use gene therapy for everything from irritable bowels to erectile dysfunction. It's a seductive vision—as if we will send molecule-sized auto mechanics into the machinery of our cells to swap out the genetic equivalent of a bad spark plug—but an absolutely false one.

Scientists have no molecule-sized auto mechanics. What they have instead are specialized viruses into which they implant "normal" genes that they want to replace the bad ones. The viruses are then turned loose with the job of inserting these genes into our own DNA. Unfortunately, these viruses not only aren't like trained auto mechanics, they're not even as sophisticated as trained circus seals. They have their own agenda, namely introducing their entire DNA into ours so they can multiply. The relationship between our DNA and the proteins that carry out a cell's everyday tasks are incredibly complex and differ tremendously among the different types of cells in the body. When a virus inserts its DNA into our cells it can wreak havoc.

So far, gene therapy has been tried for a couple of rare, terminal diseases, like Severe Combined Immune Deficiency Syndrome, the inborn condition that leaves children defenseless against nearly any infection. In these first trials, this wonder treatment failed badly. The treatments have been stopped by regulatory agencies in both the United States and Europe because the children treated with it were developing leukemia.[30] The viruses were doing what we asked them to do, that is, manipulating the children's DNA, and just as computer viruses make your operating system go haywire, the children's genes went berserk, causing their blood cells to grow and divide uncontrollably. Should we be surprised?

Granted, these are early trials of gene therapy, and it's likely that researchers will by trial and error gradually make it safer. There may come a time when diseases that are caused by a single defective gene—like sickle cell disease or cystic fibrosis—can be cured by gene therapy. But these diseases are not even close to being the major killers of our day. They are rare. Sickle cell disease affects only one in five hundred African Americans and cystic fibrosis affects only one in four thousand Caucasian Americans, and these are among the most common single-gene-defect diseases. Compare that to overweight, affecting two in three Americans, diabetes, affecting one in twenty, or alcoholism, also affecting one in twenty. The more prevalent a disease is in our modern society, the more certain we can be that the genes predisposing us to it are not so much defective as they are just operating normally in an abnormal world. The genetic patterns that influence our vulnerability to the common major killers probably involve tens, hundreds, or thousands of genes, none of which anybody could honestly call defective. It is madness to hope that we can "fix" all these genes to prevent these illnesses, let alone do it safely.

The impotence of modern medicine to cure the most common diseases of our day begins to explain the paradox of American health. Many assume that the explanation for our dismal statistics in the face of massive medical spending is that the people who need medical care the most get it the least. And in fact medical care is unfairly distributed in America, but this problem is mostly irrelevant. Why would we expect health statistics to be influenced by access to medical care if medical care itself barely influences health?

Medicine in perspective

In this chapter we have hit medical care hard, and maybe a little unfairly. Modern medicine is far from worthless. And it is not the nemesis that Ivan Illich called it years ago, or an insidious killer stalking our society. When we (the authors) get sick with anything other than a routine virus, we certainly want to see a good doctor. Doctors as a rule are trying very hard to help their patients, and within the limits of their blunt and dangerous tools, they often do well. There are many things that medicine can do that we all care about. The greatest advance—vaccination—has the potential to vanquish killer infections like polio and measles. With antibiotics, medicine also can cure infections from bacteria. Medicine can stave off death from chronic diseases for a time—time that even if small may be very precious. Coronary care units do keep heart attack victims alive more often today than they did twenty years ago. Occasionally medical care produces miraculous cures, which feel priceless when the person cured is someone we love. And maybe more important but often overlooked, modern medicine can help reduce pain and disabilities that come with many health problems. When a child breaks his arm, doctors can set it straight. When we can't see, doctors can remove our cataracts or prescribe glasses. Medicine can help people with arthritis get around, people in pain obtain relief, and people with depression get out of bed and carry on. As a society we value the relief of suffering, and modern technology can do much to achieve that. It's hard to measure the tradeoffs we might have between this relief of suffering and the risk of death that some treatments involve, but there is a fair tradeoff there somewhere. And it is likely that over time we will develop medicines and surgical techniques that are safer and more effective than what we have now.

Our mistake is not that we in America value medical care—everyone in the world values medical care—but that we have misunderstood what it can and cannot do. We need to temper our enthusiasm for care with an appreciation for the fundamental limits of the science, limits that advances in our understanding of biology will not overcome. Because of these limits, medical care operates only on the margin in improving our health. It cannot and will not transform our world, create a disease-free future, or stop the inevitable process of aging and death. It cannot come close to fixing our current epidemics of obesity, heart disease, cancer, and injuries. If we want to be as healthy as the healthiest societies on the planet, we need to look elsewhere.

The actual causes of death

We should start by thinking smarter about the major killers in America.

Government statistics list the leading causes of death as heart disease, cancer, and so forth, as if it were easy to describe what "caused" someone to die. But understanding the causes of death is more complicated than that. If a person who smoked for forty years dies of lung cancer, what "caused" her death—the cancer or the smoking? And if a person who drinks and drives dies in a car crash, what caused her death—alcohol, driving, or the crash? If a teenager becomes depressed after a fight with his girlfriend and shoots himself with his father's hunting rifle, what caused his death—a bad relationship, depression, or the gun? In fact there is never a single cause for death, but rather there are webs and chains of causes that kill a person. To understand why Americans die earlier than people in other developed countries, we need to look at some of the key strands in these webs.

A breakthrough in thinking about the webs of causation came about in a simple article published in 1993 by former Centers for Disease Control (CDC) Director William Foege and his colleague Michael McGinnis on what they called the "actual" causes of death.[31] In this paper, and in an update of the analysis ten years later by Ali Mokdad and others, the experts estimated the relative importance of these "actual causes of death" by looking at underlying factors that lead to the diseases listed on death certificates.[32] For example, a high-fat diet leads to heart disease and diabetes, smoking leads to both cancer and heart disease, and alcohol use contributes to car crashes, cancer, and heart disease. Adding the contribution of each of these underlying factors across the different diseases, the experts came up with this chart:

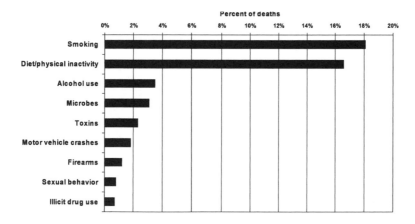

Looking at it in this way, they estimated that smoking "actually" caused 18 percent of all deaths, an unhealthy diet and sedentary lifestyle caused another 17 percent, alcohol 4 percent, car crashes 2 percent, and firearms 1 percent. The things people tend to fear most—toxins and mi-crobes—caused together about 5 percent of deaths, and the scourge of il-licit drug use was to blame for less than 1 percent.

This way of looking at the problem isn't perfect. It doesn't take into ac-count the age at which people die, and it double-counts the overlap be-tween some "actual causes" such as alcohol and car crashes. But it is a far more useful way to think about our era's modern killers than by adding up medical diagnoses, because it starts to tell us what we can do about them. A much more sophisticated analysis by a group at Harvard for the World Bank, however, showed pretty much the same ranking of leading killers in industrialized countries.[33]

Most striking about these analyses is how they show that about half of all deaths in the United States are caused by individual human behavior: too many of us smoke, drink alcohol, eat high-calorie and high-fat foods, don't get enough exercise, and use cars and guns to kill ourselves and each other. The major reason why we Americans die early is that we behave in an unhealthy way. It is what we *do* that makes us sick, not lack of access to medical care.

If we really care about our health—if we really want to be healthy—rather than worry whether we can see a doctor we should stop *doing* these everyday things that make us unhealthy. The key to being healthy in our era is changing our personal behavior.

We don't have to radically change how we behave, though. Becoming healthier doesn't mean transforming ourselves into different sorts of be-ings. The crucial behaviors are very few. Smoking, physical activity, diet, and drinking alcohol alone underlie 40 percent of deaths. McGinnis and Foege's way of looking at deaths gives us the priority list of behaviors that really matter.

Gwen Longworth is unhealthy in spite of having wonderful health care. She is unhealthy because of her individual behavior. She is obese be-cause she has consumed too many calories and expended too few for at least thirty years. She has diabetes because she is obese (combined with some genes that are unlucky but common). She has hypertension because of an unhealthy diet and a lack of exercise over the years. There is nothing her doctor, Blue Cross, or the medical care system can do to make these health problems go away. We are not *blaming* Gwen for her health problems, unless you can blame someone for being human. Gwen is not stupid, lazy, or apathetic. Right now we just want to begin to trace the origins of Gwen's health problems, which are also our health problems. And the trail begins at her behavior.

These ideas are not new. Public health advocates have been harping on the limits of medical care and the importance of our behavior to health for decades. But as a nation we have ignored their advice. The CDC—the federal government's lead prevention agency—has a budget of about three-tenths of 1 percent of national health expenditures.[34] Funding for the medical care system, on the other hand, is devouring government budgets, gobbling up one-fourth of federal government expenditures and one-sixth of state and local expenditures.[35] The enormity of this chunk of government money has real consequences. For example, during Louisiana Governor Mike Foster's eight years in office, rising Medicaid costs strangled the budget, preventing him from achieving his loudly proclaimed but modest goal of raising Louisiana teachers' pay to the Southern average, and prompting the legislature to cut public health programs.

Is prevention possible?

With as much logic as there is behind the value of prevention, we ought to wonder why we as a society pay so little attention to it. Maybe our government is hooked on medical care because we as individuals are hooked on going to doctors for disease instead of trying to stay healthy. We demand to see doctors when we get sick, and politicians respond to those demands; we don't demand that anyone keep us healthy.

But maybe we have ignored prevention because most efforts to change our behavior—individually and as a society—haven't worked very well. Between the "people's doctor" columns in newspapers and women's magazines and the health segments on television news shows, there is plenty of mostly accurate information about how to stay healthy. But it hasn't led most people to behave that way.

Anyone who doesn't live in a cave knows that smoking can kill you. But nearly one quarter of American adults smoke.[36] All Americans know that it is healthier to eat fresh fruits and vegetables than French fries and hamburgers. But only 23 percent of Americans eat the recommended five servings of fruits and vegetables a day, and 66 percent eat more than the recommended amount of fat.[37] Everyone knows that it is healthier to exercise than to watch television, but only 25 percent of Americans get recommended levels of Americans exercise.[38] Everyone knows how AIDS is spread, but less than half of adults having sex with non-steady partners used a condom the last time they had sex.[39] Gwen Longworth, a woman with a doctoral degree, understands full well how to stay thin. Over the last thirty years, though, all the expert diets and the fitness advice around her haven't prompted her to eat less and exercise more. As a society, in spite of all the health information surrounding us, we aren't much better behaved than she is: we still smoke, eat too much, exercise too little, and shoot each other and ourselves. In fact, Louise Russell of the Brookings Institution thought about this failure and asked, in a book entitled *Is Prevention Better Than Cure?*, whether we shouldn't just give up and wait for diseases to strike before doing anything.[40] We shouldn't be outraged at politicians who ignore calls for prevention if prevention doesn't work.

But *why* hasn't prevention worked better than it has? Why are we so unhealthy in our habits—especially since, as our government budgets and sales of fitness magazines attest, we seem to care so much about our health?

The truth is that prevention isn't bound to fail. There is a lot we can do to prevent disease if we are smart about it. But we have not been smart about it. To understand how we can get on the right track and make prevention work, we need to first understand where we have succeeded and where we have failed in the past.

CHAPTER 2

GREEK GODS
and
AMERICAN MYTHS

*I swear by Apollo Physician and Asclepius and Hygeia
and Panacea and all the gods and goddesses, making them
my witnesses, that I will fulfill according to my ability
and judgment this oath and this covenant*
—THE HIPPOCRATIC OATH. TRANSLATION: LUDWIG EDELSTEIN

In the classical version of the Hippocratic oath, which has stood as a kind of Pledge of Allegiance for the field of medicine for thousands of years, doctors begin by swearing to a few pretty obscure Greek characters. Many have heard of Apollo, one of the twelve great Olympian gods, who besides being in charge of plagues and healing was also the god of music, poetry, cattle, and herdsmen. But few could get exam questions right about Asclepius, Hygeia, or Panacea.

Asclepius was Apollo's son, born of a mother who was mortal. Asclepius's mother took on a lover while she was pregnant with him, which wasn't a smart move, because when it came to light the gods punished her by setting her afire soon after childbirth. Apollo then deposited his motherless infant son in the care of a centaur named Chiron to be reared. Chiron was known throughout Greece as the great teacher, and as he raised Asclepius, he taught him about health and disease. When Asclepius came of age the gods charged him with caring for the health of the mortals of Greece.

Asclepius himself fathered many children, several of whom helped him with the family business, including two daughters. The oldest, Hygeia, washed and scrubbed her father's patients. Cleanliness, it seems, was close to godliness in those days too, and Hygeia's cleansing helped protect the health of the mortals, so much so that she came to represent health itself, which gave us the word *hygiene.*

People whose diseases are prevented—as opposed to those whose diseases are cured—can never really appreciate what was done for them. Who can be grateful for what just didn't happen? The gods may have been pleased with Asclepius's use of hygiene to produce health, but with only Hygeia's powers the mortals would have barely known who he was. Asclepius solved that problem with the help of another daughter, Panacea, who represented the power to cure those who are already sick. Cures are always popular and valued, so with Panacea's powers Asclepius built his reputation as the great healer around Greece. Outside of his temple mortals waited in long lines to be cured. Besides making him famous, his cures changed the way the mortals thought about their health. Health did not occur naturally, or as the result of cleanliness. It was a gift they obtained at the hands of a physician.

The gods of the ancient Greeks were temperamental, behaving often like spoiled rich children. So when the demigod Asclepius became a celebrity, they grew jealous and plotted against him. A myth like this has to have a tragic ending, and it does, but exactly how it ends depends on the version you read. In the Greek version Asclepius's power to heal had revived many mortals that were dead, so they were still alive when the Fates came to take their souls away. This interference with the natural order of things was an affront to Hades, king of the underworld, who demanded that Zeus put a stop to it. In the Roman version the gods showed Jupiter (Zeus) that the fine print in Asclepius's contract prohibited him from accepting money for healing the mortals. And indeed the mortals had been giving Asclepius gifts to move to the front of the line in the temple, making him rich. The two versions of the myth end the same way, though. Prodded by the other gods, Zeus became enraged and destroyed Asclepius with a thunderbolt.

It's a great story, and it shows that the ancient Greeks understood better than we do about the two different ways to produce health. The Hygeian approach is to clean—not just people, but also the world around them—and the Greeks, who had pretty cities and impressive aqueduct systems before the Romans did, appreciated the value of clean water to health.

The Panacean approach repairs the health of sick people one at a time. There is something to be said for both ways of producing health, but both also have their problems. Mortals (that is to say, all of us) stay healthier when their societies follow Hygeia and create a healthy environment, but because they don't see how the environment keeps them healthy, they don't appreciate the benefit. Mortals who lose their health flock to Panacean physicians for cures. The physicians sometimes extend life longer than they should, and when they dole out cures for high fees they generate jealousy and resentment. The parable is particularly meaningful today. Americans see public health departments (which are supposed to keep us healthy) as outdated, inept, and most of all, irrelevant. And while they demand to see doctors, Americans increasingly see modern medicine as inappropriately extending life (prompting things like "right to die" initiatives), or as a for-profit business taking advantage of sick people and denying care to the poor.

Plagues

Over the millennia since the ancient Greeks lived, societies have wavered in the way they have addressed health problems between the practices of Hygeia and Panacea. Hygeia has usually gotten her due amid epidemics, when panicky citizens take drastic public action to ward off death that they can see. Plagues have bedeviled humans throughout recorded history, but probably the most famous epidemics among public health experts—in fact, the epidemic that helped found the field of public health—were the visitations of cholera in the 1830s to 1850s.

During the industrial revolution of the 1700s and 1800s cities sprang up around factories and transportation hubs. The crowding in cities was fertile ground for infectious diseases, and the increasing commerce spread diseases around the world. Originating in Asia, probably in India, "Asiatic cholera" leapfrogged relentlessly westward from city to city and then to the rural areas around them. It hit Moscow in 1830, Berlin in 1831, London in 1832, and American cities during 1832–1834. When it came, cholera invaded a city like a marauding army, massacring thousands over weeks and turning thousands more into refugees who fled in panic to unaffected areas, often bringing the disease with them.

At the time, health experts held two conflicting views on how diseases were spread. The "contagionists" believed that diseases were passed directly from one person to another, and the "miasmatists" thought that diseases wafted through the air after arising spontaneously from the "miasma" of dirt and rotting plants and animals. Doctors tended to believe in miasma rather than contagion, because they noticed that many people who developed cholera had not been near anyone else with the disease, and that people caring for cholera victims often did not get sick. Most ordinary citizens believed in contagion. Between these two opposing views, no one could agree on how to halt the cholera epidemics. Should sick people be quarantined? Or should local authorities do a better job of sweeping the streets and removing trash? Without agreement on what to do, governments didn't do anything to stop the epidemics very well.

Which brings us to the story that nearly every student of public health learns about the founding of epidemiology. In the London cholera epidemics of 1849 and 1853–54, a physician named John Snow, who had made something of a name for himself administering the new anesthetic chloroform for minor surgery, became fascinated with the disease. As a kind of hobby, he took it on himself to learn the real route of spread of cholera. His theory was that it had something to do with the water. At that time, several private companies operated water systems that drew river water from around London and supplied it to different neighborhoods of the city. In 1849 Snow meticulously put together statistics showing that the neighborhoods supplied with untreated water drawn from a site on the Thames downstream of sewage outlets had death rates two to ten times higher than neighborhoods supplied with water from reservoirs or water drawn from the Thames above the sewage outlets.[1] Even the tonier, cleaner neighborhoods supplied by water from the downstream site had high death rates. In a pamphlet he published called "The Mode of Communication of Cholera," he announced that cholera was primarily spread neither by person-to-person contact nor by spontaneous generation from filth, but instead by water contaminated with some kind of toxin in human feces.[2]

Prominent physicians didn't take Snow's theory very seriously, at least not at first. But he got a chance to demonstrate it to his doubters in the next major epidemic in August 1854, when cholera hit the neighborhood of Broad Street, Golden Square, killing more than five hundred persons in less than ten days.[3] He suspected that the source of contaminated water was a public pump on Broad Street. As others fled, he personally visited the neighborhood, knocking on doors and interviewing the sick or grief-stricken survivors as well as families who did not get sick. "On proceeding to the spot," he later wrote, "I found that nearly all of the deaths had taken place within a short distance of the [Broad Street water] pump. There were only ten deaths in houses situated decidedly nearer to another street pump. In five of these cases the families of the deceased persons informed me that they always sent to the pump in Broad Street, as they preferred the water to that of the pump which was nearer. In three other cases, the deceased were children who went to school near the pump in Broad Street.... The result of the inquiry then was, that there had been no particular out-break or increase in cholera, in this part of London, except among the per-sons who were in the habit of drinking the water of the above-mentioned pump-well."[4]

A colleague of Snow's later described the next step:

> On the evening of Thursday, September 7th, the vestrymen of St. James' were sitting in solemn consultation on the causes of the visitation.... Such a panic possibly never existed in London since the days of the great plague.... They were called to consider a new suggestion.... [Snow] was admitted and ... had fixed his at-tention on the Broad Street pump as the source and the centre of the calamity. He advised the removal of the pump-handle as the grand prescription. The vestry was incredulous, but had the good sense to carry out the advice. [The next day] the pump-handle was removed, and the plague was stayed.

Professors all over the world tell this story to showcase the power of the techniques of epidemiology: collecting statistics, comparing disease rates between two groups of persons with different "exposures," and taking ac-tion based on the differences. In fact, the national Council of State and Territorial Epidemiologists each year gives an award to the person who has contributed the most to epidemiology called the Pump Handle Award.

But there are lessons from this story that might be more important.

Snow's masterstroke was Hygeian rather than Panacean. In trying to stop the epidemic, he focused on prevention rather than cure. He could have tried to cure anyone who had already become sick from the water, but instead he acted to prevent a next group of victims from drinking it. More important, by removing the pump handle he took action on the environment, not on the people themselves. He could have educated people about his theory and suggested that they stop drinking the water or boil it first, but instead he just eliminated the handle, which protected people whether they were willing to act on his theory or not.

On top of that, Snow was able to stop the epidemic even though he had at best a vague understanding of what caused cholera. The terms "microbe" and "bacterium" weren't even invented yet. It would be a century before people understood exactly how the bacterium *Vibrio cholera* causes fatal dehydration. But even if he didn't understand the biologic mechanism of disease, he could prevent it by eliminating the "exposure"—that is, contaminated water.

Cholera wasn't the only killer infectious disease of the industrial revolution; it was simply the most terrifying marker of an entire era dominated by them. In the middle of the 1800s, the new industrial cities in the United States were not only jam-packed, they were filthy and full of garbage, dead animals, and sick people. In fact, in the disease-breeding grounds of Boston, Philadelphia, New York, and New Orleans, death rates reversed a long-term trend and *increased* 42 percent between 1813 and 1850.[5]

Doctors didn't know much about the causes of the major diseases at the time. But they noticed that the poor died off quicker and younger than the rich, and they felt that their eating and drinking habits were "intemperate." The leading experts concluded that, as public health historian John Duffy writes, "the basic problem with the poor lay . . . in their lack of moral fiber."[6] Sickness came from the package of dirty houses, dirty habits, and sin—all of which were the fault of the poor themselves. They had no one but themselves to blame for their diseases, and they would have to take responsibility for preventing them. The experts felt society's only responsibility to the poor was to teach them a combination of personal hygiene and resistance of sin.

But back in England a strident reformer named Edwin Chadwick, who knew Snow and who served as Poor Law Commissioner, took an entirely different view. Over a three-year investigation in which he enlisted a small army of district health officers, Chadwick demonstrated the connections between disease and the squalid conditions in which the poor were forced to live and work. He brought attention to these actual causes of disease in 1842 by publishing *The Sanitary Conditions of the Labouring Population.* This was the era of Dickens, and although Chadwick didn't have Dickens's way with words, he described many horrid scenes:

> Of the 182 patients admitted into the temporary fever hospital . . . 135 at least came from unpaved or otherwise filthy streets. . . . Whole streets in these quarters . . . are without drains or main-sewers . . . and are so covered with refuse and excrementitious matter as to be almost impassable from depth of mud, and intolerable from stench. . . . But dwellings perhaps are still more insalubrious. . . . The doors of these hovels very commonly open upon the uncovered cesspool, which receives the contents of the privy belonging to the front house.[7]

Anyone living in these conditions, Chadwick claimed, would get sick and die. The poor weren't inherently different from the rich except for the miserable conditions in which they lived, which they could not be held responsible for. In fact, he turned the morality theory on its head, writing that it was "these adverse circumstances [that] tend to produce an adult population short-lived, improvident, reckless, and intemperate, and with habitual avidity for sensual gratifications." To his readers who didn't care about the health of the poor, he argued that cleaning up neighborhoods would not just keep the poor alive; it would also make them morally stronger. He then proposed a truly radical idea: governments should take responsibility for fixing these problems—providing clean water, building sanitary sewers, removing animal carcasses and other refuse, and even assuring that sweatshops had decent ventilation.

When they heard his report, the Lords in the British Parliament, who were far from poor, politely buried it. They would have had to pay for sanitation with taxes—taxes that would fall more heavily on them than on those in the slums—and taxes were about as popular then as they are now. But six years later a reform government finally passed the Public Health Act, which, while greatly watered down from Chadwick's proposals, established for the first time the principle that the government would take responsibility for protecting the health of its citizens.

Chadwick was put in charge of enforcing the new law, and because he was uncompromising and generally obnoxious, it didn't take long before he was bounced out. His ideas went much further, though. Three years after Chadwick published his book, a prominent New York physician named John H. Griscom came up with a local version, *The Sanitary Conditions of the Laboring Population of New York,* in which he made the same arguments. Around that time, people in cities in the United States began to demand better water, sewers, and cleaner streets, and cities began to provide them. Philadelphia got an extensive water supply using new cast-iron pipes by 1835. New York brought water from the Croton River in 1842, and Boston greatly expanded its water supply in 1848. The major cities followed these innovations by constructing sanitary sewers in the 1850s. Smaller cities and towns then gradually built similar water supply and sewer systems of their own.

Griscom and other physicians in the port cities of New York, New Orleans, and Boston then used the success of the improvements in city water systems and Chadwick's ideas to forge a national sanitation movement. They organized a series of National Sanitary Conventions between 1857 and 1860, and institutionalized the movement after the Civil War as the American Public Health Association.[8] In the beginning they spent their time with minor reforms like drawing up standards for quarantine for cases of cholera and yellow fever, but as the movement gathered momentum they became more ambitious, taking on policies for safe water and solid waste disposal in cities and for ventilation of schools, tenements, factories, and public buildings.[9] They went on to promote vaccination against smallpox and even ventured into policies on prostitution and venereal diseases. *The Sanitarian* was launched as a monthly journal in 1873, turning sanitation into a discipline of its own. By the 1870s the sanitation movement began to incorporate nonphysicians, including leading businessmen and social reformers. Local and state boards of health grew in number, scope, and power. Toward the end of the nineteenth century the now-powerful sanitation movement further expanded its scope and took on—or aligned itself with movements for—social reform, including housing reform, control of air pollution, education reform, school-based health screening and treatment, workplace health and safety, and the abolition of child labor.[10]

It must have been an exhilarating time. The "sanitary revolution" was just that, bringing on historic advances in health. Epidemics that had decimated entire cities were quelled and the routine infectious diseases that killed many people at young ages began to fade away. After having risen in the early part of the nineteenth century, mortality rates in major cities plummeted 55 percent between 1850 and 1915.[11] Infant mortality dropped in parallel and life expectancy increased by some twenty-five years. What is most amazing is how much was done with so little knowledge of biology. What may have been the greatest improvement in population health in human history was brought about without *any* successful cures for *any* disease.

These successes put the "moralist" view of disease in decline, at least for the time. As Duffy explains it:

> Whereas sinfulness and lack of moral character were held to be largely responsible for poverty and disease early in the first half of the nineteenth century, increasingly the middle and upper classes began to recognize the role of environment in shaping people's lives. . . . [S]cience held the possibility for solving all health problems. Rather than eliminating social problems by concentrating on improving the moral character of the poor, now it seemed the solution lay in improving the environment of the poor.[12]

The victory in this era of epidemic infectious diseases belonged to Hygeia. The winning combination—clean drinking water, sanitary disposal of human wastes, mosquito control, trash removal, pasteurization of milk, regulation of food production—is now such a basic part of government services that many of us forget that in fact these were once creative solutions of sometimes desperate citizens to prevent disease. The social movements brought about improved housing and nutrition for the poor, and these Hygeian changes also contributed to the soaring life expectancy. The optimism with which Americans approached the twentieth century was based in part on the success in ending the plagues of the nineteenth century.

Cures

Toward the end of the 1800s, just as the sanitary revolution was routing the century's epidemics, science started its own revolution. In the 1880s and 1890s scientists for the first time saw under the microscope, and then grew on petri dishes, the bacteria that cause anthrax, tuberculosis, diphtheria, the plague, cholera, and typhoid fever. In 1901 Walter Reed showed how mosquitoes carried and transmitted a virus that causes yellow fever. Suddenly, infectious diseases didn't arise from mysterious "humors" but instead represented bodily invasions by tiny bugs that you could actually see. Now that scientists could train their sights on the enemy, they felt they could be much more focused and successful. As one writer put it, it looked like public health could become just applied bacteriology.

As scientific knowledge exploded, public health leaders started to view general environmental cleanup as wasteful. Filth itself did not cause disease, bacteria did. In 1904, Charles V. Chapin, the health commissioner for Providence, Rhode Island, criticized any efforts at general sanitation. As long as there were sewers to take away human wastes, "it will make no demonstrable difference in a city's mortality whether its streets are clean or not, whether its garbage is removed promptly or allowed to accumulate, or whether it has a plumbing law."[13] Other leaders began to speak of "the new public health," which concerned itself only with diseases of known cause and which distanced itself from the broad movements for social reform. As the "scientific" approach caught on, the scope of public health shrank.

In many ways the last half of the nineteenth century was the finest hour for the field of public health, and it has been in decline since. As the great epidemics disappeared, the remaining causes of death (which had always been present) became relatively much more important. With the major epidemic diseases gone, the leading causes of death in the first half of the 1900s became tuberculosis, pneumonia, and nonspecific gastroenteritis; heart disease and cancer also showed up on the list. In children, major causes of death included diseases like diphtheria, whooping cough, and measles. The sanitary reforms initiated in the previous century continued to lower rates of some of these diseases, but they did not eliminate them. The sanitary revolution appeared to have run its course. But these newly prominent diseases became treatable through the tools of modern medicine.

As the field of public health faded in the 1900s and scientific knowledge blossomed, the field of modern medicine grew suddenly in success, scope, and prestige. Some successes built on techniques developed by researchers in the nineteenth century and some were entirely new. The most important were the development of surgery, vaccines, and antibiotics.

Surgery once had been a barbarous act conducted by irresponsible men wielding knives on desperate people. It caused excruciating pain and often was followed by a fatal infection. In the original Hippocratic oath doctors pledged to "not use the knife, not even on sufferers from stone." But the scientific building blocks slowly made surgery first respectable, then glorious. On October 16, 1846, a dentist named William Thomas Green Morton went into a theater-like classroom at the Harvard Medical School and, before a crowd of skeptical medical students and faculty, rendered a man temporarily comatose with the "anesthetic" sulfuric ether, allowing a surgeon to remove a tumor from his neck.[14] The success of anesthesia caused a sensation, and soon afterward doctors throughout the United States and Europe (including John Snow) were using ether or chloroform to anesthetize people for surgery. It took doctors longer to solve the problem of infection after surgery. In 1851 an eccentric Austrian doctor named Ignaz Semmelweis noticed that the death rates on the obstetrical wards from "puerperal fever" (infection after childbirth) were over three times higher in wards maintained by medical students than in those maintained by midwives. He also noticed that the medical students came directly to the ward from the autopsy room. Guessing that they were bringing the infection with them on their hands, he started demanding that all persons wash their hands with soap, water, and a chlorinated lime solution before touching patients. This policy led to a nearly tenfold decrease in the ward death rate.[15] In the 1860s Louis Pasteur showed that disease could be caused by "microorganisms," and in 1867 a Scottish surgeon named Joseph Lister demonstrated that spraying a patient with carbolic acid killed these microorganisms and prevented the infections after surgery.[16] Other surgeons picked up Lister's "antiseptic" techniques in the 1870s and 1880s. In 1900 the differences in blood types were discovered, making it possible to give blood transfusions during surgery, which in turn enabled surgeons to experiment with extensive, bloody procedures. Improvements in obstetrics in the late 1800s, such as using forceps for difficult deliveries and Caesarean section techniques, made the complications of childbirth manageable. By 1900, doctors could put a person into a suspended state, slice him open, manipulate or cut out his internal organs, sew him back together, and wake him up, without the patient even being aware of how he had been cured. To patients and families, it must have seemed to be a kind of magic, a demonstration of the powers of the gods.

It was in 1796 that British surgeon Edward Jenner injected the eight-year-old son of his gardener with fluid scraped from a cowpox lesion of a dairymaid and showed that this "vaccination" prevented the boy from developing smallpox.[17] Doctors were slow to pick up vaccination as a way to ward off smallpox, but by the end of the 1800s, as vaccination blunted entire epidemics of the disease, they not only appreciated its potential but also began experimenting with vaccination against other infectious diseases. Between 1890 and 1960, laboratory scientists developed new vaccines to prevent typhoid, tetanus, diphtheria, yellow fever, and polio. As these vaccines were used, one by one the diseases capitulated. The death rate due to diphtheria in the United States fell from 147,000 cases in 1920 to an average of 4 cases per year from 1980 to 1983.[18] Cases of pertussis (whooping cough) dropped 91 percent from 1947 to 1960.[19] Cases of polio dropped 98 percent from 1954 to 1962.[20] To the average person, vaccines transformed these dreaded killers into ancient curiosities—symbols of how precarious life was before modern medicine arrived.

Antibiotics are chemicals produced by microorganisms that kill bacteria. The first antibiotics were sulfonamide and related "sulfa" drugs that were used in the late 1930s. Alexander Fleming discovered penicillin in 1928, but the drug wasn't manufactured on a scale large enough to matter until the early 1940s.[21] When it was, its effect of bringing back to health patients diagnosed with fatal infections seemed miraculous. Streptomycin, the first effective drug against tuberculosis, arrived in the late 1940s.[22] Before streptomycin, people saw tuberculosis as a withering, certain killer, while afterward, its cure was further proof of the divinity of modern medicine. When doctors and drug companies saw the success of these early antibiotics, they rushed to discover more. Within a few decades they had tamed the bacterial infections that killed most people.

Like the powers of Panacea for Asclepius, surgery, vaccines, and antibiotics dramatically changed the image of the doctors. In the 1800s doctors had little to offer people, and they probably killed more people than they helped. But by the 1950s doctors could manually fix or remove the diseased internal organs of sick people, give injections that would cure them, or prevent people from getting sick in the first place. People living in the 1800s avoided doctors because they suspected they would make them sick, but people living in the mid 1900s flocked to doctors because they had faith that they would make them well. In a century, doctors went from being hucksters—or at best a questionable group of professionals—to being the priests of health.

Death rates dropped from 1900 to 1960, and it's natural to think that the breakthroughs of medicine were responsible. Vaccinations definitely prevented many deaths, particularly in children. But, as British researcher Thomas McKeown showed in a careful analysis of the impact of medicine on disease, about 90 percent of the drop in death rates during this period was from diseases that were *not* preventable by vaccination (particularly tuberculosis and pneumonia), and the largest portion of the drop in death rates happened *before* either antibiotics or specific vaccines were used.[23] McKeown concluded that the overall decrease in death rates even in this time was mainly the result of better nutrition and living conditions. As in the earlier era, the cures of modern medicine had little to do with this decrease in death rates. But the wonders of modern medicine for individual people during this time convinced people that healing was the cause of health.

By the end of this era of acute individual events—1960—America's approach to health was solidly mired in the tradition of Panacea. Our solutions to the problem of disease were aimed at sick individuals rather than environments, and they were delivered by doctors rather than governments or public health agencies. Individual people became sick; they went to doctors, who cured them. The people were grateful, and the doctors were proud. As at the end of the previous era, the health problems of humans seemed solved.

Slow killers

The cures of modern medicine caused earthquakes of change in the larger society. Doctors produced health, so people demanded to see doctors. At times when the economy was strong, companies wanting to keep valued employees started paying for health insurance. The government got into the act, paying for health insurance for many citizens not covered by their employers, in particular the elderly (Medicare) and the poor (Medicaid). The flow of money to doctors and hospitals went from a trickle to a flood. Treatments and the payments for them transformed hospitals from convalescent homes for the poor to something between high-tech human repair shops and swanky hotels. Medical schools that had used poor patients to train doctors became research-based "medical centers" and then "health sciences centers." Doctors reclassified an increasing number of common human complaints (from "irritable bowels" to "anxiety") as diseases, and decided as a matter of faith that all incurable diseases were at least "treatable" in some way. With the amount of money showered on doctors and hospitals, what once was a humble calling of caring for the sick became the "health care industry," with sick people the "consumers." When industry analysts pointed out that 15 percent of Americans couldn't consume properly because they didn't have health insurance, politicians and advocates for the poor declared a crisis—not in sick care, but in health. By the new millennium the technological success of modern medicine had completed a stunningly successful transformation in image: everyone seemed to agree that "health" equaled "health care," that the *only* way to get health was through "medicine."

Throughout the twentieth century, as the stock of modern medicine grew, health departments steadily lost direction, prestige, and funding. The infectious diseases they tamed—cholera, yellow fever, dysentery, typhoid—had all but disappeared, and their tools—maintaining the city water and sewage systems, mosquito control—either had been taken over by other government agencies or seemed hopelessly old-fashioned. Citizens and politicians now tend to see health departments (if they see them at all) as anachronisms. Why do we need a health department when all we really need is for everyone to have a doctor?

In the last forty years some in public health have tried to take on the modern chronic diseases. In general, local and state health departments have not been able to drum up money to prevent heart disease or cancer, but federal agencies (particularly the Centers for Disease Control and Prevention) have been somewhat more successful. The CDC has been giving regular grants to state health departments to prevent sexually transmitted diseases, tuberculosis, and vaccine-preventable diseases since World War II. In the 1970s federal money began to flow to prevent heart disease, stroke, lung cancer, and breast cancer, and later, small amounts of money followed to prevent injuries. In general, these grants were organized around specific diseases or groups of diseases, mimicking the organization of modern medicine into specialties like cardiology and oncology. It wasn't the best mechanism for state and local health departments to get money to set up programs, but they weren't in a position to complain. To fulfill the narrow requirements of the federal grants, state and local health departments drew their organizational charts around individual diseases or disease clusters such as tuberculosis, sexually transmitted diseases, hypertension, heart disease, cancer, and diabetes.

But what exactly were health departments supposed to do with this money? They knew they were supposed to prevent disease rather than treat it after it occurred, but how could they prevent something like heart disease? Not by cleaning up the water supply. Not by spraying for mosquitoes or removing animal carcasses from the streets. These new diseases wouldn't respond to the tools public health agencies had.

Health departments gradually adopted two general tactics: screening-referral and education. The first meant screening to find people in the early stages of disease and then referring them to doctors. It included blood pressure testing in shopping malls, mobile mammography units, and "know your cholesterol" campaigns. The education approach meant first identifying "behavioral risk factors"—like a high-fat diet or smoking—and then teaching people through classroom education, posters, or brochures, that these behaviors were bad. Neither of these prevention tactics has been terribly successful. The screening programs rarely touched nearly as many people as they needed to, and as we described in chapter 1, catching these chronic diseases early often doesn't help prevent them from getting worse. As we will discuss in the next chapter, the education programs have generally foundered: some people reached listen to the advice, but most do not. Just why people continued their high-risk behavior, when they ought to know better, confounded most public health agencies. On top of that, the education programs had such meager funding that they couldn't possibly educate everyone "at risk." When public health agencies thought at all about the broader underlying environmental conditions that might affect health—the promotion of cigarettes, for example—their "categorical" federal grants and pigeonholed organizational charts got in the way of addressing them because these environmental conditions underlie more than one health problem.

This is pretty much where we stand today. The lion's share of the trillions we spend to be healthy goes as tribute to Panacea, the goddess of cures. The fact that her techniques do not work for the leading causes of death has not made us any less enamored with them. The followers of Hygeia —public health agencies—while still keeping the epidemic infectious diseases of the nineteenth century at bay, are seen by the public as irrelevant and are struggling to find a strategy to prevent the killer diseases of our time. Our death rates and disease rates have leveled off, and we are among the sickest developed nations in the world. It is time to regroup and rethink.

CHAPTER 3

HUMANS BEHAVING BADLY

Smoking may be the number one killer in America, but to Renny Lemoine and Durel Richard Jr. it's no big deal. Renny and Durel are high school juniors in a small town in swampy south Louisiana, where Cajun names like Landry, Broussard, and Breaux show up everywhere, from the car repair shop sign to real estate agents' billboards, and where everyone seems to know everyone else's cousins. Durel is six feet even and lean, a quarterback in the fall and a catcher in the spring. Renny is a little stockier, a tough linebacker who probably isn't big enough to play in college, but Durel says he feels a whole lot bigger when he hits you. They look both boyish and rugged, like they are more comfortable working outdoors than talking indoors, especially about something as trivial as smoking. They speak in sentence fragments, with the lilting Cajun accent that most Americans have heard only on cooking shows.

"Don't smoke much," Renny says. "Just a lil'. When we have a bonfire." Cajuns may be known for their ability to party, but they also work very hard. On just about every weekend Renny and Durel use chain saws and ATVs to help clear a lot that Renny's cousin is planning to build a house on. It's one of many odd jobs they do for spending money and because Durel has to pay the insurance on his pickup. At the end of the day they set fire to the pile of trunks and branches, are joined by friends, and relax with beer and Marlboro Lights. Why Marlboro Lights? "I don't know," says Durel, "that's just what everybody smokes." "They must be better, I guess," shrugs Renny. "They more expensive."

Ninety percent of smokers in America start before they are age eighteen. That means the biggest killer of our time has got Renny and Durel in its crosshairs. Odds are good that at least one of these two strapping boys will end up forty or fifty years from now wasted from lung cancer, crippled by a heart attack, or carting around an oxygen canister for his emphysema. If we can figure out how to stop Renny, Durel, and the kids across the country like them from taking up smoking, we can save more lives every year than we lost in the entire Vietnam War—times seven.

One person who cares deeply whether Renny and Durel fall permanently victim to tobacco is Cecelia Turner, a health psychologist who designs the smoking prevention programs at their high schools. Cecelia is a garrulous woman who smiles and laughs constantly, even when talking about the frustrations of fighting for declines of a couple of percentage points in addiction to our nation's biggest killer drug. She's gone through a few generations of theories about how to promote health in schools, but hasn't lost hope for the latest effort. She says her determination to succeed despite obstacles came from her mother, a harsh woman who "ruled with an iron fist." Neither of Cecelia's parents even finished elementary school, but her mother sent her to a rigid Catholic school, demanded that she obey the nuns' dictates to the letter, and cracked the whip over her studying. Cecelia resented her mother's pressures deeply, but now sees that the study habits have served her well in life. After an early career as a stenographer and a mother of two children, she started college at age forty-one, finishing in just three years, and later took on a doctoral program while working full-time, completing her PhD at age fifty-two.

For all of Cecelia's knowledge and fierce self-discipline, she has health problems of her own. She has high blood pressure for which she has to take two drugs every day and high cholesterol for which she takes one more. Her doctor prescribed these medicines after watching the warning signs grow over years. Her cholesterol, once about 185, soared to 265, and her blood pressure rose to 150 over 100. Since graduating from high school weighing ninety-three pounds and wearing size one dresses, she has gained more than ninety pounds. "The weight doesn't feel good, either, let me tell you," she admits with a sad smile. She sees where this is headed, too. Her father died of heart disease, her mother suffered from angina, and two of her three brothers have had coronary bypasses.

Cecelia's self-control at work hasn't translated into the healthy habits that she knows she needs to avoid the same fate. She exercises "very little." She has belonged to a gym for the last six years, but only makes it there about once every two months. She's tried to cut back on fatty food and calories, but can't count many successes. When she is at home she cooks fish and eats salads for dinner, but she admits that when she eats out she orders fried food, and wherever she is she eats too many desserts. Like most Americans, the rest of the day she snacks. "I'm really bad," she confesses. "If there is candy in front of me, I'll eat it."

Every high school kid in America knows that smoking is bad for you. It's part of every health class in every school in the country, and even if it weren't, kids hear it from everyone else. That hasn't stopped Renny and Durel from taking up smoking, though. Cecelia Turner knows exactly how to be healthy, and cares profoundly about health—it's her *job,* after all. But she has habits that are killing her slowly. Even her extraordinary self-discipline hasn't helped. Why do we Americans behave in such an unhealthy way? We don't *want* to be unhealthy. It's just the opposite; we are obsessed with our health. What are we missing here?

Reasonable assumptions and assumptions of reason

Humans are self-absorbed, so throughout history the question of why people behave as they do has consumed whole categories of experts, including not only psychologists, sociologists, and anthropologists, but also economists, urban planners, philosophers, theologians, advertisers, and salespeople. In the mid-twentieth century, when public health officials realized that keeping people healthy meant changing their behavior, they went to experts for help. If they had turned to anthropologists, sociologists, or salespeople our history since then might be very different, but they chose to turn to one particular brand of psychologists.

In the 1950s psychology fell roughly into two warring camps: the behaviorists and the cognitive psychologists. The behaviorists (or "radical behaviorists," as a leading cognitive psychologist calls them) were epitomized by B. F. Skinner, an iconoclastic Harvard-trained laboratory scientist. Skinner began his radical path in psychology during World War II, with the bizarre mission of training kamikaze pigeons for the military. The job of the pigeons was to guide bombs dropped from an airplane cargo bay to their targets, and the job of Skinner was to teach the pigeons how to do it. He found that by systematically rewarding or punishing a pigeon (what he called "positive and negative reinforcement") for successive approxima-tions of the behavior he wanted, he could train pigeons to peck frantically, incessantly and precisely at a target projected on a screen. Working with engineers, he then built a contraption on the bombs so that when the pigeon pecked continually at the projected target while riding the bomb through the air, the bomb stayed on track toward its actual target. Skinner's pigeons performed "beautifully," even while distracted by the sound of ex-plosions. Nonetheless, the military researchers couldn't quite get past the ridiculousness of countering Japanese kamikazes with dumb birds, so they dropped the project in favor of far more expensive and unworkable televi-sion guidance systems, but Skinner never forgot the lessons he learned.[1]

Starting with his pigeons, Skinner developed a full-blown theory that all animals, including humans, behave almost entirely based on whether the people and things around them have rewarded or punished them for what they have done before. A child learns to talk when his parents smile or clap after he makes babbling sounds, and as the parent rewards succes-sive approximations of words the child refines his sounds. People become violent, kind, curious, lazy, or flirtatious if they are "reinforced" by their friends or parents when they behave that way. Skinner, an amateur inven-tor as well as theorist, even built "teaching machines" that rewarded stu-dents immediately for getting the right answer to teachers' problems, an idea that was eccentric at the time but that is now religion for educational software developers.

In the other camp were "cognitive psychologists," whose faith was that humans behave based on how they *think*. To the cognitive psychologists, the world around us was unimportant except in how it changes the way our mind perceives it. They were fascinated with the study of *attitudes*—how positively or negatively people thought about some action they might take or what might come of it. For example, people with a positive attitude about smoking (because they think it's sophisticated) or who don't care much about whether it might give them lung cancer would tend to exper-iment with cigarettes. Human behavior followed from human thought; therefore in the field of human behavior, it was how people *thought* about the world that really mattered, not the world itself.

At what might be considered the extreme end of the cognitive group was "humanistic psychology," led by a man named Carl Rogers. He was described as "the most influential psychotherapist in American history. . . . More than any individual, he was responsible for the spread of professional counseling and psychotherapy beyond psychiatry and psychoanalysis to all the helping professions—psychology, social work, ministry, lay therapy, and others."[2] Rogers wasn't an academic, and he didn't conduct any experiments; he based his theories entirely on the case studies of his client therapy sessions. Instead of inventing contraptions, he invented concepts like "client-centered therapy" and "encounter groups" that presaged (and to an extent caused) the New Age spiritualism of the 1980s and 1990s. He believed that "man has long felt himself to be a puppet in life, molded by world forces, by economic forces. . . . But he is firmly setting forth a new declaration of independence" which therapists could help him achieve.[3] "The essence of therapy is the client's movement from feeling unfree and controlled by others toward the frightening but rewarding sense of freedom to map out and choose his personality."[4] He believed once people were "free" to "find their inner wisdom" they would make increasingly healthier and more constructive choices.

The two camps couldn't have been more different. Skinner questioned whether the "mind" (as opposed to the brain) existed at all, suggesting that it was merely an invention by people who wanted to find a cause for behavior that they couldn't understand. He believed that "the variables of which human behavior is a function lie in the environment," and that our human concept of free will was an illusion.[5] People did what they were taught (by reinforcement) to do, and everything else was rationalization. To Skinner, the only way humans could change was to restructure their environment, which would then turn around and shape their behavior. The message of Rogers, on the other hand, was wonderfully inspirational. Our minds are all-powerful: no matter what conditions we find ourselves in, we can control ourselves and our destiny, if only our helpful guides have set us "free."

Arguing against free will and comparing people to pigeons doesn't buy you many friends. Skinner's arguments were a tough sell, at least to the general public, and were made tougher by Skinner's arrogance. Even though he had far more scientific evidence on his side than the cognitive psychologists did, it is not hard to understand why public health experts looking for advice leaned to the cognitive side and haven't looked back to behaviorism since. Skinner's behaviorism is far from dead, though. It is popular and used successfully in dog obedience schools, prisons, halfway houses, and schools for wayward children. It seems that we reserve rewards and punishments for animals and for those humans we consider to have less intelligence than ourselves.

The thinking man's public health

In the 1950s the United States Public Health Service called in a group of four social psychologists on a vexing problem. Tuberculosis was nearly the AIDS of its day, a withering, fatal disease striking fear in the hearts of many. But people exposed to tuberculosis were not showing up for skin tests and x-rays to see if they had caught the disease, even when the tests and treatment were free. The four had an academic bent, so as they designed educational programs to solve the problem, they also created a theory to explain what they were doing. The Health Belief Model they invented falls squarely in the cognitive camp, arguing that people behave based on what they *believe*—about the odds they will get the disease, about how severe the disease is, and about whether their doing something about it will make a difference. They argued that the mind finds a compromise in the confusing push and pull of these three different beliefs, and from the final compromise springs behavior—what the mind tells the body to do. If people didn't believe—truly *believe*, that is—that tuberculosis might strike them, the hassle of getting to the clinic for x-rays on a busy day may just not seem worth it. Persuading people to show up for their x-rays or take their pills boiled down to persuading them that tuberculosis was not only nasty but also likely—and could be avoided if they did as they were told. The Health Belief Model's great appeal is its simple logic.[6]

About a decade later the Health Belief Model was followed up by another popular cognitive theory called the Theory of Reasoned Action, developed by psychologists Martin Fishbein and Izek Azjen.[7] These two made fine distinctions among the words *beliefs, attitudes,* and *intentions. Beliefs* (our internal estimates of the probability that something is true) and *attitudes* (how positively or negatively we feel about that something) determine our *intentions* (clear plans) to do something, and when we intend to do it, we are likely to do it. If we believe tuberculosis is stalking us, and it scares the hell out of us, we make plans to take time off work to get to the clinic, which increases the odds (but does not guarantee) we will end up there. It is a little more sophisticated than the Health Belief Model, but bears a strong family resemblance.

The titles of these two theories explain their common premise. People are reasonable. People are rational. They take action based on decisions. They make decisions based on their reasoning and their beliefs. They make these decisions individually and with their own free will. If people decide to do something stupid that will hurt them, such as smoking or refusing to exercise, they just haven't thought through the problem well, or their beliefs don't jibe with the facts, or they just don't know how to behave in a healthy way. People will make the right decisions, according to these theories, if they have the correct facts, are convinced that they are important, and understand how they should behave. To be fair, these theories acknowledge that there are factors external to individuals that influence their behavioral decisions. But the theorists argue that it is not our environment that matters but rather the representation of the environment inside our heads. As practitioners apply these theories, they accept external factors as unchangeable and work on the way people think about the world.

These theories fit comfortably in our modern "age of therapy," in which we believe that everything in an individual's life is under his control, if only his head is screwed on right. Each person decides each day whether to be fat, or lazy, or addicted to alcohol or tobacco. If he decides to do these things, the only way he can be helped is if professionals cure him (or "free" him) of his confused thinking. Although their creators don't cite his work as inspiration, Carl Rogers's influence runs through these theories. And the influence continues. To slow the HIV epidemic, for example, the Centers for Disease Control and Prevention is now promoting individual "client-centered counseling" to persuade people to curb their sexual appetites.

In a funny way, these theories have also resurrected the moralism of the 1800s. The moralists of the 1800s blamed the bad health of the poor on immoderate eating, intemperate drinking, and sin. The new moralists of our time have updated only slightly the list of sins: too much smoking, drinking, eating, and sloth. Both groups believe people have no one but themselves to blame for their behavior or their sicknesses. In the 1800s unhealthy habits were caused by laziness and immorality. Today unhealthy habits are caused by ignorance and irrationality. In either era, the only solution to their problems is through health experts teaching them the right way to lead their lives.

Of course it's also very convenient to lay the responsibility for unhealthy behavior on individual people. It absolves the rest of us from any responsibility. The problem is not with society. The problem is in the heads of a few lazy or reckless people. It makes it easier for the most cold-hearted among us to ignore people's suffering—or even feel vindicated when it occurs.

Cognitive theories like the Health Belief Model and the Theory of Reasoned Action hit their prime in public health in the 1960s and 1970s. Academic experts wrote educational curricula to teach people about disease, pump up their attitudes about preventing it, and show them how to behave differently, and public health agencies showered "high-risk" people with the educational programs. A typical program based on these models might tell people about the benefits of walking for exercise, have a healthy person give a testimonial about how enjoyable walking can be, and show them how they can work walking into their daily routine. Or it might teach people how to read a food label for its fat content and demonstrate how to cook a tasty low-fat meal.

As appealing as the theories were, they mostly failed. Or more precisely, when prevention programs put them to use, the programs at best worked to a small extent, but like New Year's resolutions, they didn't last long. Frequently these programs showed promising results in pilot trials, only to fail completely when scaled up to larger groups. A typical example: in 1963 experts from Johns Hopkins (the home of the Health Belief Model) fashioned a smoking prevention program for a Baltimore high school that hammered students with the facts that smoking caused lung cancer and that lung cancer was a very bad thing, and with encouragement to stop smoking or not start. A year later students surveyed had much more negative attitudes towards smoking but their smoking rates hadn't changed a whit.[8] Dozens of similar smoking prevention projects were tried in schools in the 1960s and 1970s, and according to one reviewer, "most attempts to influence the smoking behavior of youth have had little success." The reviewer even hinted that a reason the programs failed was that "the majority of programs seemed to accept the premise that man is a rational being and that he will act in his own best interest."[9] Similar programs to prevent drinking, teen pregnancy, sexually transmitted diseases, or unhealthy eating foundered also. These programs succeeded in teaching people how they should behave. Then—like Cecelia Turner—they didn't behave as they knew they should.

If we have learned only one thing in health education in the last fifty years, it is that the fundamental problem is not with the way that everyone *thinks*. We will not find the solution to health behavior inside people's heads. The logic of altering behavior by changing the way people think was perfect. Unfortunately, people aren't logical.

"You can observe a lot just by watching"

If thinking doesn't drive whether people take up smoking or have a high-fat diet, what does?

For Renny Lemoine and Durel Richard, there are some obvious suspects. Both boys' mothers, brothers, and sisters smoke. Both boys' fathers used to smoke, although they quit some years ago. Once Renny's father caught him smoking and told him if he caught him again he would make him eat the cigarettes. But he hasn't, and "my mama knows, and she don't do nothin' 'bout it," he says. Renny and Durel say all of their friends smoke, and Renny says that nearly the only time he smokes is when he is with them. The boys say their friends don't pressure them to smoke—they're good kids, the boys say, who wouldn't do anything like that—but admit that being around smokers all the time "must have somethin' to do" with their smoking.

Plenty of studies show that they are right: teens are somewhat more likely to smoke if their parents smoke, and far more likely to smoke if their friends smoke.[10] Teenage years are when kids reject what their parents say, when they try out different personalities and habits, so it makes sense that adolescents would also experiment with something they see friends do, even if they knew it was bad for them and even (or especially) if their parents and teachers told them not to do it. Renny and Durel enjoyed relaxing with the guys after a hard day's work, and part of the joy was behaving in synchrony, which included smoking.

Teenagers aren't the only ones who are susceptible to the influences of others. Cecelia Turner feels she can trace exactly when her health habits took a turn for the worse. In the mid 1980s, while she was in graduate school in San Diego, she spent her free time with friends who were active and ate healthy food. "People just stayed outdoors there," she remembers. With her friends she regularly rode horseback, played tennis, and walked all over town. When she ate with others—which she did frequently—they ate foods like broiled fish and fruit. "No one ate fried foods." But when she returned to the suburbs of New Orleans, "my lifestyle changed completely." None of her friends walked around the neighborhood or exercised. Cecelia loves being around people, and says now "if I had somebody who would say 'let's go [exercise],' I'd go. But for me to go alone, I won't do it." She even asked the trainers at the gym if there were a training partner she could team up with, but couldn't find one. After returning she also tried keeping up her healthy eating habits, but her family and friends back home made it tough. "When I was in San Diego, I fit right in" eating healthy foods, but when she returned "I stuck out like a sore thumb." They ridiculed her for ordering appetizer-sized portions for her entrée at restaurants or bypassing desserts. "I'd get razzed the whole meal." Soon she was eating just what she knew she shouldn't.

The failure of the cognitive theories to change behavior made health experts search for other levers, and based on stories like these, they gravitated to theories of how people influence each other. The most popular were the work of a Canadian-born psychologist at Stanford named Albert Bandura.

Bandura is probably best known for studying the effect on nursery school children of watching an adult "perform ... fairly unique aggressive responses" toward a plastic inflatable "Bobo" clown. The children were put in a room and asked to draw pictures, and then without any introduction or explanation an adult "model" entered the room and savaged Bobo: sitting on it and punching it in the nose, tossing it in the air, pummeling it with a rubber hammer, and kicking it around the room, interspersing this violence with "distinctive aggressive verbal responses." Bandura then led the children to a second room and left them alone with the Bobo clown and some other toys. Many of the children assaulted Bobo just as violently, often mimicking exactly the pummeling, tossing, kicking, and verbal abuse. Bandura went on to show that the children were just as vicious to poor Bobo if the "model" they saw was only on television, or even if the "model" on television was a cartoon cat instead of an adult human.[11]

The children had learned how to be violent just by watching—in Bandura's words, they "modeled" their behavior. Bandura's study got the most press because it showed the potential power of violence on television, but in fact it said something much more fundamental about how humans learn to behave. The children's behavior wasn't driven by how they thought —their imitation didn't seem to involve any particular thinking—so it couldn't be explained by the cognitive theories. And Bandura never had to punish or reward the children to induce them to punch the doll, so it couldn't be explained by Skinner's "reinforcement" theory either. This "social learning" was much simpler than cognitive learning and much more efficient than "reinforced" learning. Bandura's simple studies uncovered a truly new and important scientific idea.

A part of his studies that got little attention was that some children were shown adults playing peacefully with Bobo and other toys, and these children were *less* likely to show aggressive behavior afterward than "control" children not given any models. Bandura didn't show that children model violent behavior, he showed that they model any behavior. Humans are not unique in learning this way. Other researchers around that time found that many different types of animals learn how to behave by watching others. Miniature dachshund puppies that had watched a littermate get food by pulling a ribbon attached to a tiny food cart accomplished the trick ten times faster than the "demonstrator" puppies that had to learn by trial and error.[12] Rhesus monkeys who watched other monkeys solve puzzles to get raisins were able to solve the same puzzles immediately.[13] And chimpanzees raised in human homes spontaneously typed at keyboards, lit cigarettes with mechanical lighters, opened cans with screwdrivers, and did other strange things they had only watched humans do.[14]

The effect extends beyond learning. As Bandura concluded with his "Bobo" studies, watching others doesn't just teach children new behaviors, it also makes people (children or adults) more likely to repeat acts that they have already learned.[15] Overall the studies confirm this simple fact: people tend to do what they see others do. That is, behavior itself is contagious.

Contagious behavior extends to the ultimate self-destruction. Psychologist David Phillips showed in several studies that in the month after stories of well-publicized suicides appeared in newspapers or television, suicide rates jumped up. In fact, on average about fifty more people killed themselves in the month after highly publicized suicides than the month before.[16] And just to dispel any thoughts that the publicity might only have "moved up" the dates of suicides that were inevitable, Phillips showed that there was no compensatory fall in suicides in the second month.[17] When people read or see stories about others killing themselves, Phillips concluded, some who would have not otherwise killed themselves commit suicide. Phillips found that teenagers seem particularly susceptible to this.[18] Imitative suicide is common enough that occasionally single towns in America are faced with their worst nightmare—multiple suicides in teenagers, one following another. The CDC even has a name for it—a "contagion" of suicide.

The social influences on health-related behavior are at least as strong as the social influences on any other type of behavior. Teens like Renny Lemoine and Durel Richard are more likely to smoke if they are around smokers. Adults like Cecelia Turner are more likely to eat high-fat desserts if they are around others who are eating dessert, and can become paralyzed when they are around people who are sedentary.

For most of us, who feel that we are in full control, it is hard to notice this influence. We can clearly see how we differ from our coworkers and friends, and we feel that those differences are due to our own decisions. But we can never see how we would behave if we had different coworkers and friends. If we drink less than our coworkers and friends, we would likely drink still less (or not at all) if we were around teetotalers. If we exercise more than they do, we would probably exercise still more if we were around marathon runners. The influences don't feel coercive; it's just more fun for most of us to spend time with others than to be loners, and spending time with others means picking up their habits. Whether we can sense its impact on us or not, though, the contagiousness of behavior is an undercurrent that sweeps us along toward health or disease.

Our entanglement in webs of social influences helps explain why the cognitive prevention programs fail over the long term. People motivated by an informative and persuasive talk *want* to behave in a healthy way, they intend to do it, and some of them succeed. But if their social group is behaving in just the opposite way, their success won't last. Over time, usually measured not in years but in weeks, they tire of struggling against the sway of others and fall back in line. In the end, being part of the gang is more fulfilling than following some health educator's instructions. Put another way, trying to persuade someone to change his behavior without considering how people around him are behaving is a little like asking a driver in rush hour traffic to go fifty miles an hour when every car around him is crawling along at fifteen miles an hour. Even if he wants to, he just can't follow the advice for long.

Public health tries social learning

In the last twenty years, health educators have tried to manipulate social influences to stop kids from doing just about every self-destructive behavior you can imagine, including smoking, having sex, shooting each other, or eating junk food. These programs wrestle with social influences in two ways. Some train children to overcome them. Health educators don't just teach kids to "say no" to coercion from other kids to use drugs or have sex, they run through scripts of exactly *how* to say no. Girls are taught to respond to a boy's come-on of "If you really love me, you'll do it" by saying "If you really loved *me*, you wouldn't push me to do something I don't want." This "refusal skills" tactic underlies the DARE (Drug Abuse Resistance Education) program, an anti-drug education program taught by police officers. Other programs try to co-opt social influences. Instead of adults teaching children about the dangers of smoking, educators train "peer leaders" to carry the message. And the message may be more a testimonial that a lecture. "I don't smoke," a popular teen might say in front of a class, "I think smoking's disgusting."

Across the board, these "social influences" programs look a little better

than cognitive programs, but there are still many more failures than successes, especially over the long term. A typical example is "Postponing
Sexual Involvement," a project that taught middle school children how to
recognize and resist pressures to have sex. In the early 1980s, after a promising pilot test, researchers rolled it out in the eighth grade of Atlanta public schools. In telephone surveys a year afterward, teens who went through
the program were less likely to tell surveyors they were having sex and to
have become pregnant than those who didn't.[19] Health educators were ec-
static with the success, which launched PSI in the next few years as "probably the most widely implemented middle school curriculum" in the nation
to prevent pregnancy in teens. In the early 1990s, the state of California
jumped into the program with both feet, funding twenty-eight projects in
thirty-one counties for 187,000 kids. But this time the evaluation numbers
looked terrible: the program had a small effect on kids' attitudes three
months afterward, but didn't make the slightest difference in whether the
kids began having sex or in the frequency of sex, either at three months or
at seventeen months afterward.[20]

The failure of Postponing Sexual Involvement echoed the history of the
DARE program. DARE was created by the Los Angeles Police Department and the local school district in the early 1980s. An early report showed
that students in the program were more likely to refuse "imagined offers"
of drugs and less likely to report that they used alcohol, cigarettes, and other
drugs.[21] With what looked like one victory in an otherwise futile war on
drugs, state and federal governments funded DARE massively across
America. In fact it is the only drug prevention program named specifically
in the federal 1986 Drug-Free Schools and Communities Act.[22] Since then,
different groups of researchers have found in at least nine scientifically rigorous evaluations that DARE doesn't prevent kids from using drugs at all.[23]
As we write in 2004, DARE is bigger than ever in the United States, probably more because scared parents want schools to do *something* to keep their
kids off drugs, but mention it to experts and they grow livid about our stu-
pidity in wasting money on a program that we know doesn't work.

Smoking is the most destructive health behavior there is, and scores
of researchers have tried "social influences" manipulations to prevent kids
from lighting up. After years of looking at small-scale studies with flawed

methods and questionable results, in the 1980s the National Cancer Institute funded the fifteen-year, $15 million Hutchinson Smoking Prevention Project involving more than eight thousand children in forty school districts in Washington State. The kids were taught from third through twelfth grade exactly how to resist pressures from others to smoke. They didn't resist much, though, because by twelfth grade, 26 percent of kids getting the full prevention program were smoking, the same rate as kids in the "control" schools.[24]

As Cecelia Turner can testify, social influences don't end at age twenty-one. And prevention programs based on social influences don't either. Many have been tested out in adults, and they have failed also. In the late 1970s and early 1980s the National Institutes of Health rolled out three multiyear trials based on social learning to cut rates of heart disease in entire towns in California, Minnesota, and Rhode Island. The researchers distributed state-of-the-art messages about diet, exercise, and smoking through public service announcements on radio and television, newspaper columns, community fairs, direct-mail flyers, school curricula, and adult classes. A decade and millions of dollars after they started, the three research groups announced the same dreary conclusion: any improvements in behavior in the "intervention" communities compared to the "control" communities were small or negligible.[25]

These studies inflicted major damage to the idea that we can leverage social influences to prevent people from self-destructive behavior. As for the cognitive programs, the reasoning for the social influences programs was there, but the results weren't.

Looking back on it, though, maybe we should have known better. When you think of it, the reasoning *wasn't* all there—in fact, there was a pretty big hole in it. Sure, individual kids take up smoking because kids around them are doing it. But then why are *they* taking up smoking? To say that it is "social influences" that makes kids smoke is to get caught in a circular argument. Something *besides* other people must be at play here, something that encourages everyone to smoke. That something might be echoed and amplified by social influences—like a shout reverberating through an echo chamber—but the something isn't the social influence itself. The shout has to start somewhere, and the reverberating sound will die out unless someone keeps shouting. Social influences are only the most obvious and immediate causes for people behaving in ways they know they shouldn't. Changing them doesn't work because it doesn't touch the less obvious and more indirect, but ultimately more powerful forces. Or to go back to our earlier analogy, trying to change a person's behavior by teaching her to resist social influences is like trying to persuade a driver stuck in traffic to drive as if there were no cars stacked in front of her. And trying to leverage social influences through peer leaders is like trying to eliminate a rush-hour traffic jam by paying a few conspicuous drivers to drive faster in the hopes that others will follow their example. These tactics ignore the fundamental problem—the traffic is jammed not because people don't want to drive fast, but because there are simply more cars than the freeway can handle.

The wilting of the prevention programs based on social influences should make us wonder if changing our behavior to improve our health is hopeless. But something odd happened in all three of the community intervention trials to prevent heart disease, something that had cropped up in previous studies but that the researchers still hadn't expected. The trials failed not because the "intervention" communities hadn't changed—in fact they changed substantially, with the citizens showing respectable reductions in blood pressure, cholesterol levels, and smoking rates. They failed because over the several years of study, the "control" communities improved just as much (or in some cases, even more). *Something* was having an effect on people's behavior and their health. It is just that this something wasn't the program that the researchers had put in place.

CHAPTER 4

BELL CURVES
and
BAD APPLES

After nearly half a century of health education programs with feeble results, it's time to admit failure. We don't need just a different curriculum. We need a new way to think about why humans do things that hurt themselves.

Health education programs try to shape the choices of individuals —individuals who sometimes are influenced by others, but individuals nonetheless. A new way of thinking through the problem starts not with individuals but groups.

We humans evolved as social animals. We lived in bands; we gathered food, hunted, ate, and defended ourselves against predators as a group. Humans put together behave as dancers in a kind of loosely choreographed ballet, each having his or her specific role, but all taking cues from each other and keeping time to the same music. The interplay among people is so powerful that behavior itself isn't just a characteristic of individuals; it also is a feature of the group. Or as British preventive medicine specialist Geoffrey Rose wrote, "Society is not merely a collection of individuals but is also a collectivity."[1] Every collection of people shapes an average, acceptable, "normal" behavior, or what social scientists call a *social norm,* and quietly but firmly enforces it. People who stray far from the social norm of their group pay a price. The discrimination people experience when they are different can sometimes be severe, but more often it is simply the social threat of being viewed as "weird." On the other hand, people who stay within the social norm feel comfortable and supported. It's tough to swallow, but we usually behave more like herds of sheep than lone wolves.

Curves and tails

Geoffrey Rose came up with a useful way to picture the relationship between individual behavior and group behavior. He drew graphs showing the level of a health-related behavior like diet or exercise on the horizontal axis (with the people doing more of it farther to the right) and the percent of people at that level of behavior on the vertical axis.[2] For example, if we drew a graph about how much fat we eat in a year, it might look something like this:

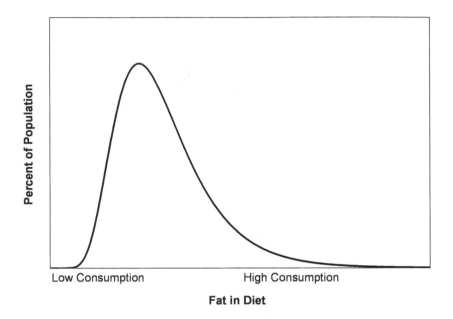

A small percentage of people are diet-conscious vegans who eat very little fat. Most people are near average—they eat meat most days, and snack on potato chips from time to time, but also eat some low-fat fruits and vegetables. And a small percentage of people pack in high-fat foods all the time—they eat bacon for breakfast, French fries for lunch, and munch on potato chips whenever they are around. So the curve is high in the middle, showing the large number of people who eat an average amount of fat, and low at the left and right ends, showing the few people who eat very little or very much. The curve reflects what we know: that while social norms are potent, we are not automatons. Most people don't stray too far from the average, but people do dance around the norms of eating behavior.

We can draw this kind of curve for all health-related behaviors, such as how much we drink, how much salt we take in, how much exercise we get, and how many people we have sex with in our lifetime. In all these curves, while most people are near the average point, a few people test the tails at either end. Usually the high-risk tail is longer than the low-risk tail.

The behavior of an individual is where he or she sits on this curve. An average person falls in the tall center of the fat-in-the-diet curve; if his father dies suddenly from heart disease and he decides to stop eating meat, he moves toward the left side. Or if he falls in love with someone with a passion for steak and adopts the same habit, he moves to the right side. In either case, the individual stays within the curve. The group behavior, on the other hand, is the entire curve. We can summarize it by measures like the mean (the average), or the median (the point at which 50 percent of people are above and 50 percent are below), or the mode (the tallest point), any of which you can think of as the social norm. If a single person in the population changes his or her behavior, the norm doesn't shift much.

The midpoints of the behavior curves are the keys to how healthy we are as a society. Since the location of the midpoint is a measure of our group behavior, it is our group behavior rather than our individual behavior that matters most to all of us. If the curve is a dog and the tail is—well, a tail—then we should care more about the dog than the tail.

As Rose pointed out, across all groups of people and all societies the general peak-and-two-tails shape of the behavior curves don't vary much. On the other hand, the *location* of the curves and the "average" person vary tremendously from one society to another. The graph on the next page is a reconstruction from different surveys of drinking in the United States and France.[3]

France has nearly four times as many heavy drinkers as the United States. That is, the right tail of the curve is higher and longer for France than for the U.S. But also the peak of the curve is farther to the right for France than the U.S., which says that the average Frenchman drinks a lot more than the average American. The basic social norm in France favors drinking much more.

Social norms not only differ between populations, they also change over time. Americans accepted heavy drinking far more in the 1950s than they do today. The two-martini lunch, not far from the "normal" range

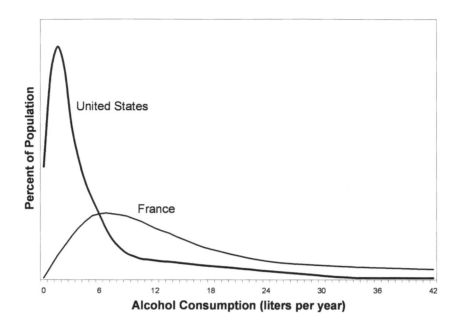

fifty years ago, is now shameful and possibly a career-killer. Today an American woman who jogs in her neighborhood three times a week is on the "fit" side of the curve, or maybe just a little strange at worst. But in the 1950s she would have been downright weird, the sort others would avoid talking to, and she might have given up jogging so as not to risk losing her friends. Or to put it more positively, to enjoy time with friends, she would spend her time doing something besides jogging.

If social norms vary between groups and over time, these norms must be changeable. But how? When the cognitive health education programs failed, we learned that we couldn't change them by nudging individuals' knowledge or attitudes. When the social influences programs failed we learned that social influences enforce the social norm, but they don't establish it in the first place. There must be other, entirely different factors at play in fixing the peak of the behavior curve.

Don't believe in magic numbers

There is something else crucial to our health that Geoffrey Rose's curves show.

Tom Farley gives a regular lecture to graduate students about strategies for disease prevention. He begins the lecture by asking two questions. First, he asks, "How many of you consider yourselves at 'high risk' of dying from heart disease?" Of a class of fifty students, only about five usually raise their hands. Then he asks a slightly different question: "How many of you think you could *lower* your risk of dying from heart disease by changing how you behave?" The response changes dramatically: about forty of the fifty students raise their hands.

The students' guesses are right. Even average people are less likely to die of heart disease if they eat less fat and exercise more. Because of the shape of the behavior curves, there are many more people at average risk than at high risk for heart disease. In fact, there are so many more, that even though they are at lower risk, *more average people will have heart attacks than high-risk people.* If we define "high-risk" as having a cholesterol level of over 240, more than 60 percent of people who will die from heart disease will be "low-risk," that is to say, average people.[4]

This effect isn't just limited to cholesterol. More people with average blood pressure than people with high blood pressure die of heart attacks, and the greatest number of people who have strokes have only slightly elevated blood pressure.[5] More non-alcoholics than alcoholics injure themselves from drinking.[6] And in general, more average people than high-risk people die from common preventable diseases, not because individually they have a greater probability of dying, but simply because there are so many more average people.

As medical care has infiltrated our everyday lives, we have all gotten used to numbers that divide people at high risk, who ought to do something different to be healthy, from the rest of us, who can relax. If your cholesterol is above 240 you are in trouble: better lay off the fries. If your blood pressure is above 140 you have a disease called hypertension: try a low-salt diet. If your Body Mass Index is above 30 you are obese: time to switch to Diet Coke. If you don't hit these magic numbers, you are healthy and can enjoy life.

These magic numbers are conjured up for a simple reason: doctors and other health experts want to persuade people to tone down their risky behavior, but because everyone has a tough time making changes like these, the health experts with scarce time and tight budgets "target" their advice to those who need it the most. They push low-calorie diets only for people who are overweight and low-salt diets only for people with high blood pressure. That is, they try to move individual people who are on the right tail of the behavior curves toward the center, while ignoring the rest who are near the middle of the curve. We call this the "bad apples" approach, because it grabs a small number of high-risk persons (the bad apples) and tosses them out.

If the "bad apples" approach actually worked, the new curve of dietary fat intake would look like this:

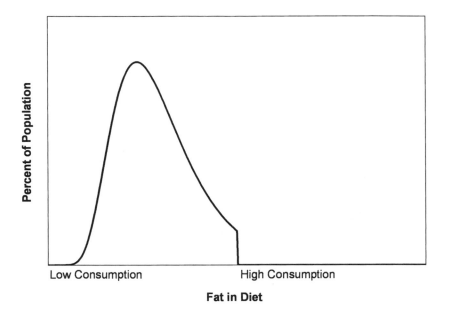

In this curve, most people's diets would be what they are now, but the small number of potato chip fiends would have cut back on their chip consumption enough to be "normal"—like the rest of us.

There are three big problems with the bad apples approach. First, a curve of this shape is not natural. Its tail has been chopped off. Curves like this have not been seen in any population, and it is hard to imagine they ever will be. Remember that behavior is contagious. If a group finds it perfectly normal and acceptable to eat one bag of potato chips a day, can it really condemn eating two as abnormal? How successful would it be in Cecelia Turner's neighborhood to start a walking club *only* for women who are obese? (Who would want to be a member of this club?) People's behavior varies naturally around certain averages; there are never sharp dividing lines between acceptable and unacceptable behavior. If no natural population has a behavior curve that looks like this one, what makes us think we can create one with a little education?

Second, people continually change their behavior. They shuttle back and forth between the main part of the curve and the tail. Some people who we find in the tail would move to the main part of the curve on their own. If they happen to be in a high-risk phase of their lives—after a string of bad luck, at an emotional low point, or on a binge—they are likely to drift back to a lower-risk phase regardless. In the words of statisticians, they "regress to the mean." More important, some people who are not in the tail when we do our targeting drift into it afterwards. They experiment with unhealthy behavior. So our targeted prevention efforts fail to help them. The curve wags a tail, and the curve will always wag a tail; even if we can successfully chop it off, another one will soon grow back.

This effect hit home—after the fact—in a failed project to prevent deaths from heart disease in high-risk men. As a researcher put it afterward:

> Even when people do successfully change their high-risk behavior, new people continue to enter the at-risk population to take their place. For example, every time we finally helped a man in the . . . project to stop smoking, it is probable that, on that day, one or two children in a schoolyard somewhere were for the first time taking their first tentative puffs on a cigarette. So, even when we do help high-risk people lower their risk, we do nothing to change the distribution of disease in the population because, in one-to-one programmes . . . we have done nothing to influence those forces in the society that caused the problem in the first place.[7]

And third, as we've said, the majority of people who die from heart attacks are not in the tail of the curve anyway. So even if we could permanently chop off the tail of the curve, we would have very little impact on the problem of heart attacks in the population as a whole. In our classroom example, if we magically prevented heart disease in all five of the students who were at "high risk," we wouldn't have made more than a small dent in the overall heart disease mortality rates in the classroom, because we would have ignored the rest of the forty who were "not high risk."

Shifting the curve

Geoffrey Rose's curves show us that our instinctive "bad apples" approach to preventing disease is bound to fail, but they also show us a different tactic that might work. Rather than trying to chop off the tail of the health-behavior curve, we can just try to shift the entire curve a little bit. That is, instead of asking a few high-risk persons to transform themselves, we try to get all people to make a small adjustment in their behavior, which moves the crucial midpoint of the curve.

For example, if we succeeded in getting everyone to back off from eating fat a little bit, the dietary fat curve might shift to the left, from the solid line to the dotted line below:

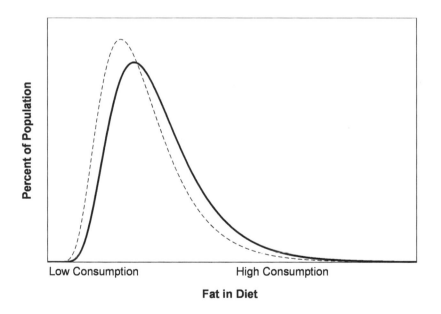

This new dotted curve may not look much different from the original curve, but in fact it is a profound change.

A group of British researchers has worked out the benefit of curve-shifting for blood pressure in detail. Eating too much salt raises your blood pressure and cutting down on salt lowers it. It can take a lot of self-discipline to cut down substantially on the salt you eat, so doctors and many public health officials argue that we should only tell people with high blood pressure to go on low-salt diets, and that the rest of us, with normal blood pressure, can eat as much salt as we want. But there is no magic number dividing high blood pressure from normal blood pressure. People with blood pressure just below the cutoff are more likely to have a stroke than people with blood pressure that is lower still. And because blood pressure in the whole population falls on a bell-shaped curve, there are many more people with "normal" blood pressure than "high" blood pressure who will die from complications of high blood pressure.

Trying out different scenarios, the researchers found that if every person labeled as having high blood pressure faithfully took medications, and if those medications all worked (a rosy scenario indeed), deaths from stroke would fall by 15 percent. On the other hand, if everyone in the *entire* population simply didn't sprinkle salt on his or her food, *even if no one were given medicines for hypertension, stroke deaths would decrease by 22 percent.*[8] That is, even a slight shift in the entire curve of salt intake would prevent more stroke deaths than chopping off the curve's tail.

This same pattern is likely to be true for the entire list of health-related behaviors that cause our era's major killers—from high-fat diets to alcohol and drug use to violent behavior. A general shift in how much fat we all eat in our diet is likely to save more lives than all of us with high levels taking cholesterol-lowering drugs. More lives would be saved if everyone got just a little more exercise than if a few obese people started a crash program. Fewer people would die from drunk-driving crashes if everyone drank a little less than if we cured full-fledged alcoholics. When the curve shifts, each individual person doesn't change his or her behavior much, but the effect on the group as a whole is big.

Curve-shifting also gets around the other problems with curve-chopping. Since it encompasses everyone, the fact that people in the high-risk tail are a moving target doesn't matter. We don't need to worry who will become at high risk in the future if we are making changes that reduce everyone's risk. And it is not a problem that behavior is contagious—

in fact, curve-shifting turns this into a big advantage. The average people—who are now healthier—exert a healthy influence on the people who are at high risk. The curve wags the tail, not the other way around. So if we shift the curve, even the tails benefit. We *all* benefit.

It comes down to this: improving our health in the United States depends on how successful we are in changing the behavior of *all* of us. As individualistic as we Americans are, we can't get away from thinking of ourselves as part of a larger group. If we want to be much healthier, we need to *all* be healthier.

Searching for the curve-shifters

But how *can* we shift the entire curve of our group behavior? How can we *all* behave in a way that is better for our health? Surely it must be much harder for all of us to change our behavior than for one person to change his. When you think of what a struggle it is for one person to stop smoking, take up jogging, or lose weight, it seems ridiculous to think that *everyone* could do these things. It's impossible.

Or is it? As we've said, different populations have different curves. Japanese people are less overweight. French people drink more. And populations change over time. People drink less now than they did in the 1950s. Smoking rates in America have fluctuated widely over the last century. The "control" communities in the NIH studies drifted toward healthier behavior over the course of the trial. Whatever nails down group behavior norms must be different between the United States and other countries and must change over time.

In the 1800s, the leading killers were epidemic infectious diseases, like cholera, tuberculosis, and yellow fever, which were spread by water, contact between people, and mosquitoes. We could blame these problems (as many experts at the time did) on individuals. People would not spread infections if they boiled their drinking water, washed their hands, and avoided contact with mosquitoes. So our society could have tried to improve its health by educating individuals about water-boiling, hand-washing, and mosquito-avoiding. But thanks to Edwin Chadwick and his sanitarians, our society learned that it made a lot more sense to just build clean water and sewage systems and to reduce mosquito breeding sites, so people drank clean water, were more likely to wash their hands, and were bitten by mos-quitoes less often regardless of whether or not they were educated. These were changes not in people's behavior, but in their environment. Chad-wick's new ideas led to the greatest improvement in human health in his-tory—not just in the poor, who were his main concern, but in everyone. As Geoffrey Rose put it, "The great public health reforms of the nineteenth century which led to such dramatic improvements . . . were undertaken *for* people, rather than *by* people [italics added]."[9] Ideas that work that well de-serve a second look.

B. F. Skinner would have predicted that health education programs di-rected at individuals would fail. He would have proposed (he *did* propose) that if we really want to change how we behave, we must change the envi-ronment in which we live. Skinner couldn't sell his ideas to health experts, but with each failure of programs based on the ideas of other psychologists, they look steadily better.

What—if anything—does our environment have to do with our be-havior and our health today? Our modern environment is made up of the streets, houses, buildings, neighborhoods, and stores that surround us, the items in them, the images we see every day, and society's rules for behavior in schools, in the workplace, and in communities. This jumble of struc-tures can make it easier or harder to smoke, drink, eat high-fat foods, or behave in a hundred other ways that affect our health. These features of our everyday world may seem innocent or trivial, but they are far from it. It is tempting to think they affect only people who don't have the money or in-dependence that we do, but in fact they affect us all.

Fast driving and fast food

Renny and Durel don't spend a lot of time watching television, but often they drive to the Lafayette multiplex to catch movies, and sometimes Durel rents videos and watches them at his girlfriend's house. The movies they see are romantic comedies, action flicks, and teen scream shows—the same big-budget Hollywood offerings teenagers see at mall theaters nationwide. Asked to name an actor he likes, Renny names Vin Diesel, a swarthy tough guy with a shaved head and hefty biceps who starred in *The Fast and the Furious* and could be Cajun if only he had the right accent. Of five movies they've watched recently, the actors smoke in four. Vin Diesel, the boys remembered, smokes on-screen.

Could merely watching actors smoke in movies possibly be more powerful than the knowledge that cigarettes kill and the "refusal" skills from years of training in school? It could. Why shouldn't teens learn to smoke in the same way that preschoolers learn to attack a Bobo doll? According to a study by researchers at Dartmouth, kids who watch the most scenes of smoking in movies are more than two and a half times as likely to smoke as kids who watch the least, even after taking into account whether their parents smoke and whether their friends smoke. In the twenty-five major movies released between 1998 and 2002 in which a cigarette brand was named or shown on-screen, for eighteen of them the brand was—don't be surprised—Marlboro.[10]

Renny and Durel offer up a clue about the source of their attitudes about smoking when asked to estimate how many kids at their school smoke. "At least 60 to 80 percent," Renny answers first. Then Durel tones it down a little. "Over 50 percent, anyway." How many adults in their town smoke? "About the same, at least 50 percent," says Durel emphatically. But in fact about a quarter of the kids in their school and 30 percent of adults in town smoke. How could they possibly get the impression that more than 50 percent, or 60 percent, or 80 percent of kids or adults around them light up? Maybe because that's about the percentage of actors who smoke in movies that they watch.

Movies are only a part of Renny and Durel's everyday world that immerses them in smoking. The first time Durel bought cigarettes on his own, he was at the Texaco station just down the road from the high school. It's a glass hut, emblazoned with the cheerful red Texaco logo, like thousands of combination gas station/convenience stores littering America, with an intermittent trickle of guys barging in and out to pay for gas and pick up beer. Inside you will find within arm's reach motor oil, magazines, potato chips, candy, and Cokes. You can't reach the cigarettes, but you don't have to, because no matter what you buy, you will end up facing the woman at the cash register, buttressed from behind by a massive display of rows of shiny cigarette packs. The top row, given extra space, is filled with Marlboro Lights, with a sign taped to it hawking the "Special" price of $3.21 a pack. Durel was nervous the first time he asked the woman for a pack, but he didn't have to be. Even if she carded him, the friend with him would have been happy to buy the pack for him.

Durel's teachers and parents have told him repeatedly that smoking is terrible for his health. But how bad could it really be, he has to wonder, if every time he buys gas for his truck cigarettes practically fall into his hands? They sure don't sell cocaine that way. The deadly drug known as tobacco isn't just easy to buy—it's "pushed" in ways that have to make street-corner heroin dealers envious.

Maybe the movies and the convenience stores aren't directly affecting Renny or Durel. But they don't have to. If the tobacco promotions merely influence the boys' *friends*—even a little bit—it could make just the difference, because it is the boys' friends who hand them cigarettes and demonstrate that the habit is cool. If the social connections create the echo chamber through which influences reverberate among the teens in Cajun Louisiana, the smoking actors and the cigarette availability in convenience stores are the shouts.

Cecelia Turner is a people person. Over the years she has always fallen in with the push and pull of her family and friends. When she was in San Diego, her group kept her healthy, but back home the group is doing just the opposite. But why are the groups so different? Are Californians really all that different from Southerners?

Or do they just live in different places? In San Diego, the weather was always pleasant, her neighborhood had sidewalks, and Cecelia lived within a few blocks of coffee shops, restaurants, cleaners, and drug stores. Everyone walked because everyone *could* walk. Walking was both fun and practical. When she returned home "the whole environment was different." She rented an apartment in a condo complex in a four-block segment sandwiched between an interstate and a major six-lane strip. It was like being trapped in an outpost on the moon; she couldn't go anywhere without a vehicle. There were no sidewalks, and a trip to a grocery store meant traveling a couple of hundred yards down the strip to a stoplight that had no crosswalks. At first Cecelia was game, trying to walk on the shoulder along the strip in the dim hours before work, but she was afraid of both the traffic and the people inside the cars that occasionally pulled up alongside her, and she quickly gave up. She could have walked around her apartment complex, which was ringed by a moat of parking spaces, "but it was all cars and concrete." This was the time when she was working full-time while studying for her doctoral degree. She could have driven to the gym for exercise, but that would mean just another chore on a "to do" list that was already much longer than the hours to complete it.

After returning from San Diego, cooking rarely got crossed off the "to do" list either. But snack foods were everywhere in her world—in grocery stores, convenience stores, drive-through fast-food joints, and vending machines. She was putting in sixteen hours a day and feeling stressed, and like all of us her biologic need for calories makes it hard to pass up food whenever it was around. So she ate "a lot of fast food" and snacked at her desk.

It was as hard for Cecelia to exercise or eat healthy food as it was easy for Renny and Durel to smoke. The everyday world around her—the condo complex, the interstate and strip, the town and whole metropolitan area—was an obstacle course for anyone who wanted physical activity, but it was jam-packed with snack foods. The social influences surely were important; maybe Cecelia didn't exercise because she had no one to go with her, and maybe she ate unhealthy food because that was the way to enjoy good times with her family and friends. But of course her family and friends, who lived very near Cecelia, didn't exercise and didn't eat healthy food, and the reasons they didn't probably had to do with the same barriers to physical activity and the same abundance of junk food that Cecelia faced. Our environment may tug at us through intermediaries—the people we spend time with—but it shapes our behavior powerfully nonetheless.

Coming to terms with ourselves and our world

Americans often bristle at the idea that our everyday world might shape how we behave. We believe—because we are Americans—that we control our destinies, that we can do anything, if only we have the intelligence, motivation, and grit. Our ancestors escaped societies in which someone born a peasant could only be a peasant. Triumph within a tough world is our collective history. Psychoanalysis, as it has diffused into our popular culture, tells us that if people can only understand themselves and their problems they can overcome any obstacles to success and happiness. Self-help books are so popular that they rate an entire category of best-seller lists. Hollywood exalts heroes who rise from poverty and adversity. We admire the successful exceptions—the rugged individuals who master their environment—so much that we believe they represent the norm. We don't sympathize with the losers who are bogged down by their surroundings; they deserve what they get. We can choose (or choose not) to smoke, drink alcohol, eat French fries, or shoot each other. To suggest to most Americans that our environment influences these choices is an insult.

Renny Lemoine and Durel Richard are as American as they come. They are convinced that the movies, billboards, store advertising displays, and magazine ads don't do anything to them. They make their own calls in life. Other high school kids in a focus group that Cecelia Turner organized were just as firm: "Who gives a damn who's smoking up there [on the screen]?" "No one can make you do something you don't want to do." Their fierce independence would be inspiring if it weren't so wrong. Cecelia Turner believes she *should* have the strength to overcome her surroundings, so when she sees that she hasn't she blames herself. It is heartbreaking to hear this woman of such extraordinary achievement say that when it comes to food, "I'm really bad."

As free and strong as we are in America, we *are* influenced by what we encounter every day. The tobacco companies understand this, or they wouldn't spend billions promoting smoking. The blossoming of the obesity epidemic in a nation of image-conscious overachievers is further evidence. The impact that any single feature of our environment has on a single health behavior might be small. But for our whole society, the effect is enormous.

Of course our environment doesn't *control* us. People do make decisions. The values and habits they bring from their families shape these decisions. Cultural differences between groups of people explain why some groups of Americans have healthier habits than others. But we now know so much about the prime dangers in our modern world (like smoking, drinking, and lack of exercise) that those among us with the extraordinary willpower to overcome their everyday world have already done so. At this point in our history, if we really want to be healthier we have to tackle the most important influence left—the world around us.

We inhabit a world that is man-made. We occupy buildings, travel through neighborhoods, shop at stores, watch video screens, and read magazines all created by humans. Our day-to-day environment isn't natural—it's designed. Since humans design this environment in a way that makes us sick, humans can just as well redesign it to help us behave in a healthy way. Governments and corporations change the world that surrounds us all the time for their own reasons and end up affecting our health one way or another. It's time for us to understand how the features of our everyday world affect us, and then to alter them in an explicit, deliberate way so that we can be healthier.

There are four features of our everyday world that influence whether we succumb to the leading causes of death in our era: accessibility of consumer products, physical structures, social structures, and media. We'll take them one at a time in the next part of this book.

PART II
CURVE SHIFTERS

CHAPTER 5

MORE IS MORE:
ACCESSIBILITY

The Winn-Dixie Supermarket #1437 on South Claiborne Avenue in New Orleans looks like a pretty standard inner-city grocery store. As you step through the automatic doors you enter a large, airy space flooded with fluorescent light, with signs shouting LOW PRICES and FRESH floating in midair. Walk past the battery of checkout stations on the left and the liquor section on the right, and before you hit the aisles you spill out into the floor-display specials. The most imposing is a stack of 12-packs of Coca-Cola Classic a yard high with a footprint the size of a cement truck. It being almost football bowl season, just beyond the Coke is a forklift-load of 6-packs of Heineken and a few refrigerator-size racks of chips, flanked by a six-foot yellow plastic goalpost, two giant vinyl inflated footballs, and a larger-than-life-size poster of a happy family on recliners snacking and drinking. Navigating past the specials, you pass a modest produce corner, with a few green-painted shelves and scattered islands of sweet potatoes and tomatoes. Behind the produce corner and taking up more space are the salty-snack aisles—four rows of forty-foot stretches of potato chips, cheese puffs, tortilla chips, and pretzels.

Next you enter the land of soft drinks. One side of one fifty-foot aisle is nothing but Coca-Cola products: Coke Classic, Vanilla Coke, Sprite, Fresca, Diet Coke, Dr. Pepper, and a few other siblings. Coke Classic here appears in 6-packs or 12-packs of 12-ounce cans and also in 2-liter bottles. The rows of the tall red bottles, standing at attention at eye level, look like sentries at Buckingham palace—*thirty-seven bottles wide,* two shelves high.

But there's more. The ends of the aisles in this region of the store are also stacked pyramids of Coke products. Round the end of the Coke aisle, making inroads into PepsiCo's territory, are rows of 3-liter bottles of Coke Classic (labeled with "50% more than 2-liter bottles!"). The rest of this fifty-foot aisle is nothing but Pepsi and its littermates, still another fifty-foot aisle is chock-full of knockoffs under the Chek label (Winn-Dixie's soda brand), and a fourth aisle is more soda pop of miscellaneous brands.

If you still have space in your cart after wading through these sections, you get to the rest of the groceries. You traverse some twenty aisles of salad dressings, breakfast cereal, cat litter, baked beans, soap powder, cake mixes, paper towels, frozen pizza, ice cream, and kitchen gadgets before you finally find the dairy section, maybe looking for that quart of milk you came for. As you round the end of the aisle your cart nearly crashes into yet another end-aisle display of Coke products. And rounding the second-to-last aisle, you come face to face with an end-aisle display of potato chips. Potato chips these days aren't a product. They are a whole genus with dozens of species. This rack has Thin & Crispy, Dip Style, Hot Flavored, Mesquite Dip, Dill Pickle, BBQ, and Sour Cream & Onion. On a thin shelf just below eye level, sandwiched between the Dip Style and the Hot Flavored, are jars of salsa, with wide mouths for easy dipping.

What are these chips doing over by the yogurt and skim milk? Why do you confront Coke Classic in three different locations—before you even get to the miniature refrigerated case of 20-ounce bottles of Coke at the checkout line? And what possessed the store manager to waste nearly a football-field length of shelf space just for soda pop in the first place?

The grocery business is not an easy one to be in these days. Profit margins are slender and competition is brutal. Stores and chains are going under or being engulfed by bigger chains with more efficiency or more marketing power. Like a creature from a horror movie, the giant Wal-Mart is wreaking havoc in the sector, and store managers know when the behemoth arrives in town there may be no survivors. In this jungle, any store manager who wastes anything doesn't hold his job for long.

And a manager's most precious resource is shelf space. The food industry today churns out about a hundred thousand "stock-keeping units" —unique items of a specific size—but a typical store can only handle about thirty thousand, so even deciding which ones to stock at all is a gamble.[1] Then an even bigger challenge in the survival game is allotting space among these thirty thousand items.

For a popular product like Coke Classic, the worst thing a manager can do is have a "stock-out"—an empty shelf because customers bought it faster than it could be replaced. But two shelves of thirty-seven columns each of 2-liter bottles Coke Classic, on top (literally) of two more shelves of 6- and 12-packs, in addition to the massive floor display, the end-aisle pyramids, and the one-for-the-road bottles in the checkout line can't possibly be just banking for a run on Coke. There must be a solid business reason for such a colossal waste of prime real estate.

And indeed there is. Grocery shopping is not something we humans plan very well. Think of it more as a modern-day analogue of gathering roots, leaves, and berries. People grab what is available. Depending on how you ask the question, shoppers will admit on surveys that they choose 30 percent to 50 percent of what's in their cart on impulse.[2] And a pair of marketing researchers studying 4,200 grocery store shoppers in fourteen cities found that people were even more impulsive than they are willing to admit: they had no intention of buying 59 percent of their purchases when they entered the store.[3] The pattern held for every age, gender, household size, and income. The researchers even delved into psychology and found that a shopper's personality type or how naturally impulsive he or she was didn't much matter. The factor that really mattered in determining the number of items shoppers bought on impulse was simply the number of aisles that people traversed in the store. In a comment that ought to make those of us who are proud of our self-control nervous, the researchers concluded, "This is good news for retailers and marketers, as shopping-trip-specific factors are much more under their control than are consumer-specific variables."

Most grocery shopping isn't rational, but it isn't exactly irrational either; it's a numbers game. The more frequently people bump into products in the store, the more likely they are to buy them. This "bump-into" factor is huge. Marketing studies show that on average, doubling the shelf space will increase sales by about 40 percent,[4] but it can be more: one study found that in high-volume stores, each additional "facing" (row of the product displayed on the shelf) meant a rise in sales of about of 60 percent.[5] The location of the shelf space is even more important. People grab items at eye level at three times the rate of the same items on the second shelf from the bottom.[6] Grocers can increase sales from two- to five-fold with a big end-aisle display.[7] Very little impulsive buying is "brand switching," so these extra sales mean people are buying categories of food they would otherwise not have purchased.[8]

This is old news to retailers. For decades they have followed the rule of thumb that share of shelf space equals share of sales. So a store manager who wants to maximize profits knows instinctively to assign more shelf space to items for which he has a higher profit margin. Over time, marketing researchers have distilled these instincts into sophisticated mathematical formulas that guide managers as to exactly how many "facings" each product deserves. Which explains why this store is a virtual obstacle course constructed with Coke. It is a high-profit product, and Winn-Dixie gets more profit per foot of shelf space with that than anything else the store manager could put there. And it also explains why potato chips have infiltrated the dairy section, because compared to milk (which spoils quickly), potato chips also have a high profit margin and are a great impulse purchase.

Of course just because we buy junk food doesn't mean we have to eat it all. But our biologic systems aren't designed to tell us when to turn down food that's right in front of us, because throughout evolution our ancestors frequently had to survive famine but almost never suffered through overabundance. Nutritionists have shown that when people are given extrasized portions of macaroni and cheese, they just eat more, without noticing that they are eating more, without taking any longer to eat it, and without feeling any more full afterwards.[9] They manage to pack it away by taking the same number of bites, but getting more food in each bite. The automatic nature of eating points a finger at "supersizing" at fast-food restaurants as a major contributor to the obesity epidemic.

So when we pick up food on impulse at the grocery store, we eat it. When a store manager doubles sales of a high-profit product by, say, tripling the facings, stacking a big end-aisle display, or moving it from the bottom shelf to eye level, as a group we consume much more of that product. If that product also happens to be bad for us—like Coke or potato chips—his reallocation of shelf space just made us unhealthier.

Conspicuous consumption

The influence of shelf space is just a small-scale example of a much larger effect—one that is so simple that it is easy to forget. The more available and more accessible any consumer product is, the more we use it. Of course at the one extreme, if we can't find a product at all, we can't use it. And if a product is in easy reach everywhere, not only are we more likely to use it at all, but also if we are already using it we tend to use it more often. Supply doesn't only meet demand; supply stimulates demand. The demand it stimulates may be "impulsive demand," but it means sales (and consumption) regardless. That's not to say that supply *determines* demand. People do not have to consume products that are widely available; no one straps us down and shoves snack foods down our throats. But when products fill a basic biologic need (for example, to consume calories) or are tempting in other ways (for example, alcohol) we can be enticed to grab them whether we believe they are good for us or not. This effect matters so much to our health because whether or not we succumb to our modern killers depends to such a great extent on the items we *consume*—particularly tobacco, alcohol, high-fat foods, and fruits and vegetables. Regardless of whether the items are inherently healthy or unhealthy, the accessibility effect works.

Maybe it isn't surprising that people will use more of something if they find it everywhere than if they have to work very hard to find it. But what is astounding is how important are the *small* gradations in accessibility to what we buy and consume. Health educators feel pretty satisfied if, with great effort, they persuade individual people to change their behavior by 10 or 20 percent. It's a little frightening that store owners can double the consumption of something just by adding a couple of more rows on the shelf, moving it to eye level, or putting in on the end of an aisle.

Some time ago we were curious about what foods were on display in New Orleans, so we sent students out with measuring wheels to a group of supermarkets. At one particular store, which serves mainly poor black people, by our measures 17 percent of the entire store shelf space—not even counting the displays by the cash registers—was stocked with snack foods like chips, cookies, and candy (not including sodas). About two miles away, at another branch of the same store chain, this one serving more middle-income white people, these snack foods filled up only 11 percent of the shelf space, or about a 50 percent smaller share of the store's shelf space.[10] It makes you wonder how much store displays contribute to the high obesity rates in poor black people.

But shelf space accessibility is also a potentially powerful tool that those of us working in health have overlooked. For example, one marketing study, buried in a business journal for the last thirty years, showed that by doubling the shelf space in the produce section, store managers could increase sales of lettuce and tomatoes by 28 percent, apples and oranges by 44 percent, and squash and eggplant by 59 percent.[11] Right now only about one in four Americans eats the recommended five servings a day of fruits and vegetables, and they are eating less all the time. With shelf space so influential in what we eat, and what we eat so important to modern diseases, the market researchers may have stumbled across solutions to some of the most important health problems of our time.

Convenient consumption

If shelf space makes such a big difference in what we buy, you would expect that the *number* of locations that sell a product in a neighborhood or a town might matter too. Partly, this is because it is much more convenient to pick up something if you find it at a store you visit every day than to make a special trip across town. But also, if you bump into that product in every store you visit, you are more likely to accept that this product is normal— what everyone else is eating or drinking—which may make you see nothing wrong with picking it up on impulse, whether it is healthy or not.

A colleague of ours named Richard Scribner conducted a whole series of studies of the health effects of neighborhoods' "density" of alcohol outlets (bars, liquor stores, and grocery stores selling alcohol). When people are drunk, they are more clumsy, hot-tempered, violent, and foolish, so you might expect more injuries, violence, risky sex, and sexually transmitted diseases in neighborhoods with bars and liquor stores on every corner. Poor neighborhoods usually have more alcohol outlets (partly because their citizens are less able to block them through local politics), and also tend to have more car crashes, violence, and sexually transmitted diseases, but Scribner showed that even after taking into account socioeconomic differences such as income, race, and unemployment, the neighborhoods with more bars and liquor stores per square mile had higher rates of these three problems.[12] The differences were big enough to stir interest by police chiefs and health departments. For example, in Los Angeles County he found that one extra liquor store in a neighborhood translated into 3.4 additional assaults in a year, and in New Orleans he found that a 10 percent increase in alcohol outlets meant a 6 percent increase in the rate of gonorrhea.[13]

These kinds of cross-sectional studies by themselves can't prove that the greater alcohol accessibility caused these health problems. Maybe more heavy drinkers just live in these neighborhoods, keeping liquor stores in business, and maybe if the liquor stores weren't there they would drink just as much, with the same nasty consequences. But other studies suggest that the supply of alcohol by itself is partly to blame. In one five-year, three-city trial in which community organizers shuttered liquor stores and pushed for stronger enforcement of bans on sales of alcohol to teens, people reported on surveys that they were much less likely to drink and drive, police recorded lower rates of nighttime car crashes, and hospital emergency rooms treated fewer people for assaults.[14] And in a study we are working on as we write this, Los Angeles County neighborhoods that were decimated in the Rodney King riots and that blocked burned-out liquor stores from reopening afterwards had larger declines in rates of gonorrhea than similar neighborhoods in which the stores started selling liquor again.

We haven't seen similar studies on the effect of the number of outlets for healthy and unhealthy food on what we eat and our health, but it is not much of a stretch to think that the pattern holds. For example, in Japan, where the foods available are low in fat, people have diets low in fat and have lower rates of heart disease than people in the United States. Among Japanese who have immigrated to the U.S., where we practically trip over high-fat foods, heart disease rates are nearly three times higher, approaching those of white Americans who were born here.[15] It is easy to trace this effect in the Japanese immigrants, but there is nothing special about the Japanese. Exposure to high-fat foods affects us all.

Healthy consumption

Accessibility means more than just shelf space and the number of stores per square mile. The more you think about it, the more variations you can imagine on where, how, when, and to whom products are offered that can make big differences in whether we buy, eat, or use them. Products can be sold (or banned from being sold) through vending machines or near schools. Stores can display products on self-service shelves, as groceries do for food, or keep them behind a counter, as they do for cigarettes. Stores can have (or not have) drive-up windows. Retailers can sell products only during regular working hours or extend sales past midnight or even twenty-four hours a day. Sales can be restricted to adults over age eighteen or twenty-one.

We restrict sales in many ways right now, and people support these limits. In most places you can't sell cigarettes through vending machines. Throughout the United States, stores can't legally sell liquor to people under age twenty-one, and for good reason: when these laws have been enacted or enforced, fewer young people drink and fewer end their lives as crosses on the roadside.[16] When the number one killer of young adults is car crashes, there is probably no worse idea than sales of alcohol through drive-up windows, so they are banned in many areas.

And people generally support limits on the hours in which businesses can sell alcohol. Most places have closing-time ordinances for bars, and some states still have "blue laws" that prevent sales of alcohol on Sundays. We can ban late-night sales of alcohol from stores. The alcohol industry itself is making the case that time-of-sale restrictions make a difference to our drinking habits: on the Web site of the Distilled Spirits Council of the United States (www.discus.org), they argue that people are more likely to buy on impulse on the weekends, and "[b]y limiting spirits sales to Saturdays only, the amount of impulse-susceptible exposure time distilled spirits customers have is cut in half. . . . By opening on Sundays sales volume will increase. This increased volume would translate into additional profits for the state's liquor business."

When one of our nation's major killers is shootings (self-inflicted or one against another), even the most fervent gun enthusiasts accept some restrictions on gun sales, such as banning sales to minors. Overwhelmed by our modern epidemic of obesity, cities are expelling junk-food vending machines from schools, and employers that cover health insurance could make a strong case for banishing them from workplaces also.

Using accessibility to promote health doesn't always involve restrictions. Back in the mid 1990s we tried to slow the AIDS epidemic in Louisiana by expanding access to a consumer product. At the time HIV was seeping into minority heterosexual networks, following in the footsteps of syphilis and gonorrhea, and people in these networks having casual sex were using condoms only about half the time. Everyone around the United States working in HIV prevention was trying to persuade people with multiple sex partners to use condoms more often, mostly by counseling them one-to-one when they took an HIV test. Few HIV experts spent much time wondering where high-risk people would get the condoms, but those who did apparently were satisfied that people could buy condoms at any drug store. Instead, we focused on the condoms themselves, buying them wholesale by the truckload—peaking at over 13 million condoms a year—and asking workers to leave them in bowls, free for the taking, not only in the usual places such as gay bars and public clinics, but also on the counters of small stores in neighborhoods in which we had mapped out high rates of sexually transmitted diseases. To check how the program was working, one day we stopped into a liquor store in Baton Rouge and asked the owner about what usually happened to the brightly colored condoms in the plastic fishbowl on his counter. Oh yes, he told us, the prostitutes working the strip outside his shop stopped by every night and picked them up. They weren't greedy—they would grab one or two, disappear for an hour or so, then come back for a couple more. We evaluated the program by giving anonymous surveys to women in the waiting rooms of public clinics and to men whom we stopped on the street, asking them whether a condom was used the last time they had sex. In the two years after the program began, condom use rose from 40 percent to 54 percent in men and from 30 percent to 48 percent in high-risk women.[17]

Increasing access to healthy products can also have important indirect effects. Storeowners have limited shelf space; people have limited budgets, limited time during the day, and a limited number of calories that they can consume. If people are "consuming" more healthy things they may be less likely to consume unhealthy ones. If someone fills up on fresh fruits and vegetables she may just take a pass on the next bag of potato chips she sees. The *relative* accessibility of a product may be nearly as important as the absolute accessibility, so we may be able to become healthier solely by expanding access to healthy things, without cutting back on the accessibility of anything else.

Elastic consumption

Economists would have a tough time explaining why doubling the amount of shelf space for vegetables makes people buy more. It takes absolutely no more time or effort to reach for an eggplant displayed on two feet of shelf space than four. The rules of these impulsive purchases are, as one other economist calls them, "uneconomic," or as another put it, "quasi-rational." But there is another aspect to accessibility that economists would have no trouble understanding, even if the rest of us sometimes do—the effect of price.

Central to economists' worldview is that people have set preferences for certain things, and the lower the price of those things, the more likely they are to act on those preferences by buying them. Lower prices of a product mean not only that more people will buy any, but also that some people will buy more. Economists boil down this relationship to a single number called the "price elasticity of demand," meaning the percentage increase in products sold for a given percentage decrease in price.

Everything people want—no matter how healthy or harmful—has a price elasticity. Most of us understand that we are more likely to buy a car priced at $20,000 than at $25,000, but many of us haven't stopped to think that we are also more likely to buy a candy bar at 20 cents than at 25 cents, a bunch of celery for $1 than for $1.25, or a pack of cigarettes at $3 than at $3.75. And sometimes we buy more of something that has a lower unit cost, for example picking up a 24-ounce bag of potato chips for $3.49 instead of a 12-ounce bag for $2.99, even if we might originally only have wanted the small bag. Just as with shelf space or outlet density, small changes in price can make big differences.

If there were any product you might expect *not* to have an elasticity, it would be an addictive drug. Wouldn't addicts desperate to supply their habit bear any cost to get it, and wouldn't the rest of us reject it at any price? But the highly addictive drug nicotine *is* elastic. Based on what happened after rises in cigarette taxes in the last thirty years, economists' estimates of the price elasticity of cigarettes run between −0.3 and −0.5. That is, a 10 percent rise in the price of a pack of cigarettes leads to a 3 to 5 percent fall in cigarettes smoked.[18] Teenagers, who have less cash, cut back even more, maybe 7 to 8 percent.[19] Some of this shrinking of demand represents nonsmokers never starting, some smokers smoking less, and some smokers quitting altogether. Tobacco is so poisonous that the impact on our health of just a few percentage points is huge: after California raised its cigarette taxes by just 25 cents in 1989, smoking fell by 5 to 7 percent,[20] slicing the incidence of lung cancer by nearly 20 percent in the next decade and preventing tens of thousands of people from dying from heart disease.[21]

Alcohol—another addictive drug—has an elasticity that varies with the type of drink. It's about −0.3 for beer, −1.0 for wine, and −1.5 for hard liquor.[22] After studying the effect of past alcohol tax increases, economists figure that raising its price by 10 percent (adding about 45 cents to a 6-pack of beer) cuts beer drinking by about 3 percent. Occasional drinkers as a group probably cut back a little more than that, heavy drinkers a little less, but the results are still impressive. A price rise of that size drops rates of drinking and driving by about 8 percent (maybe twice that in teens), lowers deaths from car crashes, reduces deaths from liver cirrhosis by about 10 percent, and even cuts rates of gonorrhea by more than 9 percent. One pair of researchers even found that a 10 percent increase in the beer tax (less than a nickel per 6-pack) cuts violent child abuse by 2 percent.[23]

With a tidal wave of obesity flooding America, some health advocates want to use the same idea by taxing snack food. If the principle works for addictive drugs like tobacco and alcohol, it surely ought to work for junk food. The idea of a "Twinkie" tax has met with outrage in some parts (particularly the food industry), but not only would it be effective, it also isn't that different from where we are right now. Many states and cities have sales taxes that apply differently to different items, and many already specially tax sodas and candy.[24]

Like accessibility, price changes work in both directions, so rather than raising prices of unhealthy food, we could cut prices of healthy, low-calorie foods, particularly fruits and vegetables. Fresh vegetables may seem cheap enough that a price cut wouldn't make a difference, but one study found that a 10 percent cut in prices led to an average of about a 10 percent increase in sales.[25] Other studies have shown that reducing the prices of low-fat foods in vending machines by 10 percent increases sales by about 10 percent,[26] and that marking down the menu prices of salads in restaurants by about 25 percent caused a doubling of sales.[27]

We (the authors) learned a painful lesson about price in the Louisiana HIV prevention project. Our initial success in getting people to use condoms was based not only on expanding the accessibility of condoms, but also on eliminating the price altogether. For a short time when our budget was tight, we tried to recoup some of our costs of these millions of condoms through sales. After people told us on surveys that they would gladly pay up to 25 cents for a condom, we sold condoms to some stores at our cost (7 cents) and asked them to start charging a quarter a piece, allowing them to keep the difference. The result was disastrous. Immediately after the price change, the number of condoms distributed by those stores plummeted 98 percent and the percent of store customers using condoms dropped from 77 percent to 64 percent.[28] The paltry returns we got from the sales clearly weren't worth it, so we went back to giving the condoms away again, and condom use magically bounced back up. The lesson: during an epidemic of an incurable, fatal, sexually transmitted disease, the right price for condoms is zero.

The big deal about small changes

For many decades, the sermons of those of us in public health have revolved around simple messages: don't smoke, don't drink, don't eat saturated fats, but do eat fruits and vegetables. During that time we have mostly ignored the fact that these behaviors involved *consuming* things. Meanwhile, convenience stores, fast-food restaurants, and vending machines have been creeping everywhere into our daily lives, so we trip over the things we are supposed to avoid and sometimes have trouble finding the ones we are supposed to use.

We learned from Prohibition about the unintended consequences of a complete ban on items that are harmful but popular. Maybe because we feel burned by that history we have been leery of even contemplating solutions to our health problems that involve tinkering with the supply side. It is finally dawning on us, though, that there are many things we can do short of banning unhealthy things that still can make a big difference in our behavior, a bigger difference, in fact, than we can make by educating ourselves or others. Nothing that we contemplate would stop anyone who wanted one from buying a beer, a steak, a bag of chips, or a pack of cigarettes—in fact, nothing would prevent anyone from getting them easily. Even within that limit, though, minor changes we can make in the number of places that sell certain products, the way they are sold, the times they are sold, or the price at which they are sold can profoundly change the mix of products we consume and can go a long way toward keeping us healthier.

CHAPTER 6

Sidewalks *and*
Falling Children:
Physical Structures

In the long, hot summer of 1967, workers in the Bureau of Health Statistics in New York became alarmed about a wave of children plunging through the air to their deaths. New York had always seen tragic deaths from falls from apartment building windows, mostly in curious preschoolers whose parents lost track of them for a moment, but in this sweltering summer as more parents left more windows open longer, the numbers of children smashed on the sidewalks hit a new peak. One patrolman later said dozens of children fell in his precinct every summer, and that he had personally picked up nine dead children in just one season.[1] By the time the annual statistics were compiled for 1967, sixty-one children had died from falls out of buildings, enough to account for one fourth of all injury deaths in children under age five.[2] And the distressed workers even found that some apartments showed up more than once in their falling children list.

The Health Department then asked hospital staff in the worst-affected borough, the Bronx, to start notifying them of all plunging children, and afterwards sent social workers to their families' apartments to investigate. In their summary report the typical child's family was poor, receiving a welfare check of $50 to $75 a month to support four or more children, and living in "a four- or five-room walk-up apartment [in a tenement, with]. many holes in the ceilings and walls, loose parts in the floor, broken windows, plumbing leaks, inadequate lighting, rats and other vermin."[3] The toddler—usually a rough-and-tumble boy—had climbed on a fire escape or near an open window and taken one clumsy step too many.

But the cause of the problem wasn't poverty and it wasn't just boys being boys. Children just as poor and just as curious who lived in the public housing projects in the Bronx at the same time weren't diving to their deaths. So Health Department investigators also visited the housing projects and found the obvious differences: instead of double-sash windows, casement windows that hinged on the side and didn't open enough to fit toddlers easily, and instead of external fire escapes, internal fireproofing. The cause of the problem was the design of the buildings.

After an initial program to educate parents about the problem, the Health Department got a little more practical. They helped design simple window guards just for the sort of tenement windows through which children were falling. Then they put out to bid the job of manufacturing them, which brought the price down to about $3 each, and bought over 16,000 a year, giving them to 4,200 families living in high-risk buildings.[4] They installed some and let families install others, later inspecting them to be sure they were installed correctly. Within two years, the Children Can't Fly program cut the number of children dropping to their deaths in the Bronx by half.[5] Then in 1976 they went further, persuading the Board of Health to pass a law requiring landlords citywide to install window guards in all apartments with small children.[6] The number of children falling in Harlem immediately dropped 96 percent.[7] Three-dollar window guards don't carry the same drama and excitement as open-heart surgery, but they can be a lot more effective in saving lives.

We spend our lives interacting with physical structures—not just windows and window guards, but also roads, cars, stairs, chairs, soda bottles, and candy wrappers—that shape how we behave, how healthy we are, and at times whether we live or die. Some influences in our modern man-made world are so hidden that we don't notice them, but for physical structures it is often just the opposite: because they are in plain view, all the time, we don't recognize how important they can be. There are three general ways that physical structures can shape our behavior and our health: by making it easier or harder to do certain things, by changing how we interact with each other, and by providing cues on how we should behave.

The path of least resistance

Like window guards, physical structures can affect how we behave by just making it harder to do dangerous things. With injuries among the major killers of our era, these "safety" features are among the most important health devices around.

A great example is that everyday-life annoyance, the childproof cap. In the late 1950s and 1960s, some 500 small children a year managed to open a bottle of pills, household cleanser, or cockroach poison and swallow enough to kill themselves.[8] Aspirin, the biggest culprit among medicines, killed 120 children a year alone.[9] Hundreds of thousands more children swallowed enough of some poison to need medical help but not enough to die. Then in 1970 Congress passed the Poison Prevention Packaging Act, which forced manufacturers to put these dangerous drugs and chemicals in bottles that were "difficult for children under age five years to open."[10] The childproof caps did exactly what Congress wanted: between 1973 and 1978 accidental poisonings in children plummeted 40 percent.[11]

Every day we see other safety devices that make it harder to do something dangerous. Left-turn lanes and guardrails make it more difficult to crash a car, and seat belts and air bags protect us if we do crash. Fences around swimming pools make it more difficult for our toddlers to drown, and automatic off switches on heavy machinery make it harder to crush or impale ourselves.

But physical structures can change our health in more ways than by putting obstacles between ourselves and bodily harm. Some physical features of objects shape our health by making it easier to do things. Some of these we can't even see, such as the chemical makeup of what we drink, eat, or breathe, which change our health without our having to plan or do anything.

One of the most successful steps in public health in the last century has been the fluoridation of drinking water. Dental and medical studies completed by 1942 had shown that kids drinking water that naturally contained fluoride had almost no dental cavities. Grand Rapids became the first city to test the idea that adding fluoride to water could have the same benefit without any damaging effects.[12] The demonstration project reduced cavities, and in spite of the bizarre reaction in some parts of the country that fluoridation was a Communist plot, by the time it ended in 1959, around 40 million people in some two thousand communities already were drinking water with optimal fluoride levels.[13] Cavities haven't disappeared in the United States, but because of fluoridation they are a tiny fraction of what they would be. Following that example, we have added iodine to salt to prevent goiter and vitamin D to milk to prevent rickets. More recently, health experts in Australia have fortified bread flour with thiamine and successfully cut rates of Wernicke-Korsakoff syndrome, a form of brain damage that happens to heavy drinkers who don't eat well.[14]

We can't see fluoride. Physical structures that we *can* see but that we often don't appreciate are the humble structures like sidewalks that make it easier to walk. We all tend to take the path of least resistance (literally), walking when it is easy and driving when it isn't. This influences not just how we get a carton of milk, but also how healthy we are. For example, compared to people in San Diego living in "low-walkability" neighborhoods, people living in "high-walkability" neighborhoods with sidewalks walked more for errands and put in about 50 percent more "moderate intensity" and nearly three times as much "vigorous intensity" physical activity—enough to keep off nearly four pounds of fat every year.[15] Over the entire nation this can make a big difference. People who live in "sprawling" counties, with scarce sidewalks and large distances between homes and stores, are more obese and have higher rates of hypertension.[16] Because they have to drive more, people in sprawling counties are also more often killed in car crashes.[17] In fact, more people in the suburbs are killed in car crashes than people in the city are killed in violent crimes.[18] It should make us think twice about buying a house in a swanky neighborhood without sidewalks.

To help us be healthier, public health experts try to make the healthiest actions the path of least resistance. But they are not the only ones using this approach. In recent years, food companies have been increasingly creative about designing food and the packaging around them to make foods convenient, that is, easy to store, carry, and eat—anywhere, anytime, while doing anything. In fact, convenience often beats taste as a food's main selling point. You now can get Squeeze-n-Go Portable Pudding in a plastic tube, which you don't have to refrigerate and which you can eat without a spoon. You can get Go Snacks, which are Doritos and Cheetos in plastic resealable canisters that fit in backpacks or car cup holders, and for which the chips are made "smaller, so consumers can chug them."[19] The slogan of Frito-Lay, which makes the snacks, is "Go anywhere but hungry."[20] You can get not only the staple of kids' school lunches—granola bars—but also handheld breakfast burritos, yogurt you can sip through a straw or slurp with an edible spoon, and gummy bears in a chug-a-lug go cup. The sales of these on-the-go snack foods are "meteoric" according to an industry analyst, up 19 percent just from 2001 to 2002.[21] And they have an impact: in the 1990s Americans took in 200 calories per day more than they did in the 1970s, and *all* of that increase was from snacks.[22] Looking at this data, a group of economists from Harvard has made the logical conclusion that the surge in snacking is entirely to blame for the obesity epidemic (and by extension, the epidemic of diabetes) in the last twenty-five years.[23] The next time you scan the snacks in a convenience store, think about how something as mundane as the packaging can change what we do, how we live, and whether we get sick.

In aging cores of U.S. cities, another type of physical structure has been the gnawing problem that everyone hates but no one seems to be able to solve: abandoned buildings. The flight of the upper and middle class from inner cities in the last half of the 1900s left cities with many more buildings than people to occupy them—or at least more than people had the money to repair. The result is urban blight: rows of decrepit houses whose owners are unknown, too poor to repair them, or too distant to care, in numbers far greater than a starved city bureaucracy could manage. If you want to sell drugs, set up a "shooting gallery" or crack house to use them, or sell sex to get drugs, these buildings are the perfect place to do it: near potential customers, easily accessible, yet hidden from police or concerned neighbors. That may explain why in studies that we published, neighborhoods and cities with more abandoned housing had higher rates of gonorrhea and homicide, even after taking into account other social factors like poverty, education, racial makeup, and neighborhood stability.[24] By making it easier to do something, physical structures make people more likely to do it—good or bad.

Getting to know you

For decades a little-known group of researchers have made academic careers of thinking about how the physical environment shapes the ways we humans treat each other. Environmental psychologists study how people respond to different physical situations, either created in a laboratory or existing in the real world. The group that laid the groundwork for this discipline carried on what may be the longest-running series of experiments in science, the twenty-five-year Midwest Psychological Field Station in the tiny town of Oskaloosa, Kansas. There, psychologists spent countless hours, with increasingly sophisticated and scientific techniques, just watching humans (particularly a group of about a hundred children) in their native habitats. Early on, they were impressed that individual people behaved differently if they were on the sidewalk, in the grocery store, at the drug store counter, at the bank, in the café, in the post office, or in the school classrooms. As the years wore on, the appreciation of the critical effect of the settings on the way people behaved grew. Summing up at the end of his career, one of the lead researchers said, "Two children in the same place behaved more similarly than one child in two places."[25]

Everything about a physical environment colors how people act toward each other. Temperature, light, noise, odors, the shape of a room, crowding, and the objects at hand—each can make us more or less likely to engage in any specific action toward those objects or toward other people. For example, men who are crowded together become more aggressive (giving harsher sentences in a simulated jury situation), but women who are crowded become more friendly.[26] One researcher showed that he could increase the amount of time nursing home residents spent talking to each other just by rearranging the furniture so that chairs faced each other.[27]

Sometimes the power of the effects can be disconcerting. One research group decided to test the effect of light and anonymity on the interactions of young adults. A control group of four male and four female strangers who were told they would never see each other again was left in a plain room for an hour. They just talked politely. Then an experimental group of the same size and gender mix was put into the same room—except it was pitch black. These young people literally reached out to each other in completely unexpected ways. Eighty percent touched another person purposely and more than half hugged another. On questionnaires later, several reported kissing others and more than 80 percent said they felt sexually aroused. The researchers concluded that "with the simple subtraction of light, a group of perfect strangers moved within approximately 30 minutes to a stage of intimacy often not attained in years of normal acquaintanceship."[28]

Humans are territorial animals, and having established their territory (in their homes, in their offices, or even at a table in the public library), they will defend it. A housing architect named Oscar Newman has shown repeatedly that by redesigning public housing projects he could use this effect to reduce crime.[29] To Newman, public spaces in these projects that belong to no one make it easier to commit crimes, from teenagers harassing other children or the elderly to drug dealers scaring up new customers. The typical nightmarish public housing projects in most American cities are big high-rises with just these no-man's-lands both inside (large interior hallways) and outside (open areas between buildings). Because no responsible adults can claim these areas as their territory, they become free-fire zones for gangs. High-rises for wealthier people don't have the same problems in part because the teens are more likely to be supervised by two parents, but also because the tenants pay for doormen, bellhops, and superintendents to guard the open spaces and chase off those who don't belong. Newman's "defensible space" solution is to mark internal boundaries and assign most of the public space to individual or small groups of residents, keeping what is left of public spaces in close view of the assigned territories. This means such things as building fences around the yards of townhouse-style projects so people have front and back yards that they can call their own, or building gates across streets to eliminate through-traffic and give residents in deteriorating neighborhoods a sense of ownership. In his examples, poor people having their own private spaces not only maintain them, improving them with prettier fences, better lawns, and gardens, but also start taking some responsibility for the public streets and sidewalks just outside their yards, picking up trash, sweeping the sidewalks, and challenging outsiders that look suspicious. Newman's designs did more than turn tenants into gardeners. They cut crime rates and made the entire area safer, *without* displacing the crime to surrounding areas. That is, they didn't just move unhealthy behavior around, they reduced it.[30]

Oscar Newman's housing projects are part of a larger movement called Crime Prevention Though Environmental Design. A group of criminologists came up with the idea that crime is often opportunistic—it happens where it is tempting and easy. Rather than trying to rehabilitate or incarcerate criminals, CPTED revamps the places where crime occurs. It redesigns buildings, grounds, and streets to mark territory, obstruct access and escape routes, and eliminate blind spots. And it works: for example, city planners in Sarasota, Florida, cut crime rates by about one half in a rundown highway strip by changing the zoning to promote landscaping that "demonstrated ownership," installing better lighting of parking lots and walkways, and encouraging the building of porches, balconies, and apartments above retail stores to increase the number of "eyes on the street."[31]

People need privacy, but they also need each other. The best building designs have not only private territory but also semiprivate common spaces where people can get to know each other. Sidewalks in front of homes, entryways serving a small number of apartments, porches, and benches let people meet each other gradually over time. When they can be viewed from people's homes, people will take some control of these spaces and keep them safe. Over time they become familiar with others in their neighborhood and tend to develop friendships. Studies have shown that people living near semiprivate common areas like this have wider networks of friends.[32]

What does all this have to do with our health? Plenty.

When health experts who are trying to get people to exercise ask them why they don't walk or jog in the neighborhoods, one of the most common answers is that people are afraid to be outdoors. The fear might be just of rowdy teens or strangers, or of genuine street gangs, or it might be a vague and seemingly irrational anxiety about being exposed in a public space. Regardless, it traps them indoors. Today it happens not just in cities but also in the wealthiest suburbs. But people trapped in their houses are taking risks to their health that they rarely think about. Because they are physically inactive indoors and the kitchen is close at hand, they are much more likely to become fat and develop hypertension and heart disease. Hunkering indoors also is likely to increase their risk of another modern epidemic, asthma. As much as we fear air pollution, the stuff we inhale indoors such as dust, dust mites, cockroach allergens, and the vapors from paints and various household chemicals may damage our airways much more than what we inhale outdoors.

As social animals, we are also psychologically damaged by isolation from other people, and this hurts our physical health. People living alone have higher risk of suicide.[33] People who have lost a spouse often become ill and die shortly after they are left alone.[34] And as we will discuss more in the next chapter, a whole series of studies has shown that people who have more social support from relatives, friends, clubs, and church live longer and healthier.[35] Fear of crime and fear of each other seems to be rampant in America these days. Anything (like actual crime) that stokes this fear is likely to make us sick, while any changes to our physical environment that reduce crime, ease our fears, encourage us to go outdoors, and bring us together with our neighbors will tend to keep us healthy.

Broken windows and other cues

The third way that physical structures can influence our behavior is by laying out visual cues about how we should behave.

Some cues are pretty obvious. Ashtrays on tables let you know that smoking is acceptable, and Coca-Cola signs remind people to drink Coke (which is why they are there). But some are less obvious.

Think about the last time you walked into a bank. The scene was probably pretty formal: the tellers dressed conservatively, speaking little and speaking quietly, and smiling only occasionally. You probably also kept still and spoke in a formal, hushed voice. Compare that to the last time you went into a bar or nightclub. The scene was probably just the opposite, with people shouting or laughing out loud, and you were probably just as rowdy. The difference between the two settings is not just the background noise or the alcohol, it is also the visual markers. Banks are designed to impress us as formidable and trustworthy—a safe place to store our money—with bright lighting, large open spaces, formal paintings and drapery, and barriers like desks and counters between us and the staff. Bars are designed to loosen us up, with dim lights, deliberately cramped and cluttered spaces, odd knickknacks everywhere, and casually dressed bartenders and waitresses. These cues work. Can you imagine someone singing along out loud with the background music in a *bank*?

Neighborhoods send cues about how to behave, too. In the 1990s a new approach to crime prevention took hold based on restoring order in communities—or what has been called fixing "broken windows." Sociologist

James Q. Wilson and police expert George Kelling coined this term with an article in *The Atlantic Monthly,* writing that "social psychologists and police officers tend to agree that if a window in a building is broken *and is left unrepaired,* all the rest of the windows will soon be broken."[36] Wilson and Kelling were inspired from an eccentric "study" performed by Stanford psychologist Philip Zimbardo in the 1960s. He bought a car, parked it in the Bronx, removed the license plates, and propped the hood up, then watched it unobtrusively for sixty-four hours. Within the first ten minutes, a family of three "well-dressed, clean-cut whites" (father, mother, and eight-year-old son) calmly stole the battery and radiator. Within the next twenty-six hours, mostly in broad daylight, a steady parade of similarly ordinary-looking citizens had stripped the car of every usable part. For the following two days random groups of children and teenagers gleefully destroyed what was left, ripping off parts that remained and smashing the windows.[37]

Zimbardo's abandoned car and Wilson and Kelling's broken windows are cues that no one cares—about the car or about the whole neighborhood. These damaged objects are unwanted, belonging to no one. The rules we have been taught about respecting the property of others don't apply. Destroying it further, which after all can be a lot of fun, is fair game. People who ordinarily play life by the book vandalize, steal, and commit other crimes. In a neighborhood that starts getting destroyed in this way a cycle of abuse, fear, and neglect gets rolling. Litter on the streets attracts more litter, graffiti stimulates more graffiti. People seeing abandoned cars, graffiti, and trash are afraid and hide indoors. When the streets are empty of responsible adults, more buildings and streets are trashed. Teenagers, the only ones who are unafraid, take over the streets. Drug dealers find they can operate in relative safety. The people who move in or who stay in these neighborhoods adopt or learn to accept behavior that is corrosive for us individually or as a society, such as drug and heavy alcohol use, prostitution, and violence. In contrast, places that are kempt and beautiful send messages of caring. We assume that we will upset someone or something if we turn this order into disorder or beauty into ugliness. Just as people in a bank tread softly and lower their voices, people in orderly places tend to behave in an orderly manner.

The problems of drinking, drug use, and violence in America seem often overwhelming and intractable. There are many factors that play into these societal problems, surely plenty of which are beyond our control. But one factor that we haven't thought much about—and that we can do something about—is the physical environment around us and the messages it sends us.

CHAPTER 7

PLAYING *by the* RULES: SOCIAL STRUCTURES

In a New Orleans neighborhood near a bend in the Mississippi River, alongside the tracks of a lazy, early-twentieth-century streetcar, is the sort of quirky restaurant that makes the locals proud: a quick-order diner, complete with Formica countertops, round vinyl-covered stools screwed to the linoleum-tiled floor, and a menu that includes burgers, chili omelets, and cheesecake, but that is also upscale, with a maitre d', linen napkins, and waiters in bow ties and short white jackets. One evening in the early 1990s a regular beside us at the counter asked the waiter about the establishment's new no-smoking policy, a radical change in a city that usually views even small changes with moderate hostility. "I think it's a good idea," he said. "Why?" the regular asked. "Because I smoke," he told her. The waiter hurried on to serve other customers and didn't explain further, but he didn't have to. The no-smoking rule did what he wanted to do but couldn't do alone—cut down his smoking.

Rules. Your average American will tell you he can't stand them. Rules are what our immigrant parents or grandparents came to America to escape. Deep in our psyche, America represents freedom—freedom from rules. The most American of American icons—the western cowboy—relies only on his wiles, needs no one, and answers to no one; he draws his strength from a land without rules. Where there are rules, we chafe. Many baby boomers took (and some still take) great pride in breaking rules.

But in America we have plenty of rules, and we seem to draw up more all the time, because fundamentally we understand that our society needs them. We need rules to protect us from each other and to protect the rest of the planet from us. They shield the minority from the majority, the future from the past, and the good but gentle from the strong but cruel. We write them to stop something bad from happening again. When we write them we express what we want ourselves to be.

Governments, corporations, nonprofit organizations, and clubs all have their laws, regulations, bylaws, policies, and statements of principle. Even street gangs have rules. Organizations aim most of their rules at their own employees and members, but the larger the organizations, the more their rules ripple through our society. These rules and the organizations behind them are the social structures that mold the world we live in. If physical structures are the hardware, then social structures are the software of our daily lives. In more ways than we realize, rules and organizations create an invisible structure that profoundly shapes how we live our lives and how healthy we are.

The rules underneath other curve-shifters

Most rules that most organizations write, including the majority of rules that affect our health, don't impact us directly. Instead they change the features of our everyday world around us that we discuss in chapters 5, 6, and 8, that is, physical structures like stores, the stuff available in them, and the pictures and sounds we soak in through the media. These rules define, constrain, or promote actions of organizations, not individuals.

Rules hide behind nearly every feature of the physical world around us. Zoning rules define where McDonald's can plant a restaurant, and where a liquor store can sell its wares. Laws restrict when bars can sell booze and to whom, whether you have to ask the sales clerk to hand you the bottle of whiskey, and whether they can sell beer refrigerated. Taxes and subsidies alter the price of products in the stores and play into managers' decisions about whether to sell them at all. Federal laws force car manufacturers to install seat belts and air bags, and they command interstate highway planners to construct guardrails and breakaway light posts. Other federal laws define what chemicals water companies can allow in the water we drink from the tap. And, as we learned in the last chapter, sometimes local health regulations require landlords to install window guards to protect children in their apartments from plunging to their deaths.

The world of media images is just as riddled with rules. The Federal Communications Commission issues rules about what broadcasters can put on television. The Federal Trade Commission tells advertisers what they can't say in ads. The Food and Drug Administration tells drug companies what disclaimers have to appear in their commercials.

Rules set the standards for nearly everything in our world that has an impact on our health. Most of the other chapters in this book focus on how we can change our world so that we can be healthier, and in the end these changes nearly always happen because some organization changes its rules. In this chapter, though, we want to focus on the specialized rules that speak to us directly—rules that tell individuals what we should and shouldn't do—and on the organizations that make them.

Just don't do it

Because rule makers draw them up after a bad incident or a pack of complaints, most rules tell us what *not* to do. Don't walk on the grass, don't feed the elephants, don't take flash pictures at the concert, don't eat in the library, and don't play radios loudly on the subway. It seems every day we see more pictographs overlaid with red circles and diagonal slashes. Of course in telling us what *not* to do, rules indirectly say something about what *to* do, but their purpose is more to constrain than to guide.

In chapter 4 we said that few people stray from the midpoint of the behavior curve, and we said a few things about why. One of the reasons people linger near the center of the behavior curve is the explicit rules we lay down. They tell us not to go past a certain line for a certain behavior. And when that behavior has something to do with our health, the rules can make us healthy or sick.

Maybe the most telling example of how we react to rules is the history of seat belt laws. In the early 1980s, after years of state "buckle up" campaigns that people ignored, seat belt use nationally was an abysmal 14 percent.[1] The idea of *requiring* people to wear belts seemed ridiculous at first, because people had always had the option to use their seat belts, and the laws would be virtually unenforceable. But safety advocates were desperate, so in 1985 the New York State legislature passed America's first mandatory seat belt law. The effect was immediate and stunning: seat belt use by New York drivers sprang up from 21 percent to 47 percent and stayed there.[2] Other states took notice and passed their own laws, and in state after state with failed education programs, the simple passage of the laws made people miraculously start wearing their belts. It wasn't the fear of punishment that made people buckle up, because cops didn't (and in most states legally couldn't) pull people over for not wearing belts; it was the statement that the law represented. Buckling up was something people were *supposed to do*. It was expected, normal, what any regular person did. These laws by themselves save thousands of lives a year, which is not bad for just a few words on paper.

As lifesaving as they are, the seat belt laws didn't always get a smooth ride through state legislatures, because they bumped into arguments about freedom of choice. Of course it is stupid to drive without seat belts, some protested, but we have no right to force people to be smarter if the only ones they put at risk are themselves. In the end, the statistics on lives saved won the arguments, but the conviction that people should have the freedom to be stupid runs strong in our national mindset. Because of this, when we do write rules that restrict individuals, we usually rely on the argument that the rules are stopping people from hurting others. That is how health advocates sold indoor smoking bans: people who are smart enough to not smoke shouldn't have to damage their lungs by breathing the secondhand smoke of those who aren't. And sure enough, indoor smoking bans do protect nonsmokers from toxic secondhand smoke, but really, the greatest benefit to indoor smoking bans is to smokers. When they have to shiver outside in the cold to do it, smokers light up less often, but—more important—they are more likely to quit for good.[3]

For all the passionate arguments about our freedom, it might at first seem surprising that the New Orleans waiter—or any smoker, for that matter—liked the restaurant's smoking ban, but in fact he was far from alone. Across a group of surveys done when indoor smoking bans were set up in workplaces in the 1980s and early 1990s, depending on how the question was asked, between 20 percent and 80 percent of smokers supported the ban.[4] It is a fair assumption that they favored it because they wanted to quit or cut down but just couldn't without a social structure that forced them to. A preference for taking *away* options goes against all the principles that economists use to explain consumer behavior, but it is not particularly strange or uncommon. Like pushing a bowl of chips away at a table so that we don't eat too many; we often deliberately put up barriers to prevent ourselves from doing things that are instinctive but that we know we shouldn't do.

Whether we like them or not, rules can be amazingly effective. As much as we Americans feel we are renegades or lone wolves, most people obey most rules most of the time. There are plenty of exceptions, but most people don't litter, park in front of fire hydrants, run red lights (even when no one else is around), or talk loudly in the movie theater. But some rules are inconvenient enough that people obey them only when someone is enforcing them.

The history of seat belts also shows how rules and their enforcement work independently and together to change how we behave. Every state that passed a seat belt law saw an increase in seat belt use, but the laws vary in how police can use them.[5] In states with "secondary enforcement" laws, police cannot ticket someone for driving beltless unless the police stop him for another violation like an expired license plate or an illegal turn, so these laws work almost entirely through their symbolism. In states with "primary enforcement" laws, police can stop people solely to check if they are wearing belts. "Primary enforcement" states have seat belt use rates that are consistently higher (on average about 11 percentage points) than "secondary enforcement" states.[6] By themselves, the laws changed what most of us do when we get into a car; add enforcement and the change has been enough to propel seat belt use in the United States to an all-time high of 79 percent.[7]

Speed limits and their enforcement are other prime examples of rules that have enormous impacts on whether we live or die. Drivers on the freeway can easily gauge the average speeds of drivers around them; as a group they drift up to higher speeds until they spot cops pulling people over. Speed limits don't have much effect unless they are enforced, but when they are, people follow the rules and crash less often. After the gasoline shortage of 1973, when Congress adopted the national speed limit of 55 and state troopers enforced it, deaths on interstates dropped 32 percent.[8] Then in 1987, when Congress reversed itself and allowed states to raise their speed limits on rural interstates to 65, the rate of fatal crashes in the states that did so jumped by about 15 percent overall, doubling in some states.[9] When Congress gave up and repealed the national speed limit altogether in 1995, many states pushed up speed limits further, and deaths on their interstates jumped by another 17 percent, killing an extra five hundred or so people per year.[10]

One study found that raising the limits, by the way, did not just encourage a few lead-footed people to open the throttle. After the 1987 change, speeds rose in Washington State by about five miles per hour, but the variance in speeds didn't change at all. That is, the entire bell curve of car speed shifted upward. *Everyone* drove faster, including, presumably, drivers who were perfectly satisfied with the 55-mile-per-hour limit.[11] Even when people are hurtling down the interstate inside metal boxes, the social pressure to be like everyone else is compelling, inducing people to take potentially fatal risks that they wouldn't otherwise take.

Not all rules that affect us have to do with driving and not all are written by governments. General Motors, the New Orleans Public Schools, the Boy Scouts, the Franklin Avenue Baptist Church, and even neighborhood book clubs are organizations that make up and enforce rules about how people within them should behave. Workers for General Motors know that they have to come to work on time and sober. And they know if they follow these and other workplace rules, they can use employee policies to take family leave after they have a baby. These kind of rules help set the average behavior for punctuality, drinking, and caring for a newborn. Schoolteachers in New Orleans know they can't hit children or smoke on campus, and their students know they should "cooperate, be a good neighbor, respect authority" and stay away from alcohol, cigarettes, drugs, and sex. Boy Scouts know they should be trustworthy, obedient, clean, and reverent. Baptist parishioners know they shouldn't smoke or drink. Many people— particularly teenagers—don't follow these softer rules, but many do. Even more than commanding laws like those for seat belts, the rules made by these organizations define what we expect of each other. And by defining what we expect of each other, they help shape the behavior curve for their employees or members, and cumulatively they help shape the behavior curve for all of us.

Even more than the other factors in our group of four curve-shifters, the social structures around us are malleable. Rules are just written words —usually voted on by a group like a committee, board, or legislature—

that take on power because the groups publicly stand behind them. When it is clear that different rules would make us healthier, these groups can redraft the policies, alter the guidelines, rescind the old laws, or add new ones. The health-related rules that most organizations already have tend to deal with drugs (both legal and illegal); they tend to avoid other important behaviors like physical activity and nutrition, but there is no reason they have to be that way. For example, to slow the obesity epidemic, workplaces could set aside time during the workday for people to exercise and could ban snack food in cubicles. School boards could require physical education every day through high school, and churches could organize adult recreational sports leagues. For each of the behaviors that underlie the major killers, there are rules like these for all types of organizations that, taken together, could make a big difference in our health.

Society's architecture

People sometimes seek out rule-driven organizations to help them do the things they want to do but can't on their own. Twelve-step groups help people stay off liquor or drugs. Churches help people act kindly toward others. Aerobics classes cheerfully flog people into exercising, which these people could much more easily and cheaply do at home.

But organizations do much more than pass and enforce rules. They are themselves social structures, and they act to define a place for us in society and provide a sense of belonging. In our hunter-gatherer days we humans probably didn't have much trouble understanding who we were or where we belonged. We were part of this small band—the human beings—and not part of the other tribes foraging nearby—the strangers. Now that we live in sprawling cities of millions and in nations of hundreds of millions, we humans have erected social institutions to know what team (or teams) we're on. Just joining an organization helps establish who we are. We have a role, a place, and a label. We work for the state, we sell shoes, we are Baptists, or we are Scouts. Workplaces are probably the most powerful structures in this architecture of our daily lives. Jobs get us out of bed and moving around, they erect a framework for our time, they throw us together with others who are different, and then they force us to work with them for a common goal. Schools organize the lives of children, telling them what to do, when to do it, what other children they have to do it with, and how they should act with them. Voluntary organizations like churches, associations, and clubs shape our nonwork, nonschool time and further spell out who we are.

Because humans are the most intelligent animals on earth, a greater percentage of our behavior than that of any other species is learned. Once we get beyond instinct, our behavior flows from the behavior and expectations of those around us, and their behavior and expectations often follow the structures in which they are embedded. People who are heavily entwined in organizations and networks tend to behave in ways we think of as "normal," but hermits or people cast aside by society tend to seem "strange."

Signing on to an organization or a club doesn't necessarily mean people will behave in a way that is healthy. Gangs, which give disconnected teenage boys a sense of belonging, are notoriously destructive, teaching them to smoke, take drugs, have casual sex with girls, and shoot other boys. Cults can set up standards that destroy members; Jim Jones's followers in Guyana probably had a deep and fulfilling sense of belonging right up until the time they drank the cyanide-laced Kool-Aid. But most organizations have corporate cultures that tend to divert people from unhealthy behavior, usually condemning drug use and violence, often discouraging drinking and smoking, and sometimes discouraging eating unhealthy foods.

There is an even more subtle effect that organizations have on how healthy we are. While businesspersons may join organizations for purely economic reasons (to make connections, to find clients or investors), all people who join organizations tend to expand their social networks. Because organizations create the space for us to meet and spend time with others, they decide how much we will interact with others, what we will do with them, and with whom we'll do it. People come face to face with each other at the office, at school, or in clubs, passing on tips about things like jobs and schools, planning strategies and events, venting about failures and frustrations, savoring victories and accomplishments, and seeking (and receiving) help and advice. Completely aside from the specific plans, conversations, and advice is just the fact that they are together—humans making contact with other humans, which we as social animals fundamentally need. In fact, many organizations spring up entirely because people need to get together, sometimes with the flimsiest of excuses. Playgroups are for lonely mothers as much as for kids who need playmates, book clubs often don't bother to talk about books, and church socials aren't about fundraising.

It isn't clear *how* organizations keep us healthy, but it is absolutely clear *that* they keep us healthy. Over the last quarter century, "social epidemiologists" have investigated the relationship between social organizations and illness in the same way that infectious disease epidemiologists study the relationship between getting bitten by a tick and developing Lyme disease or between having unprotected sex and acquiring AIDS, and they keep finding the same answer: humans thrive with the kind of social connections offered by organizations and wither without them.

Employment is an especially powerful social structure. In large-scale studies across many countries, workers who lose their jobs acquire more chronic ailments and are from 20 percent more likely to twice as likely to die in the few years afterward than others who keep their jobs. Those who find jobs again seem to bounce back, but they still do not catch up to those who never were thrown out of work.[12] Because our behavior and our health are contagious, the fate of people around us can damage us too: a Danish study recently found that people living in areas with high unemployment had a 35 percent higher mortality rate than people living in areas of low unemployment, even after factoring in whether they still held their own jobs.[13] For teens, schools are almost as potent. Kids who feel less "connected" to their schools are much more likely to smoke tobacco or marijuana, drink alcohol, have sex, act violently, and feel depressed or suicidal.[14]

Churches, associations, and clubs also keep us fit in ways that we don't fully understand. One famous example is a nine-year study of nearly seven thousand adults in Alameda County, California, which found that people were much more likely to die if they were unmarried, didn't belong to a church, or had little contact with relatives; in fact, the people with the least social support were more than twice as likely to die during the study as those with the most, making social support by itself about as strong a preventive factor as regular exercise and a healthy diet.[15] There is a spillover effect of this too: people who live in states in which fewer people belong to social organizations don't live as long, dying sooner of heart disease, cancer, stroke, and injuries.[16]

Social connections also exert effects even in the small illnesses that punctuate our lives. In one amazing example, researchers from Carnegie Mellon University recruited 276 healthy volunteers, asked them about their social ties, and then gave each one nose drops containing a virus that causes the common cold. Within five days, the volunteers with the fewest social ties were about four times as likely to get colds than volunteers with the most social ties, even when the researchers took into account their age, sex, weight, race, and education.[17]

There is something mysterious here—a benefit of human social organizations that is apart from the rules that the organizations impose on their members. Some day we may learn the biologic mechanism for this benefit. The mysterious nature of it, though, shouldn't prevent us from using it to keep ourselves healthy, any more than not knowing how bacteria caused disease prevented people in the 1860s from saving lives by constructing sanitary sewer and water lines. Social organizations, like rules, are not part of the natural world; they are things we create. If we really want to be healthy, we can create them, nurture them, and give people as many opportunities as possible to be part of them. That could mean everything from ramping up federal jobs programs to revitalizing town bowling leagues. In trying to recharge our "social capital" we wouldn't be alone. In his book *Bowling Alone,* Robert Putnam shows that not only are bowling leagues disintegrating, but our entire latticework of social organizations in America is crumbling, and he makes a powerful case of how important it is to rebuild it. "Of all the domains in which I have traced the consequences of social capital," he concludes, "in none is the importance of social connectedness so well established as in the case of health and well-being."[18]

CHAPTER 8

IT'S *the* REAL THING:
MEDIA

On October 12, 1993, in Bordentown, New Jersey, a twenty-four-year-old handyman named Marco Birkhimer of his own free will walked onto Route 206 and sat down on the yellow line that split the pavement. He died "instantly" when he was slammed by a car. Just four days later in Syosset, Long Island, a high school football star named Michael Macias lay down on Bayville Avenue as fellow teens hovered nearby. "We just turned around and he was lying in the street," one said. Macias was left with a spinal cord injury after he was struck and dragged by a car driven by a seventeen-year-old girl. That same night in the small town of Polk, Pennsylvania, a pair of teens lay down in a rural two-lane highway. Eighteen-year-old Michael Shingledecker was killed and his seventeen-year-old friend Dean Bartlett was critically injured.[1]

These teens and young men were part of a brief epidemic that fall of males who killed or maimed themselves by lying down in the middle of busy streets. More than a decade later, their behavior seems hard to fathom, but at the time the explanation was obvious. Walt Disney Studios had just released *The Program,* a film promoted as "an inside look at the gritty, action-packed world of Top 10 college football," one scene of which showed the players proving their mettle by lying down on a highway's yellow lines as cars flew by in opposite directions.[2] Reporters who interviewed witnesses of the real-world car injuries were left with little doubt that they were copying the movie—as were many others who were luckier. "My son saw the movie last weekend, and I know he was playing the game because the kids playing it with him told me," Michael Shingledecker's mother told a *New York Times* reporter just after her son's funeral. "They said about 30 other kids were playing the game a few miles up the road in another town the same night."[3]

To the families of those killed or paralyzed, Disney executives offered their condolences. They defended the movie, assuring families that the movie "in no way encourages this type of behavior," but after the bad press they cut out the key scene.[4] Some movie reviewers joined Disney in ridiculing any connection between the movie and the deaths, but others knew better. In fact, Jack Garner, a critic from Gannett News Service, wrote a month *before* the incidents that "I dread the day I read about some real high school jocks who've been inspired to duplicate that irresponsible film sequence."[5]

Violent "copycat" acts following movies and television shows are not rare. In fact, an activist in Canada maintains a Web site with a long list of them—including stabbings, rapes, mutilations of children, arson, immolations, and accidental hangings—all reported by the killers or their associates to be directly inspired by what they saw in the media.[6] (Shootings don't make the list, presumably because they are so common in the media and in real life that individual acts can't be tied to individual shows). And the risk of copycat violence and dangerous acts is so widely known to the TV networks that they have adopted the ridiculous "don't do this at home" disclaimer that has become a staple of stand-up comics.

Because often it is teens involved, people tend to attribute copycat injuries to the naiveté of adolescence, to their sense of invulnerability, or to peer pressure. But Albert Bandura, the researcher who built an entire theory of behavior starting with children's tendency to attack Bobo dolls after watching others do it on television, might have had a much simpler explanation: humans just tend to copy what they see others do. It is part of our being both social and learning animals. "Social learning" can transmit *any* behavior, no matter how destructive or self-destructive. What is astounding is the *power* of this effect. Think for a moment of how difficult it would be to *persuade* anyone, at any age, through any technique of persuasion you can imagine, to lie down in front of a moving car. Then consider this: if moving pictures can entice young men into an act so obviously stupid and so immediately self-destructive, how much power must they have in inducing all of us to do things that are more subtly and gradually self-destructive, like smoking, drinking, eating too much, or taking sexual risks?

Media, time, and space

Humans and their ancestors have communicated with each other long before the invention of language. Communication between humans face-to-face is extraordinarily rich, a performance of gestures, facial expressions, voice inflections, and the dance of cues and responses between speakers and listeners. Much more is in this than the simple transfer of information. It communicates values, intentions, and emotions. It establishes friend or foe. It transmits mental images from one person to another. In fact, spoken language is only a small part of this communication. Chimpanzees, our closest biologic cousins, maintain a complex social structure and manage to spread culture across generations by communicating only with body motions, facial expressions, actions, and just a few vocalizations.[7]

One of our main triumphs as a species has been the technology allowing increasingly rich methods for communicating across time and space. A few thousand years ago, humans developed writing, allowing words to travel. Then roughly a century ago sound began to fly through space with the telephone and radio. Fifty years later moving images were added to the sound through films and television. Each of these inventions changed the world.

The peculiarities of each technological breakthrough had profound reverberations in their own right. One of the improvements that occurred along the way was *who* could communicate with *whom*. When a group of people shares the same space at the same time, anyone can talk with anyone else, and one person can easily talk with several others at one time. Writing on papyrus enabled words to move through space, but for practical purposes it let someone communicate with only one other person at a time. Gutenberg's printing press radically changed that, enabling people to transmit their words to many others simultaneously, and it spawned huge democratic social changes. The early users of radio also thought of it simply as a means for one person to communicate with one other. The concept of one station "broadcasting" to many receivers at once was at least as revolutionary as Gutenberg's press, for example, allowing leaders like Hitler, Churchill, and Roosevelt to consolidate their power over entire nations. But these revolutions were small compared to that caused by television, a medium that not only transmitted moving images, but was also broadcast, not just one-to-many but one to many millions. Through movies and television, nearly all of the subtle and powerful methods by which humans communicate thoughts, emotions, and intentions *before* and *beyond* language leapt across space and time into nearly every household in America. Even more than radio, television gave the televised—and the ones who decided what was televised—an emotional hold over viewers that translated into enormous political and social power.

Soaking it in

The images on television wouldn't mean nearly so much to our lives if it weren't for how many hours we spend soaking them in. Depending on the survey you read, Americans watch on average three to four hours of television per day.[8] That's something like twenty-five hours per week, thirteen hundred hours per year. It amounts to 40 percent of our available nonwork time (and that's even considering time for meals and driving)—more time than we spend doing anything else besides working and sleeping.[9]

By comparison, our relationships with real humans seem small. Eight in ten Americans watch television most evenings, but only six in ten talk with family members. Husbands and wives spend about three or four times as much time watching television as talking to each other.[10] Children spend more time watching television than they do in school.[11] Increasingly, television *is* the constant activity at home—replacing what used to be the background noise of kids wrestling in the living room or relatives arguing over a meal. Six in ten Americans flick on the tube and watch without knowing what is on,[12] and 42 percent of kids say in their homes the TV is on "most of the time."[13] It is tempting to think this will all change with the arrival of "new media," particularly the Internet. Maybe it will over the long run. But studies so far show that in the Internet era people are watching as much television as ever. The time we spend on the Internet just further cuts into the non-media time we might spend sleeping or talking with other people.

What are we watching all this time? With the proliferation of cable, the number of channels available to us has grown to an average of fifty, but most of the programs we watch fall into categories that have been around for decades: situation comedies, dramas (mostly about cops and lawyers), soap operas, cartoons, sports, daytime talk shows, with the recent addition of "reality TV" shows and infomercials. These shows remain the staple of television because they draw ratings. Television networks are in the business of attracting and holding what they call our "eyeballs," which they then rent to advertisers who sell us things. Because these ratings are tied directly to what advertisers pay to place their commercials, the executives follow them religiously in deciding what shows to keep and what to kill. As CBS executive Arnold Becker told media analyst Todd Gitlin, "I'm not interested in culture. I'm not interested in pro-social values. I have only one interest. That's whether people watch the program. That's my definition of good, that's my definition of bad."[14]

And then there are the advertisements that occupy an increasing proportion of what is on the air. The most common ads are for cars, foods and restaurants, medicines (over-the-counter and prescription), movies, retail stores, and "personal care" products.[15] They sell with flashy images, catchy music, excited voice-overs, and familiar faces. Almost no one likes commercials, but we watch them, in part because the shows break off at a moment that leaves us hanging, so we'll stay tuned until they pick up again, and in part because of the draw of the blizzard of images and sound.

Selling it: the images of media

Ours has been called the information age, and when we talk about the effect of media content on our behavior, we are surprised how many people consider television to be a channel of information—facts and ideas. But television is a visual medium, transmitting to our brains moving pictures of people doing things. It is these images and the emotions behind them that give television its power, not the information spoken above the images. Michael Deaver, Ronald Reagan's PR man, taught us his principle that "sight wins over sound" in news broadcasts, meaning that it didn't matter how harsh the reporters' words were about Reagan's actions; what mattered was if Reagan appeared on the screen to be relaxed, confident, and powerful, and with Deaver's stage-managing, Reagan always did.

Because TV programmers want to nail us to the set until the next commercial, they tend to reach for images that are arousing, particularly violence and sex. The formula works, has always worked, and will always work. As media wizard Brandon Tartikoff said, "All of television boils down to excisable elements that you can put in twenty-second promos. If you can't have Starsky pull a gun and fire it fifty times a day on promos [because of citizen pressure against violent content], sex becomes your next best handle."[16]

While media critics focus on television programs, the most powerful images on television are in the advertising. They must be powerful because to the advertisers, they are everything—the entire reason they are spending hundreds of millions. Advertisers don't sell with information; they sell with images and emotion. Humans have powerful instinctive desires—for love, sex, security, pleasure, companionship, fun, and respect. Advertisers try desperately to link their products with these desires in our subconscious (called, not coincidentally, giving a product an "image"). Advertisers have long relied on social scientists, psychologists, and psychoanalysts to help make these irrational links.[17] It started in 1920, when the J. Walter Thompson agency hired John Watson, a behaviorist who preceeded B. F. Skinner and who was developing theories on how to control human emotions, to mine the latest scientific thinking. "Since the time of the serpent in the Garden of Eden influenced Eve and Eve in turn persuaded Adam, the world has tried to find out ways and means of controlling human behavior," he said in a speech. "In advertising, we call the process selling."[18] Watson preached that to sell, advertising must tap into at least one of what he considered the three fundamental nonrational emotions: fear, rage, and love.

What was at first probably seen as flaky in advertising is now core religion. In studying man the consumer, the goal of advertisers, according to advertising giant Bill Bernbach, is to learn "what compulsions drive a man, what instincts dominate his action, even though his language so often camouflages what really motivates him. For if you know these things you can touch him at the core of his being."[19] For example, the Marlboro man ads make the completely illogical but fantastically successful link between smoking and the cowboy image of freedom, strength, toughness, and most of all, independence (in particular, independence from the warnings of the Surgeon General). This potent campaign drove Marlboro from a tiny brand with less than 1 percent of the market to the number one selling cigarette for decades. If ad campaigns are successful in making emotional links like these, people—who can't tell one brand from another in blinded tests—buy the product to achieve these desires. The less objectively valuable the product is and the less it differs from its competitors, the more crucial the emotional images. Advertisers can sell washing machines by claiming they never break down, for example. But to sell subjective pleasures like cigarettes, alcohol, and junk food, they need images. As advertising philosopher David Ogilvy wrote, "Give people a taste of Old Crow and *tell* them it's Old Crow. Then give them another taste of Old Crow, *but tell them it's Jack Daniels*. Ask them which they prefer. They'll think the two drinks are quite different. *They are tasting images.*"[20]

The power of images

As with other types of behavior, there is a huge discrepancy between what we *think* about watching television media and what we *do*. As much as we watch television, we don't really like it very much. In surveys average television viewers say they enjoy watching TV about as much as they enjoy housework and cooking—enjoy it *less*, in fact, than working.[21] People watching TV often feel guilty afterward for having wasted so much time. But they can't stop themselves. One in ten Americans feels "addicted" to television.[22]

Why do these moving images that we disparage hold our attention so well? Many of us notice that when a television is in view, we can't take our eyes off it even if we try. That may be caused by the "orienting reflex," the instinct we have from deep in our evolutionary past to stop and attend to sudden motion or noise.[23] It is the instinct we needed to avoid predators or spot prey, and it is impervious to our wishes to think it away. Television producers provoke it with fast-moving images of people or animals, sudden close-ups, and jump cuts, making it tough to take our eyes away from the screen. And the more threatening or arousing the images, the more glued our eyes become.

Of course no one forces people to turn on the television in the first place. People watch so much television not because they enjoy it very much but because it is the ultimate path of least resistance: the television is always there, cost-free, summoned to life without our even standing up, happy to play endlessly, asking absolutely nothing of us. People say they watch to relax, or to relieve stress or loneliness, and this works for a short time. They enter a semiconscious state not unlike daydreaming—only with their own daydreams replaced by the producers' and advertisers'.

The more we watch television and the more disconnected we become from other real humans, the more we confuse the images on the television with reality—to the point where we trust actors on television and movies more than we trust real people. As we write, Arnold Schwarzenegger has just been elected to the governorship of California. Schwarzenegger had no experience in politics and no particular platform—in fact nothing in his past suggested he knew the first thing about how to run a government. But his media image was a hero who could solve problems through brute force, and to the voters, image was reality, so in reality, they trusted him enough to put their state in his hands.

As we absorb and react to this flood of organized images in media, it shapes our culture. Whenever a human watches another human gesture, speak, and interact with other humans, she is acquiring a little piece of culture—an example of what we come to think of as normal behavior, the rules for what we should do in different situations, and, by extension, who we are as a people. The images we see help define the average person on the behavior curve and describe how far anyone can safely stray from that average. In traditional societies the rules of behavior were spread face-to-face through customs, traditions, religious teachings, and illustrative stories. But now, as communications expert Gabriel Weinman puts it, "our children are born into homes in which, for the first time in human history, a central commercial institution rather than parents, the church, or the school tells most of the stories.... [T]elevision is the wholesale distributor of images and forms the mainstream of our popular culture."[24]

Cultural messages that originate by word of mouth don't stop after the first telling, and cultural messages that arrive through the media travel person-to-person at least as well. Think of them as contagious, like viruses (biologic or computer). They diffuse out through human networks, and depending on the networks and the messages, can have an impact that is much, much larger than the original recipients, to the point of fundamentally changing our entire society. By shaping society's views on what is normal, media messages touch each of us, no matter how much we individually pay attention to them.

Our televisions, our bodies

What effects do modern media have on the most important health behaviors of our age?

Some effects come from the media themselves, not the content. The most obvious effect is on our physical laziness. Three to four hours is a big chunk of the day to be sprawled on a couch, and that is time we might otherwise be playing with the kids or walking in the neighborhood. Any of those other activities burns more calories than watching television. In fact, the semicomatose physiologic state imposed by the TV means that even sitting doing *nothing* burns more calories than watching television.[25] Nearly every study that has looked at this has found a strong link between television watching and obesity, even after taking into account what people eat.

A more subtle but maybe more important health effect is what television watching does to how much time we spend with other people. Spending 40 percent of your free time watching television cuts back on time to visit neighbors, bowl with friends, talk to children or parents, or organize clubs. When you add in how we use the Internet and video games, people are increasingly interacting with machines and are losing touch with other humans. Unlike humans, machines are very predictable; they don't get angry when you provoke them, listen with sympathy, argue with you, or give you a hug. We humans are genetically programmed to be social animals, so it's hard to guess what effect it has on us all to lose touch with each other.

Then there is the "media content." What effect does the sum total of all the jumble of images we watch have on how we behave and our health?

Television and movies are everywhere, and for that very reason they are extremely hard to study. How can scientists study the effect of television on violent behavior when 98 percent of homes have televisions? There is no control group. Because it's virtually impossible to do clean research on something that touches all of us all of the time, researchers have done the best they could with other types of studies, like short-term laboratory studies, "correlational" studies in which they compare heavy TV-watchers to light TV-watchers, and "time-series" studies in which they see if a change in media content is followed by a change in behavior of an entire group of people. And a few researchers have been clever enough to find "natural experiments"—communities that had no television for a long time because of some technological or political quirk, allowing the researchers to compare how the communities behaved after the arrival of TV to beforehand. The best "natural experiment" was the initial arrival of television (and before that, radio) in entire countries. Taken together, these studies make a good case that the media images have a big impact on behaviors that are important to our health.

The ads

It seems ridiculous to have to make this point, but because many people we speak to don't believe it, we feel we must: advertising works. It makes us *consume*: buy cars, use shampoo, eat pizza, take pills. The more we watch ads for Coke, the more Coke we drink. That's why the Coca-Cola company spends over 100 million dollars a year on Coke ads. The company executives aren't stupid; if the advertising didn't work, they would stop advertising.

These days we are inundated with advertising, so it is tough to track how any one ad campaign affects our behavior. But the power of advertising was demonstrated well in the early days of electronic media. The first radio advertisement aired in 1922 in the form of a fifteen-minute earnest but low-key plug for a new apartment complex in Queens broadcast by a local developer over WEAF in New York City. That and five additional appearances cost the developer all of $350. Within three weeks he had sold out all of his apartments and taken in $27,000.[26] In the next few years sponsorship of entire radio programs was the basic business model, filling the air with programs like the *Eveready Hour,* the *A&P Gypsies,* and the *Palmolive Show.* In September 1928 a cigarette company tried out the *Lucky Strike Dance Orchestra,* and to test how effective this strange new medium was, they simultaneously dropped their ads in magazines and billboards. They had their answer within two months, as sales of Lucky Strike jumped 47 percent. Lucky Strike's main competition, Camel cigarettes, counterattacked with weekly, then daily shows of its own, and Camel sales soon started to approach Lucky Strike's.[27]

The early days of television repeated the lesson from radio. When *The Mickey Mouse Club* first hit television screens in 1955, a small company known as Mattel gambled its entire future that three ads a day would sell its toys. One of its first ads was for the Burp Gun, "an automatic cap-firing machine gun modeled after the machine guns used in WWI jungle fighting." Within a couple of weeks, the nation was so desperate to buy sold-out Burp Guns that even President Eisenhower had to personally write Mattel to get one for his grandson David. Within a month, Mattel had doubled its entire sales revenue from the previous year, and it soon became a giant of the toy industry.[28]

The products that rely on advertising tend to be those that we don't really need and that can get a boost from an emotional pitch. While these products aren't necessarily designed to be bad for our health, they aren't designed to be good either. The influence of these ads goes beyond the ads themselves, because the advertisers also influence the content of the programs themselves. Across the board, we consume too much of what is advertised on commercials and promoted in programs.

The powerful link between obesity and television probably isn't just the sloth of people watching. Most people snack in front of the television. Have you ever wondered why? Maybe it has something to do with the fact that TV floods us with images and references to junk food. Prime-time programs mention food about ten times an hour, and most of these references are about coffee, alcohol, soft drinks, or sweets. Characters eat snacks more than twice as often as they eat meals.[29] The ads sprinkled through the programs are even worse: they run at about four per hour, mostly for fast-food restaurants, soft drinks, breakfast cereals, and sweets.[30] Young kids are bombarded with ads for sugary cereals and snacks (two researchers estimate that kids see on average *five thousand* of these ads a year), and as they get older, ads for pizza, soft drinks, and fast-food joints.[31] Almost nothing on television shows people eating vegetables, salads, or anything else nutritionists would call healthy.

Television also teaches children (and us adults as well) how to drink. Alcoholic beverages are the most common type of drink for television characters (think *Cheers*).[32] Alcohol ads run about once an evening in prime time, but about one to three times per hour on sports shows that are popular with kids.[33] People on TV—not only in ads, but also in programs—who are drinking are usually smart, sophisticated, sexy, and having a wonderful time with close friends. They almost never get drunk, abuse their spouses, or crash their cars.[34] Children in fifth grade can recognize the cute "spokesanimals" in Budweiser ads.[35] Young adolescents who are "heavy viewers" are more likely than lighter viewers to say that "people who drink are happy" and "you have to drink to have fun at a sporting event."[36] And the few studies that have been done on the behavioral consequences overall find that the drinking ads have a solid effect on kids: teenagers who watch plenty of beer ads on sports shows or who pay attention to beer ads are more likely to drink.[37]

Television grew up advertising tobacco. Camel cigarettes sponsored one of the first running series, a 1949 drama called *Man Against Crime.* Not only did they run ads, but they also dictated what appeared in the program. The cigarette producers gave writers pages of instructions on how they should handle smoking on-screen. Characters had to smoke cigarettes "gracefully"; no one could ever grab a smoke to "calm his nerves." "Do not have the heavy or any disreputable person smoking a cigarette. Do not associate the smoking of cigarettes with undesirable scenes or situations plotwise."[38] For years tobacco companies flooded the airwaves with advertising and product image placements like this, and during those years smoking rates rose to their highest levels ever. In 1971, when they agreed to a congressional ban on advertising in electronic media, they rechanneled most of their advertising dollars into billboards, print media, and direct mail.[39] But the program images linger. Characters on television shows and in movies continue to smoke at rates much higher than in real life (even half of *cartoon* movies show characters smoking), without any character showing so much as a cough.[40]

Eyeball grabbers: violence and sex

Child psychologists and parent activists have worried aloud for decades about the damage television could be doing to our lives, but most of their worries have *not* been about advertised products. They have focused more on the images that grab our eyeballs, particularly violence and sex.

The world we see on television and movie screens is a virtual bloodbath. More than half of television shows contain violence, and those that do serve up an average of six violent acts per hour.[41] Children's shows are more violent than adult shows: twenty-five violent acts per hour in Saturday morning cartoons versus "only" eight to nine violent acts per hour in prime time.[42] As long ago as 1992, the American Psychological Association estimated that the average American child sees at least eight thousand murders and more than a hundred thousand other violent acts before he graduates from elementary school.[43] The way violence is shown is just as frightening. On the tube, killing people is fun or funny: nearly half of the time the violence is presented as being justified, more than half the time there is no pain shown afterward, and 40 percent of the time the violence is shown with humor.[44]

Movies are even more violent than television. "Action" films treat us on average to nearly fifty acts of violence against people.[45] In 1988, 18 people were killed in the movie *Die Hard;* two years later in *Die Hard 2* the death toll was 264.[46] One writer scanning a single issue of *Variety* magazine with 123 pages of ads for all types of movies found that the most common words were *kill, murder, death,* and *dead* (thirty-three times each), followed by *terror, fatal, lethal, dangerous, rage, frenzy, revenge,* and *gun-crazy.*[47]

Researchers have probably studied the connection between violent media images and violent behavior more intensely than any other single scientific question. Of more than 3,500 studies, all but 18 have found a relationship.[48] The mountain of research includes just about every type of study design you can imagine: Kids who watch violent shows in laboratories are more aggressive immediately afterward. Kids who watch more television or more violent shows at home are more likely to be violent than kids who watch less—an effect that lasts for years into adulthood.[49] Kids in a small town in Canada who were denied TV for decades because the town was in a broadcast "dead zone" became suddenly more aggressive on schoolyard playgrounds after cable TV finally arrived.[50] One study displayed this effect on a massive scale: homicides in the United States and Canada doubled over three decades after television was introduced, while homicides declined slightly among whites in South Africa where television was not introduced until the 1970s. Only in the decade after television was entrenched in South Africa did homicide rates among whites increase by more than 50 percent.[51] It would not be hard to pick apart any one of these studies based on its methods or lay the blame for the outcome on other factors, but when you take them as a group, the evidence is overpowering.

Scores of organizations have systematically reviewed these studies and reached the same conclusion, leading most recently to a joint statement in 2000 to Congress by the American Academy of Pediatrics, the American Medical Association, and the American Psychiatric Association, among others, agreeing that the studies "point overwhelmingly to a causal connection between media violence and aggressive behavior in some children," and show that "children exposed to violent programming at a young age have a higher tendency for violent and aggressive behavior later in life."[52]

Sex is not nearly as common on television as violence, but it is cropping up more often and more explicitly as cable television and broadcast networks have been competing more aggressively for the same viewers. Just between 1998 and 2002, the number of scenes showing sexual behavior increased from 1.4 to 2.2 per hour.[53] When characters on TV have sex, about 10 percent of the time they have just met and half of the time they don't have an established relationship.[54] The effect of televised sex on how we behave hasn't been studied nearly as much as violence, but the few studies that have been published show exactly what you would suspect: teenagers who watch more sex on TV are more likely to have sex.[55] We'll discuss the health effects (beyond pregnancy) of teen sex at greater length in chapter 12, but they aren't hard to imagine: teenage relationships don't last long, and teens often don't use condoms when they have sex, so in a world where billions of humans are connected in a vast sexual network, sexually active teens are perfectly placed to pick up and pass along a diverse crop of sexually transmitted diseases.

As difficult as it is to study the effect of television, then, the pattern of results from the studies is consistent: television teaches us how to behave. If people on television do things that are bad for their health, we will tend to follow them.

New media: The Internet, video games, and the future

In the twilight of a June evening in 2003, in what reporters later described as a "golf course community" of 7,200 in the Smoky Mountain foothills just outside Knoxville, Tennessee, Aaron Hamel was driving with his cousin in his red pickup truck on Interstate 40, returning from a day trip to the mountains. The cousin later told reporters that Hamel asked her,

"Wasn't this the most beautiful day?" He had moved to Knoxville two weeks earlier from Canada with a dream to live in a cabin in the mountains. "This day is perfect," he went on. Then, just as he was saying "Oh, Dee Dee, look at the beautiful flower—," before he even got to the *s* in *flowers,* his window shattered. He slumped over. His pickup careened across the median and crashed into a guardrail in the eastbound lane. A motorist driving eastbound stopped, called 911, and then used his shirt to try to stop the profuse bleeding from the bullet wound to Hamel's head, but when the ambulance arrived, Hamel was dead.[56]

At just about the same time, Kim Bede, a passenger in another westbound car on I-40, was severely injured when she was hit in the pelvis with a second bullet.

Within two days, the mystery of who had shot Hamel and Bede was answered when the local sheriff and the state attorney general produced for TV news crews fifteen-year-old William Buckner and his thirteen-year-old brother Joshua, two boys who lived about a mile from the interstate. The two boys admitted to stealing two .22-caliber hunting rifles from a bedroom closet about a week earlier and, on the evening in question, walking from their brick split-level house to a hill about fifty feet from the interstate and firing at tractor-trailer trucks. They tired of the game after about twenty-five rounds. But "at the end," reported the attorney general, "Will had a couple of shells left and fired two shots in quick succession" at cars.[57]

According to the papers, the boys were not bad kids. They had no history of troublemaking. They were just bored. And they got the idea to take potshots at passing trucks, they said, from a video game called *Grand Theft Auto.*

So far in this chapter we have focused on "old" media, particularly television, which people watch passively. "New" media—video games, computer games, and the Internet—offer an active involvement, not with another human but with a machine. Just as in the early days of television people couldn't possibly comprehend where that medium would take our society, right now we can't predict what these new media will do to us. Some aspects of this new world—like e-mail and instant messaging that revive old friendships or maintain new ones—seem very positive. Some, like the convergence of the Internet and television, may amount to just more channels of the same. But we ought to be worried about the darker side of interactive games that, rather than just letting children watch people kill, teach them exactly how to do it.

Grand Theft Auto throws players into a lawless fantasy world of gangs and gangsters at war and invites them to join the free-for-all. According to the company's Web site, in the story line of *Grand Theft Auto III,* "You've been left for dead. Now you're taking revenge, unless the city gets you first. . . . You'll have to rob, steal, and kill just to stay out of serious trouble." Players are rewarded when they deal drugs, yank drivers out of cars, beat up prostitutes, kill other gangsters, and shoot at passing cars. The company boasts that, with "a huge array of street-ready weapons and some of the seediest characters in video-game history, *Grand Theft Auto III* is a sprawling epic which will show you that sometimes, crime can pay and sometimes it can pay you back."[58]

William and Joshua Buckner are not the only children today practicing their marksmanship on a video screen hooked to a Sony PlayStation. On any given day, about a third of teenage boys play video games, and these boys average over an hour a day at the console.[59] As we write, *Grand Theft Auto III* is the second-best-selling video game in America, amid others with names like *ATV Offroad Fury* and *Devil May Cry 2.* The sequel *Grand Theft Auto: Vice City* sold 4 million copies before it was even released.[60] With these games we are training nearly an entire generation of boys to "virtually" steal, smash cars, beat up women, and shoot others.

We humans do what we've practiced doing before, which is why the military trains soldiers to kill not by just by showing them demonstrations, but by giving them plenty of practice shooting. And lately the military has found it is easier and cheaper to train killers by using video games. Back in our quiet neighborhoods, we don't know how many more of our bored virtual killers will make the exciting jump to "reality," any more than we could predict how many football players would lie down on the yellow line after watching *The Program,* but it's a good bet that it will be more than a few.

The press clippings about the Buckner boys played it as a bizarre tragedy, the final curtain of which had fallen. "At first, people were terrified that there was an indiscriminate killer on the loose," wrote the *Knoxville News-*

Sentinel.[61] But after the boys confessed and were assigned to state custody, the attorney general took credit for a spate of evil vanquished. "This should relieve the anxiety of the motoring public who were concerned about traveling through Cocke County on I-40," he said.[62] But should it?

Is it really that bad?

Ever since parents have complained about the violence on television— which is about as long as television has been in existence—people involved in the media business have been defending themselves.

A few people may claim that media images just flat out don't influence how we behave. Anyone making this argument has a lot of explaining to do: not only Bandura's kids slamming the Bobo doll and the epidemic of youngsters lying in front of cars after *The Program,* but also the effect of advertising, the studies linking sex on television with early initiation of sex, and the mountain of research showing that televised violence leads to viewers becoming violent. Exactly how many studies do we need to prove this basic fact?

And occasionally you hear advertisers arguing that *they* don't have any influence over what people do. Of course when they make their pitches to their business clients in confidential boardrooms, they must say just the opposite, or they wouldn't *have* any clients. Advertising defenders particularly cite as evidence big-budget ad campaigns that fail miserably. Of course we humans are not completely controlled by advertising, but then no one ever said we were. Some products sell better than others, and some ad campaigns resonate with our inner fears and desires better than others. But that doesn't mean that all advertising—the entire technique—rolls off our backs. In fact, most advertising works to one extent or another. The loser ad campaigns fail not because they don't make the products sell, but because advertising is expensive and the campaigns cost more than the additional profit they generate.

More often, you hear more subtle arguments about the feebleness of advertising. As advertising writer Hank Seiden put it, at best the ads can only "convince a logical prospect for a product to try it one time. No more, no less. . . . From then on, the product is on its own."[63] Advertising can't be blamed, he claims, for whatever people do on a regular basis. Think about this argument the next time you watch beer ads on television. Nothing about these hip montages of youngsters playing on beaches in bikinis is there to get you to try beer for the first time. These ads instead are a perpetual barrage of images that link fun and sex with beer, not just so people will take up drinking but also so we will all *keep* drinking.

Ad executives also plead that their advertising doesn't influence total consumption, that in fact it only changes "market share"—for example, it doesn't change how many gallons of soft drinks we drink, it only makes us switch from Pepsi to Coke. "Cigarettes can't be sold to nonsmokers," Hank Seiden says.[64] This argument just doesn't make sense. First, it is hard to imagine that advertisers care, after all. They are only trying to sell their own brand; whether their sales go up because they steal others' sales or they go up because everyone's sales go up can't matter to them. And second, much advertising seems generic—advertising the product, not the brand. In fact, a good percentage of the time, people watching TV ads remember the ad but forget the name of the product, or even think the ad is for a competitor's product.[65] Finally, there are good examples of ads that stimulate a whole product category, not just a brand. During the heyday of radio, from the early 1930s until the first health warnings on smoking, cigarette ads flooded the airwaves and sales of cigarettes as a whole category skyrocketed. In the 1950s and 1960s, Coke and Pepsi hammered us all with televised ads packed with happy young people drinking colas, and sales of *both* climbed upward.[66] When Pepsi actually did try for a short time to steal Coke's customers with the Pepsi Challenge ads, the whole industry became outraged that they were demeaning the product (suggesting people would buy soda only because of how it *tastes*), and Pepsi reverted to its upbeat image ads.[67]

Many who accept the proposition that media images influence how we behave are still willing to accept those images, because, they say with some regret, these images just reflect our society. They show the world as it is —ugly, violent, and full of casual sex. Media critic Michael Medved has ridiculed this argument, pointing out that the real world, as ugly as it sometimes is, doesn't come close to the mayhem of the televised world. If the real murder rate were that of the rate in prime time (about 2 percent of characters per night), within a few months the entire American nation would be dead.[68]

One final argument media apologists make is that television (or movies, or video games, or whatever medium you mention) is just a business in a free-market economy. They just offer a product, and if you don't like the product, then you can just turn it off. No one forces you to watch.

But we don't even need to watch. At a college forum in Rexburg, Idaho, Michael Medved asked how many students had ever been to a Madonna concert. About three students raised their hands. Then he asked how many had bought a Madonna video, CD, or cassette. A few more raised their hands. Then he asked how many knew who Madonna was. Every student raised his hand. The images of Madonna creep into our brains insidiously. Saying that if you don't like popular culture you can just turn it off, said Medved, "makes as much sense as saying, 'If you don't like the smog, just stop breathing.'"[69]

Suppose you turn off the television at home and keep your kids away from the movies. And suppose your parents had done that for you when you were growing up, too. You and your children would probably be less violent than if you had grown up on television. That might reduce your chances of being the perpetrator of violence, but not the victim. Even more so than other behaviors, violence is a plague of our society as a whole, not just of an illness we can prevent individually.

Is there good TV?

Television is so laden with health risks that some people have pleaded to just get rid of it. But television is here to stay. More important, though, television does a lot that is good in our society, and it is so powerful that it could do even more to keep us healthy.

There are plenty of good programs on television—by whatever definition you have of "good." Mixed in with the violent action shows, sexy soap operas, loud sitcoms, football games, and home shopping drumbeat are thoughtful news or talk shows that uncover and dissect important issues, documentaries on historical figures, performances of great art, and kids' shows that are truly educational. Granted, you may have to dig through piles of standard fare in the program guide to find these gems, but they are there, and the people who watch them probably end up smarter, more educated, more thoughtful—and who knows, maybe healthier in the long run.

Media's reach also has a more subtle but probably more important effect of giving our entire nation shared experiences. In a sprawling country populated with immigrants from scores of other lands, images in the media—particularly television—knit us together. A president's speech, the World Series, a president's assassination, a city riot, the moon landing, the fall of the World Trade Center, were events that we saw in the same way, together, whether we were in rural Iowa or a barrio of Los Angeles, and that drew us together as a people. People gather over coffee or lunch during the day and talk about what they witnessed the night before—a great one-liner in a sitcom or the heart-stopping play in the crucial ball game. Television has helped Americans become one people, to whom regional and ethnic hatreds of the depth seen in the former Communist states are hard to fathom. It is not a coincidence that the civil rights movement achieved its greatest gains just as televisions were arriving in nearly every living room in America. For decades beforehand, African Americans had been protesting Jim Crow laws, but they had been systematically beaten back by Southern sheriffs and political leaders while almost no one anywhere else paid attention. But when Martin Luther King and his followers skillfully used television to show all of America images of well-dressed and well-behaved teenagers set upon by dogs and fire hoses, the emotional impact of the injustice was so strong that it moved thousands of volunteers to join him and millions of other citizens to pressure their representatives to right the wrongs of the system.

But when it comes to our health, media's greatest potential may be the flip side of its dangers—its ability to shape how we behave every day. If the way that media images change our behavior is simply through "social learning"—the Bobo doll effect—then it ought to be just as effective in encouraging us to do things that are worthwhile and healthy as things that are damaging or self-destructive. Studies of television causing "good" behavior don't get the same press as studies on violence or sex, but there are plenty of them. Typically, researchers compare the effect on groups of schoolchildren of watching either an "antisocial" program with characters fighting, or a "prosocial" program with characters helping each other out. A typical "prosocial" program is an episode of *Lassie* in which Jeff risks his life to help retrieve Lassie's puppy from a mineshaft, and a typical "antisocial aggressive" program is a cartoon in which Popeye pummels Brutus. The researchers may then just watch the kids play together, or they may put them in a laboratory with a chance to push buttons to either "help" or "hurt" a child playing a game in the next room. Taken as a group, these studies are very consistent: kids who watch characters helping each other are more likely to help fellow kids.[70] In fact, it looks as though television may be *more* powerful in inducing "prosocial" effects than "antisocial" effects.[71] And true to the idea that television works through "social learning" rather than thinking, sitcoms and cartoons that show the good behavior are more effective than educational programs like *Mr. Rogers' Neighborhood* that merely explain it.[72]

The cultural messages flowing from the television can shape our behavior in as many different ways as characters can behave on the screen—including ways that most of us would say are good. Given the mix of what is on, altruism and tolerance—*particularly* tolerance—are spread and reinforced by television. The fact that racial integration has been transformed from a Communist conspiracy to a mainstream value in America may have a lot to do with the fact that the kids who grew up watching *Sesame Street,* the show that relentlessly pushes ethnic diversity some eighteen times a week, are now near forty.

Television can indeed be good. Plenty of what is on television right now is good. But as long as we pay for television with advertising revenues, which rely on ratings, and then accept what the market gives us, most television shows will be made of what pays, particularly violence and sex.

Is there anything we can do about media?

People often have a sense of hopelessness about what appears on television, thinking that the First Amendment paralyzes our collective ability to have any influence over broadcasters. But there is plenty that we can do about the images that appear in our living rooms.

Broadcasters have licenses to use exclusively a valuable piece of the nation's property—the airwaves—and from the time the system was set up in the 1930s they have been required in return to serve "the public interest." The Supreme Court has ruled that television differs from newspapers in how much is protected by the First Amendment, and that serving "the public interest" means limiting violent or indecent images.[73] So if either the Federal Communications Commission or Congress gets more demanding, they could easily clamp down on the number of murders or acts of sexual intercourse on television. The beer ads could disappear too, just as the cigarette ads have, because the Supreme Court also makes a distinction between "commercial speech" like advertising, which can be regulated, and noncommercial speech like newspaper articles and editorials, which are protected. Government's power to restrict commercial speech has eroded in recent years, but the distinction is still there.[74]

There are other options for people who get queasy with the idea of any government agency telling broadcasters what they can't put on the screen. For example, broadcasters could be taxed on the content of violence and sex in their programming, giving them the freedom to show what they want but changing the budget analyst's spreadsheet so that they might choose to cut violent scenes strictly from a business standpoint. Then there are ways to counter the damaging images that we can't or won't regulate or tax away. "Counter-advertising," such as antismoking ads, works in changing behavior.[75]

Regulation, taxation, and counter-advertising aren't popular words these days (at least not on television). But when it comes to the harmful images in the media, the ideas are not as radical as you might think. In a Gallup poll in 1999, 56 percent of Americans said they think the federal government should "do more" to regulate violence on television.[76]

Curve-shifting solutions to the health problems caused by media images are not impossible. We only need to first accept the fact that media really do influence how we behave, and second agree that we ought to do something about it. If we don't do anything about media images, those influences will not be ones that we want for our children and ourselves. On the other hand, the media can do much to help.

Fixing our everyday world

The four curve shifters described in this section—accessibility, physical structures, social structures, and media—work together to channel how we behave and how healthy we are. Rather than just being shaped by them, we can use them to remedy America's leading causes of death. In the next part of this book we pick up the problems we listed in chapter 1—smoking, physical inactivity, unhealthy eating, drinking, sexual behavior, and injuries—tracing their sources in our daily lives and laying out some of the changes we can make to solve them. In chapter 14 we look at the mysterious health problems visited on the poor, problems whose environmental causes we can't always describe but whose effects we can still lessen. Together, the changes can make a healthy landscape—or a "healthscape."

New ideas are often things of beauty, but when those ideas are turned into practical solutions to real-life problems they lose some of their luster. The solutions in the next chapters aren't all elegant, even if they are much prettier than the diseases they prevent. For readers who are uneasy with the solutions we propose or who wonder if they are unworkable, we take up the realities of health policies and politics in chapter 15.

PART III
HEALTHSCAPING AMERICA

CHAPTER 9

THE KILLER LEAF

They are very fond of smoking tobacco and they inhale the smoke,
which intoxicates them and makes them ill, but they keep on doing it.
—GABRIEL FRANCHÈRE, JOURNAL OF A VOYAGE ON
THE NORTH WEST COAST OF NORTH AMERICA
DURING THE YEARS 1811, 1812, 1813 AND 1814

Throughout history and across the globe, no drug has been more loved than
nicotine. Its effects are wonderful—the perfect antidote to the discomforts
of being human. When people are tired it picks them up. When they are
tense it relaxes them. It relieves pain and reduces hunger. It helps people
lose weight. It is easy to administer, begins acting almost immediately, and
its effects last only as long as people want them to. Every society on earth
has fallen for it, and in many nearly half of the adults soak up its pleasures
every single day. The tobacco leaf, wrote W. A. Penn in a book-length ode
in 1901, "has come to be regarded as one of the greatest boons with which
man has been blessed."[1] It is such a shame that this drug is delivered by tobacco, the greatest killer that man has ever known.

It has only been in the last few decades that health experts have grasped
the true horror of tobacco. As they gradually have uncovered the truth, they
have run the gamut of strategies to protect people from the leaf's dangers.
After many failed strategies, we finally have one that works—not one that
will ever eradicate this scourge, but one that can keep it at bay. That strategy uses the environmental levers from the last four chapters, and it is a
model for how we can tackle other major health problems.

A nicotine delivery system

Humans are captured by nicotine easily. Columbus met up with *Nicotiana*
tabacum, the tobacco plant, within days of his first island landing. At that

time, natives from what is now the tip of Argentina to Canada indulged in the drug. Those meeting him on that first landing taught his crew how to smoke it. The crew brought it back to Spain and within fifty years, tobacco was being grown in Europe for the booming market.

The tobacco leaf is a veritable nicotine factory, and smoking its leaves is a marvelous delivery system. It takes only about ten seconds for nicotine absorbed through the lungs to reach the brain—less time than it would take if the drug were injected intravenously.[2] That allows smokers to continuously regulate the amount of nicotine in their brains by varying how deeply they inhale and how long they hold the smoke in their lungs. Like Pavlov's dogs salivating at bells, smokers forge a link between the sensation of inhaling smoke and the pleasure of the wave of nicotine hitting the brain.

Unfortunately for smokers, the joys of nicotine come at a stiff price—addiction, for starters. People who smoke regularly must increase their smoking to continue to enjoy the drug's full pleasures. Monkeys given the chance to inject themselves with nicotine by pressing a bar will do so repeatedly—even after their nicotine doses are so high that they vomit.[3] When smokers stop, they have symptoms of drug withdrawal, becoming restless, angry, frustrated, and anxious; they desperately crave tobacco. Even among smokers who have broken the habit through an addiction treatment program, over 70 percent will start again within six months, the same relapse rate seen in treated heroin addicts.[4]

The smoke that delivers nicotine to the blood also deposits in the lungs a black, gooey residue called "tar," which is loaded with some 4,700 different chemicals, of which more than 50 are known to cause cancer.[5] They wreak the most havoc on the lining of the lungs—leading to a chronic hacking cough and emphysema—but they also infiltrate the bloodstream and transform cells throughout the body, causing cancer of the stomach, esophagus, bladder, pancreas, cervix, and blood.[6] Cigarette smoke also contains carbon monoxide, known for its effectiveness in automobile-exhaust suicides, which by damaging the lining of arteries leads to heart attacks and stroke.

Tobacco is not just another of the many unhealthy habits people take up. Nothing else comes anywhere close. Smoking kills 440,000 Americans a year, or nearly one in five deaths in America. That is equal to about three fully occupied 747s crashing every single day.[7] It's ten times as many deaths as occur from car crashes each year, and twenty times as many deaths as from HIV/AIDS. It isn't just smokers who die, either. About 50,000 nonsmokers die every year from lung cancer and heart disease caused by "sidestream smoke," as do about 2,000 babies from smoke-induced Sudden Infant Death Syndrome.[8] If we cured all other forms of cancer, vanquished the AIDS epidemic, prevented all murders, suicides, and car and plane crashes, and wiped out all deaths from alcohol, we still would not have saved as many lives as we could by merely cutting smoking rates in half.

Health experts become educated

To health experts who have known the facts about smoking for decades now it seems idiotic for anyone to take up smoking, or for anyone who smokes to keep doing it. It makes perfect sense, then, to think that we can win the war against tobacco by educating people. When people know about these gory statistics, they won't pick up cigarettes, and smokers won't continue.

But what makes sense isn't always true. In the 1960s and 1970s the American Cancer Society, the American Heart Association, the American Lung Association, and many other public health groups tried to dampen smoking rates by trotting out scores of variations on two types of programs: counseling adult smokers to quit and educating teens not to start in the first place. The programs employed every educational tool you can think of, including lectures, assemblies, discussions, demonstrations, posters, pamphlets, films, articles in school papers, visits by experts, and support groups, and they ranged in length from one week to several years. The educational messages were truthful and consistent, emphasizing "the health, social, and/or economic costs of smoking." But in 1976, when the American Cancer Society asked for an external review of these programs, they learned that among adults "anti-smoking campaigns have had little reported effect on smoking behavior" and that "most attempts to influence the smoking behavior of the young have had little success." Some of the programs made people adopt more negative attitudes toward smoking, but some didn't even achieve that. The report from the review even suggested why the programs were failing. "The majority of the programs seemed to accept the premise that man is a rational being and that he will act in his own best interest."[9]

In spite of this review, the education programs rolled on, and they continued to fail. A multimillion-dollar National Institutes of Health study to cut smoking through citywide education of adult smokers in twenty-two communities from 1989 to 1992 was a flop.[10] In 2000 the National Cancer Institute closed out its $15-million, forty-school-district controlled trial of school-based education about smoking that we described in chapter 3, showing no effect whatsoever on teen smoking rates.[11] Over the years, education in our society in general has met its immediate objective: in 2000, 73 percent of teenagers felt that smoking was a "great risk" to their health. But in that year 31 percent of high school seniors smoked, only a few percentage points less than twenty-five years earlier.[12] As much as we want it to, educating people about tobacco's dangers just does not prevent smoking.

Educational programs were all that most health experts could think of through most of the 1970s. And most ordinary Americans at that time saw smoking as just another unfortunate individual "lifestyle choice"— unhealthy but a matter of personal preference. In that decade, though, small groups of activists outside of medicine and public health introduced a fringe idea: people smoked not because of personal choice, but because of the massive promotion by the tobacco industry and a supportive social environment the industry created. The responsibility for smoking lay not with individual smokers but with the tobacco industry and the everyday world they created. The victims of the industry were not just the smokers but also nonsmokers forced to breathe their sidestream smoke. The activists thought the only way to cut smoking rates was by making smoking socially unacceptable, and that meant changing the everyday world.

In the beginning, the activists only asked for something that sounds pretty tame—separate smoking and nonsmoking areas in workplaces and restaurants. Because these clean indoor air laws protected nonsmokers, average citizens supported them, and initially city and town councils approved them readily.

It didn't take long for the industry to realize that these laws had real power—power that education didn't. Because they lifted smoking out of the category of personal behavior and relabeled it as an act dangerous to others, they held the potential of changing the social norm. An internal report by a polling organization prepared for the Tobacco Institute in 1978 called indoor smoking restrictions "the most dangerous development to the viability of the tobacco industry that has yet occurred."[13] After ignoring the ineffective school-based programs and individual counseling sessions, the industry suddenly became ferocious, firing off every weapon in its well-stocked legal and public relations arsenal. After Minnesota passed a clean indoor air law in 1975, the industry quietly strangled a similar California law in legislative committee in 1977, then killed a version put on the ballot through California's citizen initiative process with a $6.4 million public relations and advertising barrage, spending more than both candidates for governor combined.[14] After the Minnesota loss and the California scare, the industry was not about to be caught off-guard again. It took over state capitols with a combination of contributions to state legislators and their pet causes, contracts with lobbyists, and paid-for "support" from allied groups and front groups, managing to paralyze further state attempts at clean indoor air laws.[15] In the 1990s, when the National Cancer Institute funded the American Stop Smoking Intervention Study (ASSIST), a project that gave money to local coalitions to change policies like indoor air in cities and towns, the industry brought out its heavy artillery at every level. A Philip Morris executive showed their attitude in an internal memo: "The simple fact is we are at war, and we currently face the most critical challenges our industry has ever met."[16] The industry harassed the NCI with Freedom of Information Act requests, fed words to friendly senators like Orrin Hatch to protest the study, provoked investigations of alleged "illegal lobbying" by the Inspector General of the Department of Health and Human Services, attached language to federal laws to try to ban ASSIST activities, bought support from associations of restaurants and convenience stores, prompted two friendly academics to write a book about the "scam" of using federal funds for "political" activities, and paid a public relations firm to conjure up a "smokers' rights" organization.[17] One of the industry's most telling acts was to try to divert the ASSIST program money that was allocated to community organizing instead to schools, where of course they knew it wouldn't do them any damage. Finally, they contained the problem by lobbying in every state capitol (and succeeding in most) to pass "preemptive" laws that banned any local governments from passing strict indoor air ordinances.[18]

Changing the smoking environment

At first, most of the medical and public health leaders treated activists and their environmental approach to smoking prevention at best with indifference and at times with hostility. Now, however, nearly thirty years later, health professionals agree that the primary responsibility for smoking lies with the industry rather than the smoker and see the solution as changing our everyday environment, rather than educating kids or counseling smokers. Now that they have the fundamental strategy, they are working out exactly how effective each curve-shifter is.

Accessibility

Two ways to limit the accessibility of tobacco are taxes and restrictions on sales to children. As we pointed out in chapter 5, cigarette excise taxes work, with a 10 percent increase in the price of a pack cutting sales by 3 to 5 percent overall and 7 to 8 percent in teens. When the U.S. federal excise tax was doubled in 1983, cigarette sales fell by 12 percent, enough to save the lives of some forty thousand people per year, about as much as stopping the AIDS epidemic in the United States could.[19]

In recent years advocates and public health agencies have been trying hard to erect other obstacles to sales to teens. Teens can't buy cigarettes legally in the United States, but they can get them from vending machines or stores that ignore these laws. Cigarette sales to teenagers fall when vending machines are banned, and some (but definitely not all) studies show that enforcing bans on over-the-counter sales to teens cut sales as well.[20]

Physical structures

Since the 1950s, tobacco companies have tried to invent a safer cigarette (although, to be clear, they tried a lot harder to invent a cigarette that they could *sell* as safe), first with increasingly sophisticated filters and cooler-burning tobacco and most recently with plastic "smokeless" cigarettes that deliver nicotine by the smoker drawing air through a solution. The low-tar cigarettes may not be much safer than unfiltered cigarettes, because smokers tend to just inhale more to get the dose of nicotine they need.[21] The smokeless cigarettes are not much different from nicotine chewing gum or skin patches, which do help some smokers quit.[22] Since it's the tar in cigarettes rather than the nicotine that really does the damage, "nicotine replacement" makes sense. But because the industry's safer-cigarette attempts so far have been either shams or failures, we shouldn't hold out too much hope for a success in the future.

Social structures

The changes that the antismoking activists started with—indoor smoking bans—have still been their greatest victory. Where the term "smoke-filled room" once symbolized power and success, by 1999 79 percent of workplaces with fifty or more employees either banned smoking or confined it to rooms with separate ventilation.[23] Workplace smoking bans have several proven benefits: smokers smoke less during the workday, nonsmokers are exposed to less sidestream smoke, teenagers who work in smoke-free workplaces are less likely to become smokers, and smokers living in communities with workplace ordinances are more likely to quit. Most of all, workplace smoking bans tell everyone that smoking is socially unacceptable. The greatest decline in smoking in the history of the United States happened as these workplace bans spread across the nation.

The next areas where smoking is being banned are restaurants and bars, as in New York City and California. As we write, some communities are going further, banning smoking not just indoors but also in outdoor public places, such as beaches in California. Second-hand smoke is not a problem outdoors, of course. Activists make their case with the problem of cigarette butts, but the most important reason for these bans is to hammer home smoking's unacceptability—making people ashamed to smoke.

Media

Advertising drives smoking. As we described in chapter 8, cigarette sales grew astronomically in the first half of the twentieth century, in parallel with the powerful combination of modern advertising techniques and new broadcast media. From 1967 through 1970, the Fairness Doctrine forced broadcasters to air one antismoking ad for every three cigarette ads.[24] These ads weren't just educational; they used all of the emotional power of media image we described in chapter 8. The effect of the antismoking ads was swift and sharp: per capita cigarette sales, which had been rising beforehand, fell by about 10 percent.[25] The tobacco industry, seeing this, accepted a ban on their own advertising just to get the anti-tobacco ads off the air. They then redirected their advertising dollars to magazines, billboards, and event promotions, and within a few years cigarette sales bounced back.[26] States that have funded big, hard-hitting electronic media campaigns have slashed smoking rates: Florida's "Truth" campaign cut smoking by middle school students by 20 percent in one year and 40 percent in two.[27] California and Massachusetts had similar successes with campaigns funded by tax increases.[28] We know when antismoking programs are successful by how hard the tobacco industry works to kill them. In all three states, the drop in smoking rates was followed by the governors and legislatures dismantling the programs.[29]

The federal Office on Smoking and Health has assembled a graph of cigarette consumption over the twentieth century. The peaks and valleys in the graph coincide with the major policy and environmental changes that have taken place. The biggest reductions in smoking follow indoor smoking restrictions, increases in taxes, and changes in media portrayals of smoking, in about that order.[30] The overall message is clear: the killer leaf can be subdued, not through education, but through changes in our everyday environment.

Masters and settlement

If you paid only moderate attention to the news in the late 1990s, you might think that the agreement between the tobacco industry and the states' attorneys general over smoking-related costs dealt a mortal blow to the industry—that the war against tobacco was all but won. But this settlement was only one battle in the war, and it is looking more and more as though it is a battle that the industry won. Whatever this settlement will do in the long run, it will *not* put an end to smoking in America, and it may not even put a dent in it. The path the settlement took shows the immense power of the tobacco industry's profits and gives us a glimpse into what future battles might look like.

Even though they've known for decades that smoking is addictive and fatal, the tobacco companies managed for about a century to maintain a golden immunity from government regulation or penalties. But in the late 1990s Mississippi attorney general Michael Moore led a group of state attorneys general to sue the tobacco companies for state Medicaid costs rung up by smokers. Using confidential documents showing that the industry lied about tobacco's dangers, this group had an angle that looked to everyone as if it might actually work. In 1997 the big tobacco companies, seeing both a threat and an opportunity, surprised everyone by agreeing to a proposed settlement that would pay the states $368 billion over twenty-five years and allow some restrictions on tobacco sales and promotion—in return for immunity from all other lawsuits and sharp restrictions on how the Food and Drug Administration (FDA) could regulate them.[31] While the states (and the press) nearly burst with pride over the huge dollar amounts, public health advocates screamed bloody murder: in one pass the tobacco companies were buying off the entire system of federal and state governments, taking away the best tools our society had to prevent smoking—regulation and litigation—for a cost that would mean a price hike of only 72 cents a pack.[32] Both the Federal Trade Commission and industry financial analysts predicted that the industry would not just survive with this settlement, it would thrive by raising prices and by passing on much of the costs of the tax-deductible settlement to taxpayers, making as much as $123 billion in additional profits even after paying the settlement costs over the subsequent twenty-five years.[33]

Because the federal government was part of the settlement, it had to be approved by the U.S. Congress, so public health advocates mobilized in Washington to fix it. Instead of going along with the plan, Senator John McCain introduced a bill that would give the tobacco industry limited liability protection, but would allow the FDA to regulate them. The McCain bill passed out of his committee with bipartisan support, nineteen to one.[34] The reaction of the industry to this bill laid bare the fact that what the industry really feared wasn't a big financial settlement, which they could always pay off with their big profits, but rather regulation of how they could promote smoking. The big five tobacco companies announced—

acting as if they constituted a fourth arm of government—that they flat out would not accept the McCain bill.[35] Within days the Republican support for the bill mysteriously turned to opposition, and in another two months the bill was dead.[36]

The states' Attorneys General, afraid to lose the money they had so painstakingly negotiated, tried again, this time giving up on the idea of the support of the U.S. Congress or federal immunity. Just five months after the McCain bill died, in November of 1998, the Master Settlement Agreement was unveiled. In this settlement, the tobacco industry agreed to pay the states $248 billion over twenty-five years if the states dropped their claims for smoking-related Medicaid costs.[37] The tobacco companies also agreed to marginal limitations on how tobacco was promoted, but the settlement does not restrict advertising in magazines, by direct mail, through the Internet, through point-of-purchase ads, or by brand-naming sports on television.

Since the point of the settlement was to compensate the states for the deceitful promotion of smoking on the part of the tobacco industry, you might think the states would use the money to prevent smoking, which was, after all, the biggest killer of their citizens. But even though the settlement barred the industry from lobbying to divert the settlement dollars to other purposes, the state legislatures suddenly found other needs more pressing. Only 6 percent of the settlement funds in 2001 were used for tobacco control programs, and the states with the highest smoking rates often spent the least on smoking prevention.[38] In Louisiana, the first $200 million in settlement money was used to build prisons, repair roads, and cover Medicaid's deficit. About $2 million was allocated to smoking prevention, but when a new deficit showed up, it was the first to be cut.

The war rages on

We've learned a few things during all this political and legal wrangling. First, selling an addictive drug like nicotine is immensely profitable, so much so that no amount of taxes or court settlements will hurt the business—let alone drive it into bankruptcy. Second, the industry knows that to continue to create new smoking addicts it must continue to promote smoking—glamorizing it with advertising, littering our world with brand names, and placing packs at nearly every cash register—so it will fight regulation with every weapon it has. Third, unless we demand otherwise, the flood of tobacco profits can buy more than enough U.S. congresspersons, senators, and state legislators to pamper the industry.

Tobacco is still heavily advertised, promoted, and marketed in the United States. The year after the settlement was announced, tobacco companies bumped up their marketing expenditures by 22 percent to $8.2 billion, enough to plaster the nation with magazine ads, billboards, point-of-purchase displays, sponsorships of events (such as the Marlboro Grand Prix), direct mail ads, hats and T-shirts, and free product giveaways.[39] Cigarette ads are the biggest source of income for many magazines and newspapers, and tobacco companies don't mind using this leverage to manipulate magazine content. The ads associate smoking with our greatest desires—even if they are just the opposite of the effects of smoking—such as the Marlboro cowboys' strength and independence (meant to hide smokers' weakness and dependence) and the Virginia Slims models' health and happiness (meant to hide smokers' debilitation and nervousness). These images are powerful. They sell smoking to us all—but they sell most effectively to teenagers who are trying to establish their identity.

The most galling promotion of tobacco might be product placements in movies. Although the tobacco industry claims that it does not pay film producers to show actors smoking, the facts tell us the money must be getting there some way. Smoking in movies has been on the rise for the last ten years, so much so that actors are as likely to smoke on-screen in 2002 as they were in 1950, when actual smoking rates were twice as high as they are now.[40] Movie product placements rarely show a brand name. They don't have to. The tobacco companies aren't selling particular brands. They are selling smoking itself.

When tobacco companies spend billions a year to get people addicted to nicotine, can we do anything to prevent the deaths from smoking? Yes, plenty. The steps we should take are fixing our everyday world to make smoking more socially unacceptable. We can:

- run hard-hitting ads on television and radio which deglamorize smoking and point out the industry's lies;

• limit all tobacco advertising to appropriately named "tombstone" style (lettering only, with no human images or logos) and ban all outdoor and point-of-purchase ads;

• limit the number and type of retail outlets that can sell cigarettes (maybe to licensed pharmacies), and tightly control sales so that teenagers cannot buy them;

• assign the FDA the job of regulating tobacco as the drug that it is, so that new industry promotional tactics can be countered quickly;

• tax cigarettes $1.50 per pack to drive up the cost and pay for the cost of counter-advertising and regulation;

• ban smoking in all buildings except private residences and in all public outdoor areas.

Some of these ideas may strike some people—even those against smoking—as too intrusive, too heavy-handed. But tobacco is killing at least twenty times more people than the most dreaded addictive drugs—heroin and cocaine.[41] Would we feel comfortable watching our movie stars healthily and happily sticking heroin in their arms in every scene? Would we accept magazine ads showing a handsome, macho "Crack Man"? Do we think it is good policy to allow 7-Eleven to sell cocaine to fourteen-year-olds? Would we allow crack users to light up in front of our kids in the town square? Given the nearly half-million dead bodies piled up by tobacco every year, these changes are actually very modest. More important, they will work.

We've got the basic strategy for this epidemic: environmental changes. Now the question is not whether we know what to do, or whether it's practically achievable, it is whether we can outmuscle the tobacco industry to make it happen. Trying to overcome the tobacco industry is a little like trying to overcome the Colombian cocaine cartel. The opposition has limitless resources, is unprincipled, and its core existence (selling tobacco) is the direct opposite of our goal (preventing smoking).

Before we despair, though, we should remember that the United States is supposed to be a democracy, our elected leaders are supposed to represent the will of the people, and Americans *overwhelmingly* support regulating tobacco. To say that we cannot protect our children and ourselves from tobacco is to say that we no longer have a democracy in America. The actions that we need to take as a society are clear; we simply need to demand that our elected leaders listen to us.

CHAPTER 10

HABITS
of the HEART

On a Tuesday evening, in a brightly lit, carpeted classroom at West Jefferson Medical Center in suburban New Orleans, ten people gathered for their weekly meeting under the guidance of three gently encouraging group leaders. One by one they reported their victories and lapses. "I lost one pound since last week," said Robert. The group answered with polite applause. Next, Tiffany said, "My weight was the same." She was met with sympathetic nods. "But I bought a new skirt and I went down three skirt sizes." The group erupted with cheers and clapping.

This group was a behavioral-modification program for obesity. But this one was not typical, because the participants were all children. Young children at that, some as young as five.

Unfortunately, these fat kids themselves were pretty typical. In 1999–2000, 15 percent of children aged six to nineteen were overweight.[1] That's about three times the percentage twenty-five years earlier, and it translates to more than 7 million overweight American children. About the only thing that set the kids in this program apart from kids all over this country was that their parents could pay for the program.

The mushrooming of obesity in children is the latest grim news in the larger epidemic of obesity in the entire U.S. population. In 1999–2000, nearly a third of adults were obese—about two and one-half times as many as in the early 1960s—and nearly two-thirds were overweight.[2]

The children at this clinic were worried about being teased by classmates, but the leaders—a pediatrician, a psychologist, and a dietitian—had far greater fears, knowing that their patients were headed fast toward several linked killer diseases. Obesity is only the most visible marker for a cluster of pernicious health problems linked to our eating and exercise habits that kill hundreds of thousands of Americans a year, including diabetes, heart disease, stroke, and kidney failure.

In the 1950s, after surviving the starvation of the Depression and the horror of World War II, America woke up to an epidemic of heart attacks. Heart disease was the cause of over 40 percent of deaths, three times higher than the next biggest killer.[3] The medical establishment responded with a flood of tests, studies, and advice. In the last half-century it has continued to hammer home the basic prevention message: exercise more and eat healthier. The explosion of obesity in the last few decades despite this advice ought to tell us that our fundamental approach to preventing these chronic diseases has failed. Like the 1970s-era smoking-prevention activists, we need a new strategy.

The deadly quartet

In the late 1980s Norman Kaplan of the University of Texas coined a phrase for four major health conditions that often ran together: obesity, hyperlipidemia (excess fat in the blood), hyperglycemia (high blood sugar), and hypertension (high blood pressure).[4] If you have any one of the members of this "deadly quartet," you are asking for heart disease. (This discussion does not consider smoking, which is an extremely important risk factor for heart disease and stroke, but which we covered in the last chapter.) If you have more members of the quartet, the risks are compounded. These conditions are densely intertwined:

• In people with hyperlipidemia, cholesterol settles out under the lining of the arteries, especially those that supply the heart and the brain. The narrowed arteries can starve the heart muscle slowly, causing congestive heart failure, or kill it suddenly through a heart attack. Blood clots can also suddenly block off narrowed arteries leading to the brain, causing a stroke.

• In people with hypertension, small arteries supplying the brain sometimes burst under the increased pressure, causing a stroke. Hypertension also puts a chronic stress on the heart and arteries, making them more susceptible to narrowing. Long-term hypertension also hammers away at the kidneys, sometimes leading to kidney failure.

• High blood sugar, caused by a resistance to the hormone insulin that is supposed to keep blood sugar low, is an early marker of diabetes, which worsens all of these other conditions. People with diabetes don't metabolize fat well, so fat levels rise in their blood and clog their large arteries sooner. Their small arteries also get damaged, leading not only to hypertension but also to kidney failure, blindness, and chronic ulcers and infections of the feet, necessitating amputations.

• Obesity increases the risk of all of these other conditions and diseases. Obese people get high blood pressure and high blood cholesterol. And overweight people—after years of needing extra insulin to metabolize the extra food they eat—finally become resistant to insulin and are much more likely to develop diabetes. Obesity also increases the risk of cancer of the colon, breast, and prostate.

All of the members of the quartet are so common in America today that even though they are killing us, it might be fair to call them normal. One in four men and one in five women in America are labeled as having full-blown hypertension, but over half of the population would be healthier if they had lower blood pressure.[5] Likewise, one in five American adults meets the official criteria for high blood cholesterol, but the overwhelming majority—maybe over 90 percent—of Americans would be healthier if they had lower blood cholesterol.[6] When nearly two-thirds of Americans are overweight, we are not dealing with a genetic problem of a few but a population-wide phenomenon. One in sixteen Americans have been diagnosed with diabetes, and an even greater number have either undiagnosed diabetes or "pre-diabetes."[7] It shouldn't be surprising, then, that the final crash at the end of the long skid of the deadly quartet—dropping dead of heart failure or stroke—is a common event in America. In 2000, ischemic heart disease was the cause of 21 percent of the deaths among Americans, with stroke responsible for another 7 percent; together they bury hundreds of thousands every year.[8]

Why us?

Why is it normal in America to be sick with obesity, diabetes, and hypertension?

The specific behaviors that lead to these conditions are few and familiar. They are eating too many calories, fat, and saturated fat, taking in too much salt, and not being sufficiently physically active.

Americans get about 33 percent of their calories from fat right now, up from 27 percent a century ago.[9] Fat and saturated fat in our diet probably peaked in the 1960s, and since then Americans have been eating foods with less saturated fat and less total fat. This surely has contributed to the lowering of blood cholesterol in America and an easing of the epidemic of heart disease. But the *amount* of total fat we are eating is as high as it was thirty years ago, because we are just eating more of everything.[10]

Salt—sodium chloride—causes hypertension. In fact, it is beginning to look as though hypertension, which not long ago was mysterious in origin, is just chronic salt intoxication. Like fat, salt is something necessary to life that throughout our evolution has been in short supply, so we crave it. Now that it is everywhere, we overdose. Americans consume about ten times as much sodium per day as people from tribal societies that don't have any members with hypertension.[11] Any decrease in salt would cut rates of hypertension, the lower the better. A review panel of the National Institutes of Health was emphatic that all of us, not just people who already have hypertension, should be on low-salt diets.[12]

Obesity is the easiest of the deadly quartet to understand, at least in theory. As complicated as our metabolic processes are, the basic equation of energy balance is simple: we gain weight when we eat more calories than we burn off. It doesn't take a lot of imbalance in our calories to make people obese, just consistency. It is the little things we do every day that make us stay lean or gain weight. If a person sits in a car instead of walking slowly for only twenty minutes every day for a year, he will store about 26,000 calories and gain about five pounds.[13] If a person drinks only one extra can of Coke every *other* day, she'll store enough calories to gain about four pounds,[14] Researchers at the University of Minnesota estimated that if a person spends only five minutes each workday for a year sending e-mails to coworkers instead of walking to their offices to talk to them, he or she will gain about a pound.[15] This weight gain won't continue indefinitely, because as we put on more fat we have to expend more calories just to lug those extra pounds around every day, but small energy imbalances continue to add to our body fat. Most of us gain weight like this—a few grams a day, a couple of pounds a year.

The current national panic about carbohydrates and the desperate search for the magic diet to fight obesity is missing the point. Rather than *what kind* of food we eat, the problem is simply *how much* we eat, which is increasingly a reflection of *how often* we eat. Men are now taking in 168 more calories a day than they were thirty years ago, and women are gobbling up 335 calories more.[16] A greater percentage of these calories comes from carbohydrates than was the case thirty years ago, but the basic problem is not the carbs, it's the calories.

Americans no longer eat just three meals a day—they graze constantly. Young adults now eat on average two snacks per day—which means that many snack far more than that.[17] The most common snacks—desserts, chips, candy, and soft drinks—are calorie-dense and in every other way distinctly unhealthy.[18] With the average snack containing more than 300 calories, close to one-fourth of Americans' total calories now come from snacks.[19] If it weren't for snacks, we would not be eating any more than we were thirty years ago, and we probably would not be facing an epidemic of obesity. This snacking pattern may also in a funny way partly explain why Americans are eating less saturated fat; snacks are replacing meals, and people rarely snack on steak.

Diabetes simply follows in the wake of obesity. If we weren't overweight and got plenty of exercise, the adult form of this disease would be rare.

While a "sedentary lifestyle"—or lack of physical activity—contributes to obesity, it also contributes to high blood cholesterol levels, high blood pressure, and resistance to insulin.[20] Inactive people are more likely to die of heart disease and stroke, even after you take into account body weight. Only a quarter of American adults get the recommended amounts of exercise during nonwork hours, and about 30 percent are completely inactive.[21]

American smorgasbord

On a health blog,[22] a person named Larry Anderson wrote:

> The reason I am obese is both obvious, and at the same time, deeply mysterious. It is obvious because it is clear that I eat too many calories and I expend too few calories. I don't deny it. I don't offer excuses that defy reality. But, why I eat too many calories, and why I don't exercise, is a mystery.
>
> It is not because I am not aware that I overeat and under exercise. I know it. It is not because I am not aware of the consequences. I have a heart condition and diabetes and take several medications, every day. It is not because I don't suffer as a result of my obesity.
>
> At times it seems to me that everyone else has the answer except me. "You're lazy," I've been told by some.
>
> "You're undisciplined," others have explained. "You must get control of yourself. It is a matter of will. A question of choice. You are fat because you choose not to do something about it."
>
> "You have unresolved emotional issues, and until you resolve them, you will always be fat," the more gentile [sic] advise. "Perhaps you should consult a psychiatrist."
>
> Still, I don't know why I do what I do that maintains my obesity. Does anyone have any ideas?

When two-thirds of Americans are overweight, Mr. Anderson is in good company. The mystery would be less mysterious if he were to look around him rather than, as his friends suggest, look inside himself. The external source of his problem is not hidden. It is in plain view, but he can't see it because it is everywhere.

After 3:00 P.M. on weekdays in New Orleans, children carrying backpacks and wearing the plaid school uniform of Warren Easton High School drift into the Burger King on Canal Street near the intersection of Broad Street. They order drinks or fries at the counter, or just hang out, swapping stories and flirting.

At this Burger King a Whopper costs $1.99. A "Value Meal" that comes with a Coke and fries costs only $3.39 and packs 1,190 calories, which is more than half of the recommended daily calories for a teenage girl. If you "King Size" your Value Meal (more fries, 32-ounce drink) by tossing in 80 cents more, you can bump it up to 1,570 calories, or more than 70 percent of what a girl needs. It is hard to imagine that anyone having polished off a Value Meal will then fast for the next 24 hours, so it is easy to imagine that frequent visits to places like Burger King have something to do with the excess fat that kids (and the rest of us) are carrying. That same King Size Value Meal also carries with it 2,080 milligrams of sodium, nearly 90 percent of what is recommended for the whole day, leading any customer well on his way to hypertension.

The flow of kids in the door of this particular Burger King doesn't seem heavy at first, maybe fifteen kids over fifteen minutes, at what ought to be peak time for schoolchildren. But then this Burger King is not alone. Next door, within maybe thirty feet, is a McDonald's. And around the corner on Broad Street, with a parking lot adjacent to Burger King's, is a Rally's, a local low-cost burger-and-fries chain. The schoolkids are milling around all three, making up the largest group of customers—if you don't count the steady queues of cars at all three drive-up windows.

Even beyond fast-food burger joints, America is littered with outlets for high-fat, calorie-dense, salty junk foods. "Convenience" stores pop up on nearly every corner. A typical one we visited in New Orleans had over 40 percent of its shelf space devoted to snack foods, all in easy reach, close to the ground for youngsters.[23] Typical snacks here are potato chips— a tiny, 1.5-ounce bag loaded with 23 percent of the recommended daily allowance (RDA) of fat and 11 percent of sodium—and chocolate bars— a 2-ounce bar stuffed with 22 percent of the RDA of fat and 6 percent of sodium. There are no fruits or vegetables in any form in sight.

It doesn't end there. Supermarkets also devote more shelf space to snacks than fruits and vegetables.[24] Vending machines have sprouted like mushrooms everywhere (including schools). At a gas station in New Orleans we found Coke vending machines not at the indoor cashier but on every outdoor "island"—with one island having two—so drivers didn't even have to walk the few steps to the cashier to grab 150 calories of dissolved sugar. So, like the rest of us, Larry Anderson of the health blog is swimming in a sea of calorie-dense snack food.

Our newly acquired habit of constant snacking can only take place in an everyday environment such as this, where ready-to-inhale food is always in arm's reach. Between 1955 and 2004, according to industry statistics, the percentage of Americans' total meal dollars spent away from home nearly doubled, to 46 percent, and within the next few years it will top 50 percent.[25] Between 1977 and 1995 the percentage of meals eaten at fast-food restaurants tripled.[26] Sales of snacks from vending machines grew 150 percent from 1990 to 2000, to $41 billion.[27]

Some will argue that the industry behind all this junk food is just meeting demand. People just like high-salt, high-fat foods; if they wanted more fruits and vegetables, they would ask for them and the food industry would sell them. But that argument has at least two holes in it. First, according to Advertising Age, besides putting their junk food where we practically trip over it, the food industry spends $10 billion each year in advertisements persuading us to eat it.[28] McDonald's alone spends over $1 billion a year.[29] They spend these billions not to meet demand, but to manipulate demand. Of course these investments pay off, or they wouldn't spend the money. This advertising overwhelms health messages like the federal government's 5-A-Day fruit-and-vegetable campaign, funded at $1 million a year.[30] Second, studies have shown that our tastes for food are acquired—or as one put it more clearly, "you eat what you like, but you like what you eat." Japanese people grow up eating raw fish, and they love it. As the food industry has learned, if we grow up entirely on Happy Meals we come to expect food to taste like that, and we continue to buy it as adults. If we have never seen fruits and vegetables, why would we demand them?

Certainly, we have natural cravings from our evolutionary past that make high-fat and salty foods appealing, but the food industry pushes this weakness of ours as far as it can. The food industry chooses what foods to sell based not on demand but on how much profit it can make. Junk foods, which are cheap to produce and have a long shelf life, are much more profitable than fresh fruits and vegetables, which have neither of these advantages.

Locked in our cars

At a scientific meeting we attended, a speaker asked some hundred nutritionists if they walked to school when they were young. About two-thirds raised their hands. Next he asked them how many of their children—or if they didn't have young children, how many of their nieces, nephews, or grandchildren—currently walked to school. About one in ten raised their hands.

Everything about our modern American world forces us to be physically lazy. We don't walk anymore. If we want to move, we drive. We drive on streets without sidewalks or crosswalks, from culs-de-sac through traffic-clogged multilane arterials to strip malls, "big-box" retailers, and office complexes. Neighborhoods are fortress enclaves walled off from commercial and industrial areas. In some places it is attempting suicide just to walk across a major street, as we learned once when we were forced to take a cab to traverse a six-lane wonder in Atlanta. And as the speaker at the scientific meeting showed, most children don't walk to school any more. The National Personal Transportation Survey showed that people traveled on foot or on bicycles for a pitiful 5 percent of trips in 1995, down from 7 percent in 1990 and 9 percent in 1983.[31] Meanwhile, drivers spent nearly an hour a day in their cars.[32]

And wherever we go in our cars, we spend our time there in front of a video screen of some kind. The Internet is today's transformation of our world, but the really big change occurred in the 1960s, when televisions invaded first living rooms, then dens, "family rooms," bedrooms, and kitchens. When a person watches television her body downshifts into semi-comatose mode, her heart rate and muscle activity dropping to about what they are during sleep.[33] Even a minimal activity such as sitting and talking with friends burns about 35 calories more per hour than watching TV.[34] Multiply that by just three hours of TV a day and you can estimate that television could increase an average person's weight by as much as seven pounds a year, even compared to a completely "sedentary" activity.

Schools used to make up for some of the sedentary behavior at home with physical education classes. But of the children in the New Orleans obesity clinic, only two said they had physical education classes more than one day a week in school. National surveys showed that the percentage of high schoolers who attended physical education classes five days a week decreased from 42 percent in 1991 to 27 percent in 1996; in any given week 79 percent of adolescents do not have physical education at all.[35]

Actions of the heart

What as a nation have we done to respond to the carnage from heart disease, stroke, diabetes, and kidney disease?

Of course we've spent a lot on medical treatment. Estimates are that the medical costs related to hypertension run about $110 billion, those related to obesity run about $75 billion, and those related to diabetes run about $92 billion per year.[36] The cost of keeping patients with kidney failure alive through dialysis is running about $16 billion a year and growing fast.[37] Even with some double counting these numbers are huge. About a half of these medical costs are paid by the government in programs like Medicare and Medicaid, and another third are paid by private insurers, which is to say that we all pay these bills in one form or another, whether or not we personally get the diseases.[38]

Drug companies are pushing a variety of drugs to lower our blood pressure, reduce our blood cholesterol, and treat our diabetes. For all the direct-to-patient advertising about these drugs, though, as we discussed in chapter 1, treatments for the deadly quartet as a means to prevent cardiovascular diseases fall far short of the hype. Drug treatment of hypertension lowers mortality, but only about a third of people labeled as having hypertension are effectively controlled by drugs,[39] and of course these drugs do nothing for the majority of us who are at increased risk from having "high normal" blood pressure. Treatment of high blood cholesterol with new "statin" drugs can lower mortality rates for people who are at high risk, but the benefit is small and the costs high for most people, so the National Institutes of Health considers the use of these drugs only "an 'adjunct' to lifestyle changes," concluding that "the lion's share of the effort to prevent coronary atherosclerosis [heart disease from high cholesterol] falls to the population (public health) approach."[40] Diabetes treatment is particularly disappointing: in the best-run trials, intensive treatment for type 2 diabetes doesn't affect mortality at all.[41]

Medical treatment for obesity is a near complete failure. Most drugs that have been tried as obesity cures have been dangerous enough that the FDA has kept them off the market or withdrawn them after approval. The effectiveness of drugs that have been used is, in the cautious words of experts at the National Institutes of Health, "modest"; they may cut weight by about five to ten pounds, after which people usually stop losing or gain weight back.[42] Diets and exercise programs to shed fat don't fare much better. An expert panel at NIH concluded that people following strict low-calorie diets can lower weight by about 8 percent over six months, but they gain half of that back within the next two to three years.[43] And these less-than-modest successes are for people in intensive programs with researchers giving them constant monitoring, education, and encouragement; the rest of us, left to our own devices, don't do even this well.

If people and their doctors can't cure these risk factors once they happen, as a nation we ought to prevent them in the first place. And health experts *have* been trying to prevent heart disease with education programs. They have been telling people to eat low-fat, low-salt foods and to exercise more. But failures of large-scale education programs to prevent heart disease have been so dismal that they've prompted lively discussions in medical journals about whether we have the basic biology wrong, or whether we should just give up on the idea of prevention.

We haven't got the basic biology wrong. We just need to apply the lessons we've learned from the tobacco wars.

First, we need to reformulate the basic prevention message, which until now has been too much, too late. It extols "dieting" and "exercise" for people with "risk factors" rather than "healthy eating" and "physical activity" for all of us. "'Exercise' is something you *go do*," says Bill Wilkinson, Executive Director of the National Center for Bicycling and Walking. "It means shoehorning another responsibility into a busy day." Most of us just aren't going to do it. There may seem to be a lot of joggers out in parks these days, and health clubs may be booming, but the number of Americans who say they are deliberately exercising hasn't increased in the last decade.[44] The only way the majority of Americans are going to get moving is if activity is part of their daily routines. It has to be as unavoidable as an encounter with a vending machine is now.

The same idea applies to diet. Americans try valiantly to lose weight by dieting—just look at the mountains of diet books in stores. But almost no one keeps on a "diet" for long. It means denial. The temptations of forbidden food within our reach are too great. We don't need another diet. We need a way to make healthy eating simpler.

Everyday fixes for everyone's problems

How can we change our everyday world to make it easier to eat healthier food and be physically active? The problem is so huge that we need to push on several fronts.

We're stuck with the invention of junk food—that genie is out of the bottle. We can't ban it, and our appetites won't let us ignore it, but we can regulate it. We have already made tremendous gains in health by regulating what we eat and drink: fluoride in water has made Generation X the first generation virtually without cavities, iodine in salt has practically eliminated iodine-deficiency goiters, and grains and breads enriched with vitamins have vanquished vitamin deficiencies—all without most people even knowing about these benefits. These successes tell us that there is no reason why we cannot, for example, require the fat content of hamburgers to be no higher than 15 percent, or set a limit on the salt in French fries or frozen pizza. And we can also set some rules or incentives to limit portion sizes in fast-food restaurants—no "supersizing." These kinds of regulations would not stop the dedicated overeater from eating too much high-fat or salty food, but it could make overeating less convenient, more expensive, and therefore less frequent in the general population.

Or we could tax food based on its fat content or calorie density. Kelly Brownell of Yale University was the first to seriously propose slapping a tax on junk food as a way to blunt the obesity epidemic.[45] Nineteen states and cities already have some kind of tax on specific junk foods, such as soft drinks, candy, chewing gum, or snack foods, usually as a sales tax of 5 percent to 7 percent, so the precedent is there.[46] It would mean defining what we consider as junk food (which is not easy but not impossible either) and varying the tax according to whether it meets that definition.[47] Brownell estimates that even as small a tax as 1 cent per can on soft drinks would generate $1.5 billion a year.[48] We could use the money to counter-advertise against junk food and to promote fruits and vegetables with the same level of slickness and saturation as the "got milk?" and "Beef: It's What's for Dinner" campaigns. We could also subsidize healthy foods like fruits and vegetables. The federal government is already in the food subsidy business through the Women, Infants, and Children (WIC) supplemental nutrition program for low-income women and children; why not expand the program to subsidize fruits and vegetables for a larger group?

Besides taxing junk food and using media to counteract its advertising, we ought to think about regulation of food advertising itself. At the very least, we should ban advertising of junk foods to kids, starting with Saturday-morning cartoon shows.

We can also limit the places in which junk food is available. No one will tell Burger King they can't run their business, but in the middle of an obesity epidemic killing hundreds of thousands of people a year, is it really a good idea to have *three* fast-food high-fat burger joints within half a block of a high school? There is no reason we can't, through local-level zoning and planning, regulate the location, density, or hours of junk-food outlets. We also ought to put limits on the location and number of snack-food and soft-drink vending machines.

In every town in America businesspeople need a permit to sell food in a store, whether that store is a giant supermarket or a corner convenience store. That provides a mechanism to require or provide incentives for all food stores to sell fruits and vegetables. A requirement like that wouldn't force people to eat fruits and vegetables, but it would at least give them the choice to buy them—a choice the poor living in inner cities and rural areas may not have at their corner groceries now.

We should strengthen and enforce the USDA regulation of the foods sold in schools. Since the 1960s, federal law has required that school lunches be nutritious, but the law has huge loopholes—among them that schools can sell "competitive" foods like soft drinks as long as they are not sold in the cafeteria during lunchtime—and its enforcement is lax.[49] What can parents of the kids in the New Orleans obesity clinic do when their school cafeterias serve French fries every single day? Soft-drink companies sign contracts with school systems guaranteeing hefty payments to schools in return for putting vending machines in front of kids.[50] The school systems themselves—starved for money for basic programs—are some of the staunchest defenders of these contracts, but they bring in funds at the cost of cutting short the life spans of the children they educate. When we teach children about nutrition in health classes and then make money by plying them with Cokes and other junk food in school hallways, the children learn only about our hypocrisy.

We have to put walking and bicycling back into our daily lives and temper our addiction to cars. For starters, we can require that when developers build neighborhoods they put in sidewalks and bike paths, and we can direct federal and state highway funds to building them on existing streets; at least then people will have a place to walk and ride if they want to. A little progress has been made here. The major federal transportation bill—the Transportation Equity Act for the 21st Century, or TEA-21, like its predecessor ISTEA—includes language allowing the use of federal highway funds to build bicycle paths and sidewalks. As a result of these laws, in the 1990s federal expenditures for bicycling and walking projects grew from almost nothing to over $400 million per year.[51] Still, this represents less than 1 percent of federal highway dollars. Future versions of the transportation law should have stricter requirements for bikeways and walkways.

We also need to reinvest in parks. New communities—often laid out more by developers than they are planned by citizens—rarely seem to build parks these days, and old communities seem to let theirs deteriorate or (in the case of schoolyards) lock them up because of fear of lawsuits. Parks, "the lungs of the city," are about the only places that people in urban areas can exercise without paying a membership fee, and they are needed even in the suburbs if children are to play basketball or soccer. In high-crime neighborhoods, parks can become places to fear, but paying community police or park attendants to keep them safe and prevent vandalism can change them back into community assets.

Building recreational bikeways and walking paths makes it easier for people to exercise, but if we really want to make physical activity routine, we need to change the way we organize and build neighborhoods. If we want people to get out of cars and on their feet regularly, we need more than sidewalks. We need sidewalks that go somewhere useful—like a store, school, or workplace. "I don't want to build bike paths so kids can ride five miles to a big school on the outskirts of town," says Wilkinson. "I want them to ride to smaller schools in their own neighborhoods." That means creating more densely built mixed-use neighborhoods. Attempts to recreate neighborhoods like this—going under the name of "traditional neighborhood development" and "new urbanism"—have been very successful, but they are drowned in the flood of sprawl throughout America. This kind of change will require altering the approach of developers and often rewriting local zoning ordinances, but there could be state or federal incentives for these changes attached to transportation, housing, or other grant funds.

We need to take a new look at our buildings too. We (the authors) are frequently frustrated when, arriving in an unfamiliar building, we can't find the stairs, or we become discouraged when, once we do find them, they are dark, dirty, or behind forbidding doors. Stair-climbing is a great way to get exercise: Brownell has estimated that walking up and down two flights of stairs just once a day for a year instead of taking an elevator prevents us from gaining six pounds of fat.[52] People are likely to use them more if stairs are more accessible and more attractive.

Beyond the physical redesign of our environment, we can put in place social structures to encourage people to get more physical activity. In the middle of this epidemic, there is no excuse for schoolchildren getting physical education only one day a week. Recreation programs don't have to stop at age eighteen, though. Community recreation programs that get twenty-, forty-, or sixty-year-olds out of the house and moving around are a lot cheaper than routine cardiac catheterization.

Most people believe that maintaining their body weight is a matter of personal responsibility, and that being overweight represents a personal failure, a lack of individual discipline and willpower. Accepting that argument, when six out of ten Americans are overweight, means believing that we are a nation of losers. Americans are not irresponsible or lazy; they work harder and are more productive and creative than people from any other nation on earth. The character of Americans has not changed in the past forty years—our environment has.

Why would we want to do this?
Back in the kids' obesity clinic, the professionals were stuck trying to teach young children how to fight back the overwhelming pressures of a world they don't understand. In spiral-bound planning notebooks, the children wrote their goals ("lose 5 pounds by June," or "make the cheerleading team in the fall"), actions they would take to reach these goals ("stop eating cookies after school"), and the rewards they would get if they met them ("Mom will buy me a new dress that I want"). The medical staff sat beside them,

patiently helping them choose these goals, actions, and rewards, and giv-ing them ideas on how they could control themselves enough to make their plans work. In the process the children, all seemingly earnest and commit-ted, learned to blame themselves for their personal failures.

Christine had been in the program for nine months. She lost fourteen pounds in the first few months, but then regained much of it. The preco-cious nine-year-old explained the weakness that she was ashamed of. "I have a problem with carbohydrates." The psychologist gently walked her through situations to help her with her "problem." "What are you going to do if you eat one cookie, and it tastes good, and you want more? You can smell the cookies, and the bag is on the counter, calling you. What are you going to do?" Get away from the bag, the girl said. "Get out of the kitchen and go upstairs." The psychologist was pleased. The girl was learn-ing to resist.

On the other hand, Kaitlyn, about ten, just starting the program, who dreamed of making the middle school cheerleading squad, was worried that she wouldn't be able to stick to the rigorous program. "I want to just be my-self and be with my friends and not have to worry about being overweight."

Now is that really too much to ask?

CHAPTER 11

TO OUR HEALTH?

An accident investigator estimated that the Nissan Sentra was going a hundred miles an hour when it hit the utility pole. The teenagers were driving north on Santa Fe Drive in Littleton, Colorado, at about 3:00 A.M., passing drivers on the right, when the car spun out of control. After it crashed, a half-empty sixteen-gallon keg of beer flew out of the trunk.[1]

Behind the wheel was eighteen-year-old Christian Workman, and with him in the car were fellow Englewood High School seniors Adam Devereaux and Adam Neyer and fifteen-year-old Nicole Scott. Workman and Devereaux survived their injuries, but Adam Neyer died at the scene. Nicole Scott was taken off life support thirty-six hours later, her organs taken for donation. Workman had a blood alcohol level above the DWI threshold, and Devereaux and Neyer had been drinking also, but the police refused to release the exact numbers. Nicole Scott, whom Devereaux later said "was like a little sister to all of us," had no alcohol in her system.[2]

The teens had gathered to drink with about a dozen others where kids do, in the brush a short drive away from town, on a Saturday night just one week before their high school graduation. Workman had bought the keg from Warehouse Liquor Mart at about 10:00 P.M.. A videotape captured him paying cash; the store owner's lawyers claimed he must have shown a fake ID.[3] Nine months after the teens died, Workman pled guilty to two counts of vehicular homicide and one of vehicular assault. He was sentenced to five years parole, ten years probation, three hundred hours of community service, and classes in alcohol abuse.[4] The Warehouse Liquor Mart was not charged with anything.

The teens were from Englewood, Colorado, just next to Littleton. That year—2001—was not kind to teens in Arapahoe County. At the Englewood High graduation, the seniors left not one but two symbolically empty chairs: one for Adam Neyer and one for cheerleader Heather McQueen, who was killed about a year earlier when her car was hit by a drunk driver.[5] Less than three weeks after the crash that killed Adam Neyer and Nicole Scott, nineteen-year-old Jeremy Patrick Falkner, a former football star at Arapahoe County High School, was crushed to death when his pickup rolled.[6] Three months after that, seventeen-year-old Jade Castenada of Littleton died when his drunken nineteen-year-old friend who was driving slammed his pickup into a concrete retaining wall on the way home from a party.[7]

In fact, 2001 was a grim year for teens in all of Colorado. In December the state Department of Transportation reported that alcohol-related crash deaths had jumped 19 percent compared to the year before. For the year as a whole, the state racked up 137 deaths for ten- to twenty-year-olds, 35 more than the year before. In July and August alone 58 people died in crashes involving alcohol.[8]

Few Americans have heard about Christian Workman or the Warehouse Liquor Mart. But nearly every American has heard of the most famous teens of Littleton, Dylan Klebold and Eric Harris, who two years earlier gunned down twelve fellow students and one teacher before killing themselves in Columbine High. The Columbine killers and their twelve teen victims provoked national anguish and self-examination about disaffected teens, but the 137 teens who died in car crashes barely made a ripple in local papers.

The fact that alcohol is a killer drug is easy to forget when you are sipping wine with dinner or cooling off with a beer in front of a football game. But it is a drug, and it kills plenty of people—estimates hover around a hundred thousand Americans a year—through many different mechanisms. That pales in comparison to tobacco, which rings up over four hundred thousand per year, but it still makes alcohol one of the major killers of our time.

Brain juice

Take nearly any sweet liquid—juice from berries, honey, or fruit, or starches broken down to sugar with enzymes from saliva—leave it in the sun, and before long airborne yeast will convert the sugar to a solvent called ethyl alcohol, or ethanol. It may not taste wonderful, but it gets you high. Fermentation is so easy that nearly every primitive human society managed to discover both how to do it and the joys and dangers of drinking the product.

The two effects that make the drug so popular happen within thirty minutes: euphoria (it makes people feel happy for no good reason) and an easing of anxiety (it helps people "unwind"). Rats, for example, are far less anxious after drinking than teetotaling rats when presented with a collar that smells distinctly like a cat.[9]

Anxiety is a tortured state of mind, and everyone appreciates having it lifted. But anxiety is so common in humans and other animals that it obviously must be there for a reason. Throughout evolution, any rats that routinely *didn't* get edgy after smelling a cat wouldn't have lasted long before they ended up as one's meal.

Driving is the most dangerous act that most of us do. Directing a two-ton vehicle along an obstacle course amid a herd of other two-ton vehicles careening in diverse directions is a complex task involving processing a torrent of stimuli every second and making continuous decisions about steering, acceleration, and braking. At these times, when alcohol helps us relax it puts our lives on the line. We are more likely to ignore traffic rules and we take risks we wouldn't otherwise take. At the same time, alcohol gums up our ability to drive a car by slowing our reaction time, dulling our attention and concentration, and making our movements clumsier. These effects don't just happen to people who are falling-down drunk; in laboratory studies people tested on driving simulators are subtly impaired after less than one beer (blood alcohol level less than 0.01 percent), and they flunk most tests of coordination, attention, and reaction time at a blood alcohol level of about 0.04 percent, which an average-size person achieves after a little more than two drinks and which is well below the 0.08 percent DWI limit.[10] Alcohol also has a nasty side effect of making people—particularly men—more aggressive. For example, in laboratory experiments, compared to men who are sober, men who have been drinking are far more enthusiastic about inflicting painful electric shocks on imagined opponents in a competition.[11] That is why barrooms are famous for brawls and husbands who beat their wives do it when they are drunk. And why teenager boys tanked up on beer pass on the right and drive a hundred miles an hour. Interestingly, even though drinkers get more aggressive, in laboratory studies they say they don't *feel* more aggressive — in fact, they believe they are friendlier and less angry than do people who are sober.[12] If the impaired coordination caused by alcohol is the effect that kills people in cars, aggression is the effect that kills people who have access to guns.

There is yet another psychological effect of alcohol that is often fatal. While alcohol makes people happy in the short term, it tends to do just the opposite as the effect wears off and over the long term. A drinker can get acutely despondent or chronically depressed, sometimes just enough to prompt her to swallow a bottle of pills or turn a gun on himself.

People have a reason to be chronically depressed if they are addicted, and alcohol is an addictive drug. The more alcohol people drink, the more they need to drink. Regular heavy drinkers don't just suffer from a hangover the morning after; they get anxiety and the shakes, which are temporarily cured by another drink. Alcoholics abruptly deprived of booze go through cold sweats, tremors, sometimes seizures, and in the worst cases "delirium tremens"—a racing heart rate, fever, profound confusion, agitation, and vivid and horrifying hallucinations. Heroin addicts going through "cold turkey" withdrawal are in agony, but they live through it; by contrast, about one in twenty alcoholics going through delirium tremens dies. Of course not everyone who drinks becomes addicted to alcohol, but then not everyone who snorts heroin becomes addicted either.

Drinking healths?

Some people assume that the major risk of alcohol is to our livers, and alcohol does kill through cirrhosis, but statistically alcohol cuts its widest swath with injuries. About 40 percent of the bodies carted from car crashes—or about seventeen thousand per year—can be attributed to alcohol[13] Of those, a third are people who, like Nicole Scott, are not themselves drunk drivers but rather are hapless passengers, drivers of other cars, or pedestrians.[14] Alcohol is also to blame for about a third of deaths from fires (a thousand per year), falls (five thousand), and drownings (fifteen hundred).[15] Alcohol causes just short of half of the deaths from homicides (ten thousand per year) and more than a quarter of the deaths from suicides (eighty-five hundred per year). No one has put a number on it yet, but by making us take risks we otherwise would not take, as any college student can tell you, alcohol also increases the risk of sexually transmitted diseases, including HIV. And then alcohol is in fact toxic to organs besides our brains. It not only causes cirrhosis, but also increases the risk of high blood pressure and stroke, cancer of the stomach and esophagus, and cancer of the liver. Finally, each year about twenty thousand Americans just flat out drink themselves to death. Most of these are chronic alcoholics, but some are just kids who are found dead in the morning after guzzling a bottle of whiskey or rum.

To be fair, we have to say that alcohol at lower doses is good for your heart. Several big studies have now shown that people who drink have about a 30 percent lower risk of heart attacks.[16] This benefit stops after about one to two drinks per day, though, and it mostly helps men who are at higher risk for heart attacks because they eat too much saturated fat, don't exercise enough, or both. Some might argue that this makes drinking something we should encourage, but it is hard to be enthusiastic about recommending one dangerous habit solely because it helps offset the damage from another one. And at higher levels this heart benefit is more than counterbalanced by increases in cirrhosis, cancer, and injuries.[17] On top of that, any savings in years of life from the heart disease benefits of alcohol among the elderly are swamped by years of life lost from injuries among the young.

Beyond human costs, all of us—even nondrinkers—pay for the damage caused by alcohol. The National Institute of Alcohol Abuse and Alcoholism estimates that alcohol cost society $184 billion in 1998, including $26 billion in health care, $134 billion in lost productivity, and $24 billion in other costs like damage from car crashes, which we pay for with taxes and insurance premiums.

One of the best ways to measure the total effect of alcohol on a society's health is to see what happens when for one reason or another people suddenly drink less. The impact is stunning. In 1985 the Soviet government, which controlled alcohol distribution, raised prices by about 50 percent and cut production. As sales fell sharply in the city, hospitalizations for alcohol-related mental problems dropped 63 percent, deaths from cirrhosis fell 33 percent, deaths from alcohol overdose plummeted 51 percent, and injury deaths fell 33 percent. The government reversed course in 1987–88, and over the next couple of years, as alcohol consumption rose back to its 1984 levels, so did the death rates.[18]

The same huge health benefits happened a few years later in the tiny Arctic town of Barrow, Alaska, after it tightened rules on alcohol availability. Before 1994, alcohol sales in Barrow were illegal, but people could and did import alcohol. In October 1994 the residents voted to ban importation also, and in the next year the number of people showing up in the Public Health Service Hospital emergency room for alcohol-related health problems like injuries (unintentional and intentional), domestic violence, gastrointestinal problems, and suicide attempts plunged 85 percent.[19]

Shifting the alcohol curve

A medical school professor once told us that the definition of an alcoholic is someone who drinks more than his doctor does. So many of us feel comfortable drinking that we are quick to believe that the health problems only happen to those other people—the alcoholics or heavy drinkers. But in the last twenty years, alcohol researchers have shown that Geoffrey Rose's prevention paradox rings true for the drug: most of the health problems from alcohol come not from alcoholics but from "moderate" drinkers—simply because there are so many more of them. For example, in a general population survey in Scotland, researchers found that while the 12 percent of people who drank more than the Royal College of Physicians recommended were very likely to have any of a list of psychological and physical problems stemming from alcohol, 64 percent of the people who had these problems were drinking below the limit.[20] The damage is tied more to how often people get drunk than how much they drink on average,[21] but when even "moderate" drinkers drink, they often put away five or more drinks, which is when they crash their cars, play with guns, or decide life isn't worth living. True to the curve-shifting principle, the studies show that more health problems will be prevented if everybody cuts down on drinking by about 20 to 30 percent than if *all* of the heaviest drinkers cut back to become merely "social drinkers."[22] Thus even forgetting for the moment that drinking is a group behavior, if we want to limit the carnage from alcohol, it makes more sense to focus on average drinkers than alcoholics.

But then drinking *is* a group behavior: like other behaviors, it is contagious. People drink more if they are around others who are drinking. When everyone is drinking "moderately" it gives license to a few to get drunk.[23] The more we all drink and the more acceptable drinking is among friends and neighbors, the more people will become alcoholics.[24]

Anywhere and everywhere

Imagine what alcohol looks like through the eyes of a suburban teenage boy. The drug is everywhere in his town: in liquor stores, grocery stores, convenience stores, daiquiri shops, bars, restaurants—a typical town of thirty thousand will have more than fifty different places to buy booze. Not only are there shelves full of brilliant bottles of wine and vodka, but there are cans of beer in 40-ounce bottles, 12-packs, 6-packs, and singles on ice, ready to grab near the cash register. Grocery stores where he might pick up a carton of milk have six-foot standup displays reminding him how much fun it is to drink beer. Budweiser logos adorn the local football stadium. Happy young people drink beer on billboards on the town's strip. It's a good bet that there is beer and wine in his family's refrigerator. When he picks up a magazine—say *Rolling Stone* or *Sports Illustrated*—he finds scenes of sexy folks quaffing Bud or Bacardi.

But he really gets pounded with alcohol images when he turns on the TV. His favorite characters on sitcoms or cop dramas drink nightly, and that is just the beginning. With the industry lavishing $1.7 billion per year on advertising, if a kid watches three hours of television a day, depending on how much of his time is spent on sports shows, he will see about five hundred beer commercials a year. These beer ads are loads of fun for kids, with cute animals like talking frogs, lizards, and chickens, celebrity endorsers, and mini-comedies. By age sixteen kids say alcohol ads are among their favorite commercials.[25] The alcohol industry doesn't exactly suffer from this. Junior high school students and high school students drink 1.1 billion cans of beer a year, giving the industry over $200 million in revenue.

What a teenage boy learns from this barrage—and for that matter what we adults also constantly relearn—is that drinking is fun, exciting, cool, and most of all, normal. It's what anyone whom he wants to be like does. It is part of growing up, of breaking away from his nagging parents. In fact, if his friends were watching, he'd be ashamed to ever turn down an opportunity to drink.

Undoubtedly, many of us would drink if there were no advertising, but the advertising elevates the habit into a national crutch. About 85 percent of Americans drink at some time in their lives, and at any time about half of American adults are current drinkers. That acceptance of drinking as normal enables people to drink too much: more than 20 percent—that's 54 million people—"binge" (drink five or more drinks on one occasion) at least once a month, and 7 percent binge five or more times a month.[26] Over 4 percent of American adults, or about *10 million,* meet the psychiatrist's criteria for "dependence" on the drug.[27] If you doubt that it's a big problem, try to count how many friends, coworkers, or relatives you have who are alcoholics or who have gotten into a car wreck from alcohol.

Regulation and deregulation

For about as long as we have had human civilization on this earth, our societies have tried to control the damage from drinking by regulating it. The oldest known laws, from Babylonia about four thousand years ago, included regulation of drinking establishments. Over the millennia and across the globe the regulation has ranged from barely a hint of oversight to the complete banning of drink. In between, governments have taxed liquor, limited where and when it could be sold or consumed, and taken monopoly control of the business.

America, founded both by people desperate for freedom and by people trying to forge a perfect society, has veered between extremes. In 1633 the Plymouth Colony banned sales of alcohol "more than 2 pence worth to anyone but strangers just arrived."[28] Throughout most of the colonial period, though, people drank freely. The temperance movement had its first stirrings around the birth of the United States, as the founding fathers of the new democracy spotted politicians buying drinks at taverns. Over the next hundred and fifty years, individual states went through spasms of prohibiting drinking, only to repeal the prohibitions a few years later.[29]

Of course the grandest experiment in alcohol control in Western history was the fourteen-year national Prohibition. The bedtime story that we all have heard about Prohibition is that a bunch of joyless and fanatical schoolmarms in the Women's Christian Temperance Union tried to force their morality through heavy-handed government on normal folks, giving license to Al Capone to grip the nation in a gang-ruled crime wave, until everyone came to their senses and sent them back to their churches. One factoid that everyone knows is that people drank more than ever during the ban, because Prohibition made drinking the forbidden fruit. The moral to the story is that it backfires to try to influence human nature, so we should never tamper with alcohol regulation again.

But it's a story that has been falsely spun. The truth is that alcohol use plummeted during Prohibition, initially to about 30 percent of pre-Prohibition levels in the early 1920s and then to about 60 to 70 percent by the late 1920s.[30] And the lower drinking rates caused deaths from alcohol-related health problems such as cirrhosis to drop by about 50 percent.[31] Prohibition was definitely unpopular in some quarters, but it was repealed less by a popular uprising than by the urging of wealthy people like Pierre DuPont, John D. Rockefeller, and S. S. Kresge, who hoped that by legalizing and taxing alcohol the government could collect enough revenue to repeal the income tax.[32] In fact, after Prohibition was repealed at the national level, it was still popular enough that it was retained by many individual states. Prohibition *did* cause a black market that spawned gangland violence, but gangs were present in the big cities before and afterwards. That black market bore a striking resemblance to the illegal heroin-and-cocaine industry today, but you don't hear many people who consider Prohibition to have been self-destructive folly arguing for legalizing and deregulating heroin or cocaine.

In fact, Prohibition taught us that if we tighten up the availability of alcohol, people will drink less and be healthier. It also taught us that a total ban on drinking causes our society more problems than we are willing to bear. It didn't teach us about the effects (good and bad) of all the many policy options between a total ban and an unregulated free market, which are exactly the options we ought to be thinking about.

Choosing our poison

Think for a minute about how we deal with alcohol in America versus how we deal with other intoxicating drugs. Using marijuana, cocaine, or heroin in the privacy of your own home is illegal and often a felony. You can drink alcohol not only in your own home but also in plenty of public places. Selling marijuana, cocaine, or heroin can put you in jail for decades. Selling alcohol is a business conducted by corporations that sponsor our children's favorite sports teams and pay for our election campaigns. Producing marijuana, cocaine, or heroin will make you a target of the military attack helicopters. Producing alcohol may give you tax breaks if you dangle your distillery in front of local politicians cleverly enough. Enticing young people to use marijuana, cocaine, or heroin will put you on the socially valued list somewhere near child molesters. Enticing young people to drink alcohol (through advertising) will get you countless friends in the media companies who want your business. The federal government spends $13 billion to enforce laws in the "war" against illegal drugs. The same government spends less than 1 percent of that to enforce alcohol sales laws and boasts that it "has established beneficial working relationships to minimize regulatory burdens on businesses."[33] But the best estimates are that all the illegal drugs combined kill about forty-five thousand Americans per year (including deaths linked to drug trafficking), less than half of alcohol's hundred thousand.[34]

Alcohol is a powerful, dangerous drug. It's time we started treating it as that.

The art of the possible

Humans are drawn to alcohol so strongly that it is tempting to assume that nothing we could do would change our drinking habits much. But by using curve-shifters, there is plenty we can do short of banning the drug to curb the destruction caused by alcohol.

Accessibility

Alcohol sales should be legal, but does the drug have to be on sale everywhere? Two stores pushing alcohol in a neighborhood make it easier to buy booze than one, and four easier than two. When there are more stores, not only are sales higher, but also drinking feels more acceptable and normal. Storeowners need a permit to sell alcohol in most places, so the machinery is already in place in every city and town for citizens to cut back on the number of places that sell it. *Where* the liquor outlets operate may matter too. We can stop them from opening where they will attract kids and teens, like near schools and parks. To cut drunk driving, we can ban sales of alcohol from any stores that also sell gasoline. We can also limit *when* people can sell liquor, not just by banning Sunday sales (as some states and towns still do), but also by banning sales late at night, when people are most likely to get drunk and drive. And we can limit *to whom* stores can sell, by enforcing the bans on selling alcohol to teens. These kinds of restrictions work: since they were enacted in the early 1970s, the laws establishing a minimum drinking age of 21 have prevented tens of thousands of deaths from crashes, suicides, and other injuries;[35] if these laws were enforced vigorously, they would probably prevent thousands more deaths.

By providing cheap beer by the gallon, kegs are popular with kids. To maintain some control on the spigot, some states have passed laws requiring that the sellers register each keg they sell. In these states, buyers not only have to show ID, they also have to write down their name, phone, and address, as well as sign a statement agreeing not to serve beer to people who are underage and to take legal responsibility for any problems caused by the beer. Fewer people die in car crashes in keg registration states.[36] If Colorado had required keg registration, when Christian Workman showed up at the Warehouse Liquor Mart he would have had to do a lot more than just flash a (possibly fake) ID. Maybe the clerk wouldn't have trusted him enough to fill out the paperwork, maybe Workman wouldn't have risked giving the clerk so much information, or maybe, if he'd had to promise in writing not to give the beer to underage friends, he would have thought twice about doing just that. If any of those things had happened, maybe Nicole Scott would be alive today.

Probably the simplest and single most effective step we could take to cut drinking is to raise prices by taxing alcohol more. As we pointed out in chapter 5, economists have shown that when alcohol prices rise, not only do people drink less, but fewer people die from car crashes or violence.[37] As with tobacco, taxes on alcohol have the biggest impact on teens, who have are often strapped for cash. Taxes on alcohol have barely been touched in the last few decades, while the dollar has shrunk. In 1991 federal taxes were set at 32 cents per 6-pack of beer, 21 cents per bottle of wine, and $2.16 per fifth of 80-proof spirits. Because of inflation, this level of tax for beer and spirits is far lower in real terms now than it was in 1951.[38]

Physical structures

Anything that makes it easier to grab and gulp down a quick drink is likely to tempt some people to drink in places where they shouldn't or to drink too much at a time. For starters, maybe we should ban store sales of drinks that are already cold. The extra step of having to wait for a 6-pack to chill in the refrigerator might be enough to deter some people from drinking while driving. Then there is the size of the containers. What do people do with a whopping 40-ounce non-reclosable bottle of beer after they've popped off the cap? No one likes to waste anything they've spent money for, so they are likely to drain it. Smaller containers encourage less drinking than larger ones; we could put an upper limit on container size. Many places sell beer in single cans, which are easy to pick up on the way to the cash register. Requiring beer be sold in 6-packs, in the same way that we require cigarettes be sold in packs of twenty, might cut down on these impulse buys and on buying by kids with little pocket money. We can probably cut down the impulse buying even more by requiring stores to stock all their alcohol (including beer and wine) behind a counter, so people have to request it from a sales clerk.

The most infuriating physical structure is the drive-through liquor outlet, which is still legal in many jurisdictions. In Louisiana you can, by just reaching out of your car window, get daiquiris with clever names like Jet Fuel and Kami Kazi. If you had to design a structure to trigger drinking and driving, could you come up with a better one?

Social structures

The number of drivers killed in alcohol-related crashes has fallen in recent years, thanks mostly to social structures to prevent drinking and driving. States have been pressured by the federal government to drop the legal DWI blood alcohol limit from 0.10 percent to 0.08 percent. The states that have done this already have cut alcohol-related roadway deaths on average by about 7 percent.[39] The laws work better when police take away drunk drivers' licenses. Since people are clearly impaired at lower levels, it probably makes sense for the limit to be lowered further to 0.05 percent, as it is in France and Germany now. Because under-twenty-ones can't drink legally, another law that some states have tried makes any amount of alcohol in the blood of teen drivers illegal; these "zero tolerance laws" cut alcohol-related crashes in kids by about 25 percent.[40] Another tactic that has caught on is sobriety checkpoints. No one likes the inconvenience of waiting to be checked, but it is hard to argue that people who are drunk and are actually driving should be allowed to continue. When these are large-scale and well publicized, they cut alcohol-related crashes by about 20 percent.[41]

These laws and policies save lives, but they are only part of the solution to the death toll from alcohol, because they only address driving after drinking, not drinking itself. But as long as people get drunk, some will still find a way to drive and some will be clumsy or violent and will hurt others or themselves. One social structure that may reduce the number of people who get drunk is legal liability for bar owners who sell alcohol to intoxicated people who then injure or kill others. If toy manufacturers are liable when kids injure themselves with their toys—even if the kids were using them in ways the manufacturer didn't dream of—why shouldn't bar owners be liable for selling a drug everyone knows makes people inept, aggressive, and reckless behind the wheel? This idea isn't just the latest scheme of greedy trial lawyers. "Dram shop liability" laws were passed in many states in the mid to late 1800s, as a way for wives and children of drunkards to sue tavern keepers for the support lost when they sold booze to their husbands and fathers. Lately they have been used to compensate victims of drunk drivers. Since about half of drunk drivers that crash have been drinking in bars and restaurants, if liability cuts the number of drinks bartenders sell to people getting publicly plastered, they could make a big dent in the overall drunk-driving deaths. The lawsuits have been too haphazard to consistently change the ways that bartenders operate, but there is some evidence they work: in Texas, after two highly publicized lawsuits against restaurants for serving intoxicated patrons who then killed people in car crashes, the number of nighttime single-vehicle crashes that hurt people dropped by about 10 percent.[42]

Indoor smoking bans have changed our whole image of smoking. Twenty years ago lighting up was normal and smokers had to be accommodated, but now because smokers are banished to parking lots and garages, we view the habit as shameful. Right now we restrict where people can drink. In most places, you can't drink in movie theaters or on school property, and drinking a beer in the office cafeteria, if not against explicit policy, might shorten your career. To make drinking less acceptable, we can further limit where we can drink, banning it (if it isn't banned already) in parks, beaches, amusement parks, college dormitories, and other places packed with kids or teens. It is outrageous that in a few states, people can still drink in cars. When alcohol-related crashes kill about seventeen thousand people a year, how can we justify *not* banning open containers in cars?

Media

The alcohol industry runs some ads purportedly to discourage people from drinking too much or from driving drunk. But the ads, with slogans such as "Know when to say when," play on what one author has called "strategic ambiguity"—not ever defining what is "when," for example.[43] After watching these ads, teens tell researchers that the ads send the message of permitting "liberal alcohol consumption."[44] One ad that we saw showed a group of happy young people toting beer to a wild party, and just before entering slashing their own car tires. The message: go ahead and get sloshed, but then don't drive afterward. It is difficult, in any case, to imagine that these ads can have much effect because they are lost in the flood of standard get-drunk ads. In alcohol-heavy sports shows, less than one half of one percent of the companies' alcohol commercials contain these "moderation" messages, and there are nearly seventy times as many alcohol ads as anti-alcohol public service announcements.[45] We shouldn't really be surprised. Why would a manufacturer advertise against its own product?

More often—much more often—the industry does just the opposite. The National Beer Wholesalers Association advertises their members as "Family Businesses Distributing America's Beverage," to drive home the point that beer is as wholesome as a Fourth of July picnic.[46] By sponsoring nearly every major sports league and sporting event, having picturesque horses march in local parades, and then pumping out a torrent of commercials during football games, beer companies hammer us with heartwarming images. Why should we allow them to use happy pictures to push an addictive drug that kills a hundred thousand people a year? Unless we can run hard-hitting counter-advertising campaigns at a reasonable ratio to the pro-alcohol ads, linking alcohol to images that are not cute, wholesome, or sexy, but truthful, like teens vomiting out of car windows, violent drunks hitting their wives, and cars crumpled with people inside, we should ban the alcohol ads from the airwaves.

That bottle of beer or glass of wine you had for dinner seemed so innocent. It helped you relax after a tough day at the office or squabbling with the kids. It didn't feel the least bit dangerous, and if that is all you had, it wasn't. Alcohol will always be part of our lives. The problem with the drug is not its existence; it is its omnipresence and the relentlessness with which the industry promotes it. When alcohol is everywhere and our televisions constantly sing its praises, when we all accept it as an innocent accoutrement of a life well lived, plenty among us will drink way too much. In this world it is hard to blame a Christian Workman for having a grand time with a pack of friends and a keg of beer. As long as we leave things as they are, our newspapers will always be sprinkled with stories of teens like him dying or having to live with the deaths of their friends.

CHAPTER 12

WHEN SEX IS LETHAL

We remember back in the 1970s watching on television an educational special on venereal diseases that was as innovative as it was emblematic of the time. Instead of interviewing somber medical experts on biology, the special had the feel of *Saturday Night Live*, flipping between comedy skits and the lighthearted chatter of its host, Dick Cavett. In one Woody Allen–like skit, two comedians costumed as the bacteria that cause syphilis and gonorrhea commiserated about the tough life of VD microbes these days. Afterwards Cavett cut in, telling viewers that while syphilis and gonorrhea were bad news, people could easily be cured by a shot of penicillin. "Yes, penicillin," he told the camera, "the gift for the man who has everybody."

People don't tell silly jokes about sexually transmitted diseases any more, not on network TV anyway, now that sex can be lethal. As of 2002, more than 886,000 Americans had been diagnosed with AIDS, about half a million of whom had died.[1] That means AIDS has killed more young Americans than died in World War I, World War II, the Korean War, and the Vietnam War combined. Approximately a million are living with HIV infection, about a third of whom don't know it yet.[2] And the virus finds some 40,000 new victims every year.[3]

You might think, then, that someone would have to be crazy to have unprotected sex with anyone who hasn't just gotten a clean bill of health from a sexually transmitted disease clinic. But millions of Americans, not all of whom can be certifiably insane, are still having casual sex without condoms. In national surveys about one in ten adults say they have more than one sex partner a year, and a third of these say they did not use a condom the last time they had sex.[4] In neighborhoods with high rates of sexually transmitted diseases (STDs), the fraction of adults who have multiple partners is closer to 70 percent, and only half use condoms.[5] It is not just adults who are at risk: about a third of ninth graders and over 60 percent of twelfth graders have had sex, and when they have sex they use condoms less than 60 percent of the time.[6] Gay men in America, after backing off from casual sex from the mid 1980s to the mid 1990s, are rediscovering it; bathhouses and gay pickup bars are thriving again. Thirty percent of gay men surveyed in gay bars in Louisiana had had anal sex without a condom in the previous month.[7] Most ominously, after a fifteen-year hiatus, outbreaks of syphilis and gonorrhea resurfaced in gay men in the late 1990s.[8]

I don't know why I love you like I do

It isn't hard to understand why casual sex was popular in the 1970s, with the pill and penicillin seeming to make it risk-free, or in the early 1980s, when Americans hadn't yet grasped the catastrophe of HIV. But why on earth do so many Americans risk getting AIDS today?

One thing is clear: it is not because people are ignorant about HIV. Nearly 90 percent of teenagers have been taught about HIV/AIDS in school, and well over 90 percent of both teens and adults answer correctly on surveys that AIDS is incurable and that it can be spread by sex or sharing needles.[9] These high levels of knowledge don't do much, though. There is only a weak relationship at best between people's level of knowledge about HIV/AIDS and how likely they are to have high-risk sex.[10] Gay men who pick up partners in bars are at just about the highest risk, and a good proportion of them have college degrees.[11]

In fact, people seem to believe that their risk of getting HIV is extremely high. In one study, college students asked to estimate risks thought the likelihood that a typical young heterosexual would get infected was about 30 percent—a few hundred times more than it actually is, and a figure that ought to terrify even people who like to live dangerously.[12] It should make us wonder, though, whether more education about HIV would do any good. After all, if people were truly aware about the low chance of catching HIV, and if their thinking drove their behavior, they might take even more risks.

There is a better explanation: what we know and what we think don't really influence our sexual behavior very much. This is tough to accept. While we think of ourselves as *rational* beings—people who act based on our knowledge and reasoned judgment—often we are *rationalizers*—people who act first and afterward come up with excuses for why. So on surveys when people are asked why they had unprotected sex, they say they didn't really believe what they were doing was risky. In fact they knew it was risky. They did what they did; they don't really know why.

Of course not everyone's sexual behavior is irrational. Since AIDS arrived in America, plenty of people have become more cautious in choosing with whom or how to have sex. But in trying to explain why millions of Americans *haven't* become cautious, and therefore in trying to stop the AIDS epidemic, the idea that sexual behavior is not rational is the most useful place to begin.

Curve-shifters for sex

If the large majority of people stayed with only one partner, the HIV epidemic would die out fairly quickly. It is not a strong sex drive that puts people at risk for HIV, it is their tendency to stray from a single partner. If we are looking to understand why we as a society are at risk for HIV, we need to understand why our relationships fall apart and why we have sex with people outside of steady relationships.

Sexual behavior seems to be like other behaviors in that it follows a single-curve pattern. Just as there are behavior curves for how much salt we eat, how much alcohol we drink, or how much we exercise, there are behavior curves for how many sex partners we have. About a third of adults have had no more than one sex partner in their entire lives, another 30 percent have had two to four partners, and about 5 to 10 percent have had twenty or more lifetime partners.[13] These curves shift just like the curves of other behaviors. For example, the graph on the next page shows these curves for California and Massachusetts. People in California are about four times as likely as people in Massachusetts to have had forty or more sex partners over a lifetime. But the difference between the two states isn't just a difference in the high-risk tail: people in California are also a little more likely than people in Massachusetts to have had between five and nine lifetime sex partners, and a little less likely to have had only one. The entire populations in the two states are different, and the differing tails of the curves are just a reflection of the shifting of the entire curves. This pattern isn't limited to California and Massachusetts. Across forty-five states, we found that the proportions of a population that had very many sex partners

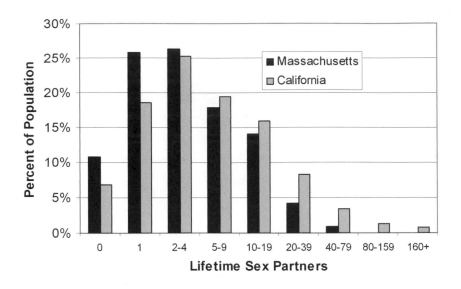

(defined in different analyses as over ten, over twenty, or over forty) had strong straight-line mathematical relationships to the average number of sex partners of that population, even after we removed the people at the extremes from the calculation of the average. For example, a population with an average number of lifetime sex partners of 2.5 (instead of 2.0), will have 30 percent more people with 10 or more lifetime sex partners. The study suggested that if all "average" people are even just a little more likely to change sex partners, it makes it more acceptable for the few people at the extreme to have casual sex. We learn to have casual sex from each other. Sex, that most private of acts, seems to be a "collective" behavior.

The tail of the sexual behavior curve is central to the epidemic of AIDS. The amount that HIV spreads in a population has a lot to do with the mathematics of who comes in contact with whom. Because most people with HIV have only one partner (who already has HIV), or they don't change partners often, or they have unprotected sex infrequently, they are "dead ends" in the chain of infection. A small number of people with HIV infect many other people; these are the few that continue to practice high-risk sex and change partners frequently. People studying the mathematics of STD epidemics call these people "core transmitters." If an infected core transmitter comes in contact only with "dead ends," he may infect a few people but he won't ignite an epidemic. On the other hand, if an infected core transmitter pairs up with just a few other core transmitters, something akin to a nuclear chain reaction gets started, and an epidemic explodes through an entire community. The health director in Portland, Oregon, developed a computer model that suggested that as few as a couple of dozen core transmitters could have driven an entire citywide epidemic of syphilis in the late 1980s.[14] Researchers in Colorado Springs found that 20 percent of the entire city's gonorrhea cases were in six closely linked sexual networks embedded with core transmitters.[15] And CDC epidemiologists were able to trace 40 of the first 248 AIDS cases in gay men in the entire United States to a single flight attendant—labeled "Patient Zero"—who frequented gay bathhouses and boasted that between 1979 and 1981 he had sex with 250 different men, most of whom had hundreds of partners themselves.

If our brains don't tell our bodies when or with whom to have sex, what does? What features in our physical and social environment pressure, sway, or induce us to pick up new sex partners? For all the studies on sexual behavior that have been done over the years, no one really knows. But we can think of a few possibilities.

Media

As prudish as we Americans become in serious discussions about sex, we are drenched with casual images of sex. In the late 1980s a Lou Harris study found that the average American teenager views nearly fifteen thousand sexual references, innuendos, and jokes on television each year.[16] According to studies by the Kaiser Family Foundation, in 2002, of the twenty television shows most popular among teens, over 80 percent had sexual content and half had scenes that showed or strongly implied sexual intercourse.[17] The sex our kids are seeing is exactly the kind that propagates sexually transmitted diseases: unprotected sex between people who don't know each other very well. Nearly half of the characters having sex are not in an established relationship (married or otherwise). Only 1 percent of scenes mention condoms, and only 2 percent mention any risks or negative consequences of sex.[18] The risky sex is nearly always portrayed in a positive light. For example, Ally McBeal, a model for young professional women on the Fox Network in the late 1990s, has intercourse with a stranger in a car wash. The scene flashes back to the couple, writhing in different positions, naked and soaking wet. And she's thrilled by it, announcing to a coworker, "And that's what I want to do to him again!"[19]

Television isn't the only medium overflowing with sexual images. The Internet has upwards of a hundred thousand subscription porn sites in the United States and a half million globally, and there are plenty more you can scan for free.[20] The industry estimates that every week 20 million different adults view pictures from porn sites in the United States or Canada.[21] This medium is too new to know what the sexual images on it do to us, but you have to wonder about the "modeling" effect. One study of a thousand young women in a family planning clinic in Sweden found that 84 percent had viewed pornography and that many explained they did it because it gave them "new ideas" and "tips on new positions" so that they could "experiment a little more." Those who had watched porn were nearly twice as likely to try anal sex as those who hadn't.[22] The modeling is especially frightening because porn stars rarely use condoms.

But television and porn are just slivers of the sex industry. Movies, music videos, video games, and computer games all sell themselves with sex. Magazines push the sex buttons also, and we are not just talking about *Playboy* or hard-core porn. About a quarter of magazine covers on newsstands sell themselves with seminaked men and women in seductive poses, alongside headlines like "The Best Sex He's Ever Had," "Jump-Start Your Sex Life," "Ultimate Orgasm Secrets," and "Sex on Ice: 15 Remarkable New Positions to Try at Home." These images and articles say a lot more positive things about sex with an unfamiliar partner than they do about any kind of long-term relationships. Does this immersion in images of casual sex encourage our teens to start having sex and adults to stray from spouses or steady partners? As we discussed in chapter 8, it's certainly possible. The age at which teens start having sex is not hard-wired in our genes: it is earlier in the United States than in France, and it is much earlier now than it was forty years ago.[23]

Decline in marriage

The most stable sexual relationship is marriage. As cynical as modern Americans can sometimes be about marriage, the vast majority of married couples are mutually faithful. Only 3 percent of married people say they had sex with two or more partners over a twelve-month period, versus 18 percent of people cohabiting, 14 percent of people widowed, and well over 30 percent of adults divorced or never married.[24] Married people are only about one-tenth as likely as unmarried people to have sex with a stranger.[25] Marriage, then, clearly protects people against HIV. But marriage is breaking down as an institution in our society. Divorce rates more than doubled between the 1960s and the early 1980s and have remained high since, and now about half of all marriages end in divorce.[26] People are getting married later in life, and an increasing number of Americans are choosing to never marry. The decline in marriage is a conundrum in itself that has bothered many experts. Regardless of its cause, though, the breakdown of marriage helps establish sex outside of marriage, and even casual sex, as normal, which may influence how often people as a group change sex partners and how widely HIV spreads in America.

Opportunities

Some situations simply make it easier to have casual sex than others, and while we usually think raw determination will overcome any barriers to a tryst, people are influenced by opportunities (or the lack of them) to have casual sex. In agrarian developing countries in Africa and southern Asia, where villagers still know each other and gossip is rife, studies have found that truck drivers—the few members of these societies who can practice casual sex without word getting back to friends and family members—may be a main cause of the spread of HIV between towns.[27] Closer to home, there is probably some truth underlying the jokes about the flings that happen at conventions—where attendees are distant from married partners and beds are easy to find. Teenagers are the best example of this: even in the most troubled neighborhoods, big, tough kids have told us that they have sex in secret because "My mom would kill me if she found out what we were doing." But increasingly in America, mothers and fathers aren't around, either because both parents are working or because there is only one parent to begin with and that parent is working. Surveys we did in New Orleans found that more than half of teens were free from adult supervision every day after school, and that more than half of this group were left unsupervised for more than five hours in a day. Many children are virtually raising themselves. In this world, teens don't have to hide in the back of a parked car to have sex. Eighty percent of sexually active teens told us that they had sex at home.

Because of the mathematical importance of core transmitters to STD epidemics, places that provide opportunities for core transmitters to have sex with each other are especially dangerous. The AIDS epidemic started out in America in gay bathhouses, and these clubs thrive today. Bathhouses are little more than warrens of dark rooms designed for men to have anonymous, one-time sex. They are magnets for gay men who want nothing more than sex from a partnership, and that want to constantly experience new partners. Because bathhouses are a core transmitter's fantasy, they are an epidemiologist's nightmare.

Alcohol and other drugs

The press has made a lot during the AIDS epidemic about the link between the use of drugs—particularly crack cocaine—and risky sex. But although it has devastating consequences, crack isn't at all a popular drug: less than one half of one percent of adults admit to smoking crack according to national surveys.[28] On the other hand alcohol, by far the most popular drug in America, gets a pretty free ride in the press, even though it may be causing more HIV infections than crack is. Drinkers are about twice as likely as abstainers to have multiple sex partners, and the 15 percent who are the heaviest drinkers are nearly five times as likely to have multiple sex partners or to have sex with a stranger.[29] The heaviest drinkers are about three times as likely as light drinkers to have an STD—about the same increase in risk as for illicit drugs—but because there are so many more heavy drinkers than cocaine users, alcohol is responsible for more STDs than illicit drugs in the United States.[30]

This is not to discount the importance of crack, heroin, and other illegal drugs on the spread of HIV. Intoxicated people are more likely to have risky sex than sober people, regardless of the drug that intoxicates them. Cocaine or heroin addicts—especially women—also find that prostitution is the quickest and most reliable way to raise cash to keep the drugs flowing. And a major route of spread of HIV is through needles shared by drug users who don't have clean ones.

Sex, drugs, and politics: the state of the art

In the early 1990s, a reporter interviewing Kristine Gebbie, the White House AIDS czar in the Clinton administration, asked how she balanced the two imperatives of research and treatment. She immediately corrected him, pointing out that he had missed a third imperative: prevention. This reporter isn't the only person to completely overlook prevention of HIV infection. If you follow the mainstream media, you might think that the only stories in this epidemic were the frantic race for the cure and the desperate search for money to pay for drugs to treat HIV-infected people. Given that AIDS will likely be incurable for at least another decade but that it has always been easily preventable, this media obsession with cure and neglect of prevention is bizarre and infuriating. But even if few people notice them, there are many programs in America funded by the federal, state, and local governments to slow the spread of HIV and other infections spread by sex. The CDC alone spends nearly $800 million each year on prevention of HIV infection and another $170 million a year on prevention of other STDs.[31] But what exactly are they doing, and how effective are they?

Besides providing general information and promoting screening of blood for donation, the first step the CDC took in prevention of AIDS in the mid 1980s was to set up offices where people could be counseled and get tested for HIV free of charge. Later CDC and state health departments ventured further, distributing information to the general public and paying outreach workers to go where high-risk people met each other, like gay bars and neighborhoods where drugs and sex were traded. This is pretty much the range of tactics used now. The messages of these counseling and outreach sessions are pretty clear and consistent: when you have sex, use a condom; if you inject drugs, use a clean needle. The CDC and a few health departments tried out a few public service announcements on television and radio, but because the political right didn't like blunt messages about condoms, most of the PSAs were vague ("AIDS Kills. Get the Facts."). At the time of this writing, CDC has given up on promoting condom use through the electronic media, and condom manufacturers—who ought to be promoting sales through advertising—aren't airing many ads either.

The fights over public service announcements about AIDS are part of a larger political war between public health experts and social liberals on one hand and the political right on the other over how to respond to the epidemic, the main battleground of which is promotion of condoms. Here are the facts: Condoms are extremely effective in preventing the spread of sexually transmitted diseases, including HIV. In an individual exposure they reduce spread by at least 90 percent and probably closer to 99 percent. As Ward Cates, the former director of the STD division at the CDC pointed out, the fact that condoms are not perfect is beside the point.[32] No devices used in medicine or public health are perfect—not vaccines nor antibiotics nor seat belts—but that doesn't stop us from encouraging people to use them if they save lives. Victories in public health are never absolute. The millions of Americans who are having high-risk sex would be a lot less likely to get HIV if they used condoms every time. In fact, given the "tipping point" effect of epidemics like AIDS, if everyone with more than one sex partner used a condom every time, even if condoms were only 90 percent effective, the entire AIDS epidemic would quickly burn out.

The public health programs and social liberals don't spend much energy trying to get people to stick with one partner or refrain from casual sex. Whatever social trends or biologic facts are causing people to have many sex partners are basically out of our control, the thinking goes, so the best we can do is limit the damage by encouraging people to protect themselves and their partners when they do have high-risk sex.

The political right, on the other hand, cares more about the trends toward declining marriages and increasing extramarital sex, seeing them as part of a greater moral decay with many dire consequences. They want to change society's norms to make sex before marriage or outside of marriage rare and shameful. Anything that presents extramarital sex as acceptable works against this, in their view, not only sex on television and movies but also handing out condoms. Their latest initiative has been federally funded abstinence campaigns, media messages, and classes using an absolutist "just say no" approach.

Studies show clearly that various programs to promote condom use work—that is, they increase condom use and cut rates of sexually transmitted diseases, including HIV.[33] The abstinence programs haven't been scrutinized much, but to the extent that they've been studied, as with school-based education programs, they don't seem to work very well.[34]

Unfortunately, as in many other political battles of our time, the battle lines in this war are artificial, the only winners are politicians who make careers out of confrontation, and the heaviest casualties are borne by ordinary people. The political right has successfully blocked the most effective way to promote condoms—through frank messages on television and radio. In Switzerland, a straight-talking condom promotion program using television, radio, and billboards increased regular condom use among casual partners from 8 percent to 56 percent among young adults over seven years, *without* increasing the number of people having casual sex, an effect that could probably save thousands of lives in the United States.[35] At the same time, the liberal passion for freedom of speech (certainly backed up by campaign donations from media companies) has prevented us from making serious attempts to moderate the barrage of casual-sex-promoting images in the media, or from even thinking seriously about how we might encourage people to cut down on the number of people they have sex with. In the middle of this political fight, we are missing out on important ways to stop a killer epidemic. There is no reason we cannot discourage casual sex *and* promote condom use. There is absolutely no conflict between the two goals.

In our meetings with citizens about how to stop the AIDS epidemic, the most common pleas we hear are for AIDS education or sex education in school. If that were the answer to this epidemic, AIDS would be nearly gone by now. These days sex education or AIDS education in school is routine, factual, and surprisingly detailed—more than 90 percent of teens say they get sex education and AIDS education in school, and this education usually includes detailed talk about STDs, AIDS, and how to avoid them, including the use of condoms.[36] For all the parental gnashing of teeth about sex education—either as a magic cure or as a risky scheme that can backfire—it has confounded everyone by having very little impact in either direction on when teens start to have sex, how often they have sex or change partners, or whether they use condoms.[37] The best example of this is the middle school program Postponing Sexual Involvement which we wrote about in chapter 3, which when rolled out didn't meet parent's hopes *or* fears. A sympathetic reviewer of PSI concluded that the program "may be too modest in length and scope to have an impact on youths' sexual behavior."[38] But the flaw is much more basic than that: nothing we can teach kids in the school day can overcome the bombardment of other sexual influences on kids during the rest of the day and the rest of their lives.

One little-appreciated weapon in the battle against the HIV epidemic is treatment of other sexually transmitted diseases that are easily curable. STDs such as syphilis, gonorrhea, and chlamydia, by making the genital tract inflamed, act as powerful "cofactors" for the spread of HIV between partners. Studies from populations all over the world have found the same effect, estimating that HIV is anywhere from two to over twenty times more likely to infect an HIV-negative person if he or she has one of these other STDs.[39] A study in Africa found that when basic STD clinics were set up in villages to provide simple and cheap STD treatment, HIV infection rates were cut in the entire population by an astonishing 40 percent.[40] It is a shame that this way of preventing HIV has been so neglected in America: although the CDC has enthusiastically endorsed it, federal funding for STD control has barely budged during the massive AIDS epidemic.

Breaking the epidemic wave

There are many things we should do to slow the epidemic of AIDS. Some work over the short term while others may take many years to put in place but promise to have a more lasting effect. We are in this for the long haul, though, so we need both.

Short term

Given that the other sexually transmitted diseases have such a central role in promoting the spread of HIV, and that they are so easily curable, there really is no excuse for us to not put more money into screening and treatment for them. Screening can take place in jails, drug treatment centers, hospital emergency rooms, workplaces, colleges, high schools, medical clinics, doctors' offices, and mobile clinics in high-incidence neighborhoods. Treatment can take place on the spot, using cheap, safe, single-dose medicines. People with STDs can be given extra doses of medicines to bring home to their partners. This entire strategy could cut HIV infection rates sharply, even if people did not change their sexual behavior the tiniest bit.

We need to do more to encourage people to use condoms, employing all the tools of modern marketing. Networks that run ads for Viagra and dramas depicting fellatio during prime time are in no position to be squeamish about running ads for condoms. A nation that mourns AIDS victims with massive quilts on the mall and whose government spends billions treating people for AIDS cannot argue that it doesn't have a few million dollars for a decent condom ad campaign. And as long as pornography is providing models for how we have sex, why not provide safer models by demanding the porn stars use condoms? As for worries about condom promotion condoning extramarital sex, we think condom promotion sends the opposite message—that sex is risky.

As serious as the decision is about using condoms, we (the authors) have found that people are influenced by the most mundane of issues. They are more likely to use a condom if they happen to have one at hand when they are ready for sex, and they are more likely to have one at hand if condoms are widely accessible, easy to find, and free. Shockingly, sales of condoms in the United States have not risen during the AIDS epidemic. As we discussed in chapter 5, when we put condoms in bowls, free for people to pick up without asking, people picked them up by the millions and used them more.[41] It would cost very little by the standards of the U.S. government to have a nationwide program that bought condoms in bulk at cheap prices and distributed them for free in many sites throughout any neighborhood with high rates of STDs.

Among the many sites where we ought to put condoms are high schools. Only 2 percent of high schools provide condoms to students.[42] When they have been made available, though, in places such as New York City, Philadelphia, and throughout Massachusetts, they do not increase the number of kids who are sexually active but they do increase the frequency of condom use among kids having sex.[43] If they are freely available in bowls so students do not have to go through the embarrassment of asking for them, students pick up more of them.[44] National polls have found that a majority of parents support distribution in schools.[45]

Long term
Over the long term we need to change the influences in our society that are putting our lives at risk by promoting unstable relationships and casual sex.

Let's start with the mass media. Why not use television and radio to promote more stable relationships or to encourage people to stick with one sex partner? This type of campaign doesn't need to be prudish or even negative; the message would not be "don't have sex," it could be that sex is better if you have only one partner or if you are married. It would nicely complement a media campaign promoting condoms.

Even if we have solid ad campaigns pushing condoms and faithful relationships, they might be overwhelmed by the torrent of images on television and in movies promoting just the opposite. These sexual messages don't come from artists practicing free expression, they come from corporations that make lots of money selling sex and selling products with sex. As important as the freedom of individual speech is to our democracy, we shouldn't let them do this much damage. The ratings systems for movies and television are a joke, and the media industry has shown that it can't police itself. We should more tightly regulate the sexual images on television—with clear programming standards. Because the specter of government censorship may scare us as a nation away from this, and because in any case the Supreme Court may rule that it violates the first amendment, another possibility is putting a tax on movies and television shows with sexual content (such as those with R or NC-17 ratings), and earmarking the money for the ad campaign promoting stable relationships.

Some of the blame for the AIDS epidemic lies with alcohol. We discussed how to deal with the problems of alcohol in the last chapter. After injuries, a reduction in the spread of HIV would be the clearest benefit of tighter restrictions on alcohol. Gonorrhea rates are the best marker at the neighborhood level for high-risk sex, and as we discussed in chapter 5, the more accessible alcohol is, the higher the rates of gonorrhea.[46] States with higher alcohol taxes, and thus higher alcohol prices, have lower gonorrhea rates, and when states have increased their alcohol taxes, gonorrhea rates have fallen.[47] The studies suggest that a 20-cent increase in the price of a 6-pack of beer leads to a 9 percent decrease in rates of gonorrhea, and by analogy, probably a decent reduction in HIV rates also. We already tax and regulate alcohol, so the levers to express the public will are there. Prevention of AIDS is an important reason to pull those levers harder.

What about sex among teens? If teens have sex when they are unsupervised, then we should be able to cut down on the number of times they have sex by supervising them more of the time. Plenty of these programs exist already, but there are many more after-school programs for preteens than for teens, and teen programs are much more common in wealthy communities than in poor communities.

An empty house at 4:00 on a weekday afternoon is not the only opportunity for casual sex worth thinking about. Adults engage in very risky sex in one-hour motels, which make their money on prostitution. The one-hour motel business can be banned or closely regulated at the local level. In Thailand, strict regulation of brothels increased condom use to an astounding 97 percent and was probably a major contributor to a turnaround in the HIV epidemic there.[48] Obviously this regulation won't end the world's oldest profession, but by making it more difficult to practice prostitution, it can cut it down some.

When it comes to the mathematics of HIV spread in a population, there is nothing worse than a gay bathhouse. If we want to stop the AIDS epidemic in America, we have to get rid of sites designed and operated specifically to allow core transmitters to meet each other and exchange bodily fluids. Is closing bathhouses too draconian? Does it inhibit gay men from expressing their identity? We don't think so. But if as a society we think it does, an alternative is to regulate and closely monitor these bathhouses to ensure that men are using condoms. The idea of "condom inspectors" showing up at random while men are having sex may seem ridiculous. But remember that these men are infecting each other with an incurable, fatal virus. If they were playing Russian roulette in a bathhouse nightly, wouldn't we close the bathhouse, jail the owner, or at least make sure they were using blanks?

Our society changes so fast that it is hard to follow—let alone understand and change—the forces that influence sexual behavior. AIDS as a disease will likely be with us until an effective vaccine arrives, and even if modern medicine ends the epidemic with a vaccine, a panoply of other STDs will still be around to make sex dangerous in a globally connected world. Rather than just waiting for a biomedical breakthrough which may never come, we should act to dampen the epidemic now.

CHAPTER 13

INJURIES,
NOT ACCIDENTS

If a mother turns to look at her baby and she goes off the road and
hits a pole that shouldn't have been there, that turns a mishap into
a fatal event. I think that's too high a penalty for being human.
—WILLIAM HADDON, M.D., M.P.H.

Early one foggy Sunday morning, when we were on a bike ride in a local
park, we came upon a late-model Nissan sedan resting just off the road on
the grass, its front end pressed into the trunk of a stout oak tree, the hood
crumpled into a V. Its horn was braying constantly. The windshield was
cracked but not shattered.

There was no driver in the car, and no blood. Hanging limp from the
middle of the steering column like a big white shriveled grape was a spent
air bag. Papers were scattered across the floor mats and passenger's seat.
On the top of a pile was an opened sleeve for an Allstate insurance policy
brochure. The driver, apparently, not only walked away from the crash with
skull intact, but also with his brain functioning well enough for him to plan
how he would buy a new car.

When our everyday world fails us spectacularly, we achieve in death a
measure of fame through our obituaries. But when our world reaches out
and saves us, we continue on as anonymously as before. The driver's name
didn't appear in the newspaper the next day. It was a non-incident. Chalk
up an anonymous life saved by the people who redesigned cars for safety
nearly half a century ago.

But the pioneering car safety advocates actually did much more than
that. They gave us a new way to think about injuries. Now that people are
scouting around for new ways to prevent diseases from diabetes to AIDS,

it is suddenly obvious that we *have* been using environmental approaches to preventing deaths from injuries for decades, and that they have worked spectacularly. We just need to use them more.

Counting the causes and mechanisms

In raw numbers, injuries kill roughly 150,000 Americans a year—more than any cause of death except heart disease, cancer, and stroke.[1] More important, injuries kill us when we are young. In fact, injuries are the number one killer in America for every age group from one to thirty-four.[2] Put another way, every single week, injuries cause more deaths in America than the terrorists did on September 11, 2001. And for every person who dies from an injury in America, about one more survives with a permanent disability.[3]

Violent deaths can happen in three basic ways: a person can kill another (homicide), a person can kill himself (suicide), or a person can be killed by accident (unintentional injury). Of these, the unintentional deaths are by far the most common. Among teenagers and young adults, the top three causes of *all* deaths are unintentional injury, homicide, and suicide, in that order.

It is natural to think of these different types of injuries as completely unrelated. Homicides, we think, are caused by criminals, not by ordinary people like you and me. Suicides are an affliction of the mentally ill. And accidents are, well...accidental.

Injury epidemiologists, on the other hand, tend to classify injuries not by who inflicts the injury or why, but rather by the mechanism. That is, they think about injuries caused by cars, by guns, by knives, through falls, by poisoning, and so forth. Deaths caused by guns can be intentional or unintentional, but classifying them all as gun-related injuries helps epidemiologists think of ways to prevent them that otherwise we might not think of.

When we summarize injury deaths in using both of these descriptions simultaneously, we get a graph like the one on the next page:

The most common mechanism of fatal injury in the United States is still the car crash, killing about forty thousand Americans a year. A not-too-distant second is death by firearms, killing nearly thirty thousand people a year.[4]

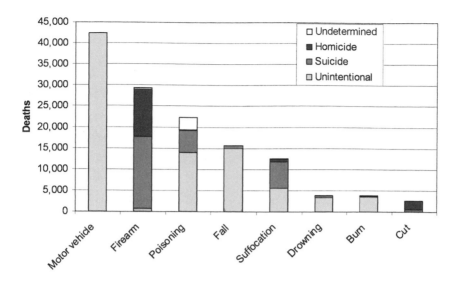

These deaths aren't an inevitable fact of modern life. America is not a fundamentally dangerous or violent place. They are at least as preventable as medical illnesses. They are not accidents.

Accidental thinking

As prominently as car crash deaths lead the list of injuries, they would be even more devastating if it weren't for the changes we have made in building safer cars and safer roads in the last fifty years. These changes didn't just evolve; they arose from hard-fought victories by an odd collection of people who started with the then-eccentric idea that we can prevent people from dying on the highways if we change the world around us.

In the 1950s, Detroit designed cars for good looks, power, and speed. The car companies' faith was that "safety doesn't sell." In a crash, car doors popped open under pressure, and with seat belts an "option" chosen by fewer than 5 percent of car owners, drivers were often flung out onto the pavement.[5] Steering columns were single steel rods running from the front axle to the steering wheel; in a head-on crash the rod shot backward and upward, slamming the steering wheel into the driver's chest or head and often snapping his neck. The interiors of cars were bedecked with sharp edges and knobs that punctured skulls and sliced other body parts when drivers were thrown into them. The interior of a car was so dangerous that even a fifteen-mile-an-hour crash could cut a driver deeply enough for him to bleed to death. Crashing in a typical car was, as one writer put it, "like going over Niagara Falls in a steel barrel full of railroad spikes."[6]

Anyone wanting to do anything about car safety was fighting a pervasive and paralyzing way of thinking about accidents. From the origins in 1914 of the National Safety Council, the leading safety experts preached that the cause of deaths in car accidents was bad drivers. The National Safety Council bolstered this way of thinking with seductive statistics from accident reports on "driver error." Drivers were driving over the speed limit. They drove through stop signs or red lights. They failed to yield to oncoming traffic. They were tailgating. Or, on a rainy or foggy day, they were just driving too fast for road conditions. Some accident investigations automatically classified any single-car accident as caused by driver error. The National Safety Council reported variously over the years that 74 percent, or 80 percent, or 90 percent of car crashes were "caused" by driver error.[7] Then the NSC and the car industry took these analyses one crucial and illogical step further by subtracting these percentages from one hundred to estimate the fraction of accidents caused by *anything other* than driver error. This left about only 10 percent caused by problems with roads or cars, which they argued was hardly worth bothering with. If drivers caused nearly all accidents, then the solution was to make better drivers, not better cars.

The first real challenge to this faith came in the late 1950s from a little-known congressman from Alabama named Kenneth Roberts. After being injured himself in a bizarre shooting in the U.S. Capitol, Roberts decided to commit himself to preventing deaths from injuries, and he saw car crashes as his greatest opportunity. He thought many lives could be saved if, rather than rattling around loose inside cars, people were packed like fine china in shipping boxes—strapped into a smooth, padded interior without sharp edges or knobs that stick out, and with objects like steering columns that did stick out designed to collapse on impact. Roberts wasn't much for heavy-handed government regulations, and at first he thought he could coax the car companies to voluntarily make cars designed like this by publicizing the problem. Trying to do just that, Roberts led a subcommittee through eight frustrating years of hearings on car safety.[8] Over that time, as the car companies brushed him off, Roberts gradually took to using the clout of the federal government. After several failed attempts, he finally got the House and Senate to pass a bill in 1964 requiring that all of the thirty-six thousand cars bought annually by the General Services Administration for federal agencies have seventeen different safety features.[9] His plan was to force these same requirements on all cars sold in the United States in the next Congress, but he lost an election before he had a chance.

The argument that safety could only be brought about by producing safer drivers was ultimately trampled not by Roberts but by an intellectual doctor named William Haddon. A graduate of MIT and Harvard Medical School with training in epidemiology from the Harvard School of Public Health, Haddon had the look and temperament not of an advocate but of a scientist. During his training in the late 1950s, he began to apply the science developed to investigate epidemics of infectious diseases to the problem of car crash deaths. One of his first studies, an investigation of fatal crashes in Manhattan, had him collecting data from crash scenes, then stopping randomly chosen drivers to serve as "controls" for the killed drivers and asking them to complete an interview and take an alcohol breath test. "Despite some initial apprehension and occasional hostility," he wrote, "and in one case an initial plea of diplomatic immunity, only one of the 259 drivers stopped (0.4 percent) refused to complete the interview and breath specimen."[10] In 1964, as Congressman Roberts finally pushed through his requirements for safety features in government cars, Haddon published *Accident Research: Methods and Approaches,* in which he attacked what he saw as previous sloppy research in accidents.[11]

Haddon was, first of all, incensed that people considered accidents to be bad luck, chance, or "acts of God." "Accidents remain the only major source of morbidity and mortality which many continue to view in essentially extra-rational terms," he wrote.[12] Second, he took aim at simple categorization of the "causes" of accidents. An accident wasn't "caused" by any single factor—such as driver error—but instead resulted from "a combination of forces from at least three sources . . . the host [driver], . . . the agent [car], . . . and the environment in which the host and agent find themselves [road]." Driver error, he argued, was present "to a greater or smaller extent in virtually every accident," but the characteristics of the car and the road still had enormous influence on the outcome. On the one hand, a driver error might be obvious (such as running off the road), but that error might be "greatly favored if not . . . inevitable," if, for example, there was a crater-sized pothole in the road. On the other hand, even if there was an obvious mechanical failure such as a blowout, that could be assigned to "driver error" for not inspecting the problematic part of the car before driving. Asking how often car crashes were caused by driver error, he later told a reporter, was like asking the post office "how often broken china in shipment is the result of somebody dropping the package."[13] It was almost impossible to know, but more important it didn't get you any closer to solving the problem.

An inattentive driver, a fallen branch on a slippery road, a car without seat belts: the driver swerves, skids, hits a light post, is thrown through the windshield, lacerating an artery and bleeding to death on the roadside. Earlier safety experts would classify this as caused by the driver, and it is in part. But it makes more sense to say it happened as a result of the interaction among the driver, the road, and the car. And the beauty of this new way of thinking about accidental deaths is that it leads to many different steps (beside just driver education) that could prevent the death. Sure, the driver may not die if she is more alert. But she also may not die if the fallen branch is not on the road, if the road is less slippery, if the light post is "padded" to cushion her crash or breaks away when the car hits it, if the driver is wearing a seat belt, or if the car is equipped with an air bag. Some of these factors might be easy to change, some might be difficult; some changes might save many lives, some might save a few. To Haddon, then, the study of accidents was not an exercise of finding a single cause but a measurement of how many lives we could save by each of the many different specific changes that could be made in the car, the road, and the driver.

Haddon favored any change that worked, but his schooling in epidemiology led him to suspect that changes to the car would save more lives than attempts to change the driver. He described "active" versus "passive" changes that might prevent injuries or deaths. "Active" approaches meant encouraging individual people to do something repeatedly to lower their risk of injury—like drive below the speed limit, or not drive after drinking. "Passive" approaches meant making changes to protect people whether they take deliberate steps to protect themselves or not—like installing light posts that break away when hit. Because people often just don't do what they ought to, Haddon was inclined to passive approaches. "Long experience in the prevention of diseases shows that, other things being equal, the less people do to be protected, the more successful is the prevention measure," he said.[14] It just plain worked better to have dairies pasteurize milk than to ask people to boil it at home.

So Haddon argued that instead of educating to erase "driver error," safety experts should fix roads so that crashes are less likely to occur (or less damaging when they do occur) and redesign cars so that they wouldn't crush drivers who crash. Haddon reprinted data in his book that 45 percent of fatal crashes occurred when the car was moving at forty miles per hour or less, speeds which needn't kill if cars were well engineered.[15] The paper also noted that stunt drivers "repeatedly crash cars head-on at 35 mph without sustaining any injury. Actually without knowing it, these professional drivers who elect to earn their living by avoiding injury in daily crashes apply practical principles which are used by every packaging engineer to protect goods in transit." The principles were basic: cars should have a hard outer shell that does not spill its contents on impact, those contents (people) should be held in place rather than rattling around, and the structures they hit against in the collision should be flat to distribute the force, rather than sharp and penetrating, and should give a little to cushion the impact. So cars should have doors that stay closed in a crash. The interior of the car should not have any knobs, screws, or edges that stick out. The instrument panel and doors should be flat and cushioned. And cars should have lap-and-shoulder seat belts, which people should wear. These kinds of cars could easily be built and should save lives, but in the 1950s they weren't.

Haddon's ideas take over

Haddon's shift in focus from drivers to cars picked up in Washington where Roberts's committee had left off, among characters who would remain influential for years afterward. While working for the New York State Health Department in the late 1950s, Haddon met Daniel Patrick Moynihan, then an aide to the governor of New York. Moynihan was excited by Haddon's ideas on car safety and pushed them in a 1959 magazine article called "Epidemic on the Highways."[16] Moynihan then brought his ideas to Washington when he joined the Kennedy administration in 1960. Then, a young activist lawyer named Ralph Nader, who caught hold of Haddon's ideas, traced the root of the problem back to the car industry in his muckraking book *Unsafe at Any Speed.*[17] And in 1964 a freshman senator named Abraham Ribicoff became a convert after reading a review of Haddon's book. With Nader as a staffer, Ribicoff chaired a subcommittee that in 1965 held new hearings on car safety, this time with a toughness that shamed the Detroit executives.[18] Jumping on their embarrassment, President Lyndon Johnson threw his support behind two bills establishing federal mandates for what Roberts had wanted for so long: safer cars and safer highways. With Johnson's political muscle, the bill sailed past objections by the car companies. The first director of the agency that was set up to specify and enforce these requirements (now called the National Highway and Traffic Safety Administration) was William Haddon.

The car design requirements Haddon initially came up with echoed the requirements Roberts had put into the GSA cars and wherever possible were faithful to his "passive safety" principles: safety latches on doors, recessed or padded interiors, collapsible steering columns, seat belts, and headrests. The car companies complained about some of the specifications, argued that customers wouldn't be willing to pay the extra cost for others, but grudgingly accepted most of them.

Haddon's rules did exactly what he thought they would. The cars that met the initial federal safety standards had about 20 to 40 percent fewer fatalities in crashes than cars that didn't.[19] The Government Accounting Office estimated that from 1966 to 1974 alone, Haddon's rules saved twenty-eight thousand lives, or about half as many as died in the Vietnam War.[20] Overall, between 1966 and 1990 deaths per vehicle-mile traveled fell a whopping 62 percent.[21]

The safety rules mandated that cars be equipped with seat belts, but there was no way of forcing people to buckle up. Haddon and others at the National Highway Traffic Safety Commission, true believers in passive approaches, were skeptical that enough people would ever wear seat belts, so they favored laws that required air bags in cars. The auto industry fought mandatory air bags ferociously, forcing a stalemate between 1970 and 1985 in which cars were not equipped with air bags and seat belt use was still abysmally low.[22] But in the late 1980s most states passed laws requiring that drivers and passengers wear seat belts.[23] These social structures that we discussed in chapter 7 have pushed seat belt use to an all-time high of 79 percent in 2003.[24]

Some of the decrease in car-crash deaths per mile traveled over the last four decades is due to the safer cars and seat belt use, and some is because traffic experts also put safety features on roads, including limited-access highways, acceleration lanes, median strips, better delineation of curves, breakaway light posts, and guardrails. But very little—if any—of the decrease has anything to do with safer drivers. Some people drive recklessly, most don't. Most young people are educated to drive safely in high school and almost no one gets additional education afterward. But then, as with high school education about other behaviors that affect health, driver education doesn't do much; studies generally indicate that teenagers who get driver education don't drive any more safely than those who don't.[25] So the focus of five decades of safety programs—"driver error"—has proven a useless way to reduce deaths from traffic crashes.

Haddon's contribution could be measured in saving hundreds of thousands of lives, or it could be measured in giving us a better way to think about injury, disease, and health, with the potential of saving hundreds of thousands more. His focus on addressing the dangers of the world around us, rather than our individual behavior, has produced what may be the greatest public health achievement of the twentieth century, and it points us toward how we can make the greatest health advances of the twenty-first.

We haven't by any means solved the problem of car-crash deaths in this country. There are many more steps we ought to take to save the forty thousand people who continue to die on the roadways. Besides cutting down on the number of drunk drivers (see chapter 11), we can, for example, require better safety standards for sport-utility vehicles (which currently don't have to meet car standards), lower highway speeds, and do a better job of enforcing seat belt use.

Then there is the car safety issue that people almost never talk about:

our reliance on driving to begin with. The main reason the number of deaths from car crashes is so high in spite of our safer cars and safer highways is that we go everywhere in our cars. That's not because people like to drive, it's because in the suburbs and exurbs to which people move it is nearly impossible to get around any other way. People can't walk to the store or take the train to work, and kids can't ride their bikes to school. And the more miles people drive, the more likely they are to crash and to die in a crash, no matter how well we design our highways and cars.[26] This relationship is so strong that it outweighs the injuries that people in cities tend to worry about: homicide by strangers. Comparing deaths by car crashes and by street violence, it turns out that it is much safer to live in inner-city Chicago or Baltimore than in the swanky, far-flung exurbs around them.[27]

Getting people out of cars and moving around in other ways can make a huge difference. Cities with good commuter train systems have two-thirds the traffic deaths of those without trains.[28] A step that will not only prevent injury deaths but also cut respiratory problems from air pollution (as well as deaths from obesity) is building compact, walkable neighborhoods with many destinations and then constructing mass transit systems to connect them to each other.

Guns and butter

In the late summer in suburban Washington, DC, two teenagers were hanging out after their first day of school at the home of one of their grandfathers. Fourteen-year-old Stephen Harris and a thirteen-year-old friend liked to ride bicycles or play basketball together. The thirteen-year-old attended Gwynn Park Middle School and Harris had just begun at Gwynn Park High. No one else was at the grandfather's house, a split-level brick house in a quiet neighborhood. They were in the basement. The thirteen-year-old found his grandfather's shotgun and shot Harris in the head, killing him.[29]

In Maple Grove, Minnesota, Brandon Block, a "blond fourteen-year-old with great shoulders and a winning smile" decided one day to play hooky with a fifteen-year-old friend. They went to his friend's house. His friend pulled his father's handgun from a desk drawer, "waved it around, cocked it, pointed it inches from Brandon's face, and pulled the trigger. . . .

The bullet went straight into Brandon's open mouth, and didn't even shatter teeth."[30]

In Detroit, Terry Gaines was washing dishes in his house at about 4:00 P.M. He heard a shot inside the house. He ran upstairs and found his son, Terry Jr., still standing. "Daddy, I'm shot," Terry Jr. said before he collapsed and died. One of Terry's six-year-old twin daughters had found the gun under her father's pillow.[31]

In Prince George's County, Maryland, a police officer for the District of Columbia was at home with his wife and family. His three-year-old daughter was in a room by herself. The officer's service pistol, a Glock semi-automatic, was stored high up, out of reach, but the three-year-old climbed on top of a piece of furniture. "It's still very sketchy at this point, but it looks like she found the gun and started playing with it," a spokesman for the county police office said. A neighbor said afterward, "It was terrible; there was a lot of blood everywhere."[32]

Every year in America about two hundred and fifty children perish from unintentional shootings, the trigger pulled by themselves or their friends. Another six hundred or so adults die the same way. And every year about thirteen thousand more children and adults are injured but not killed in accidental shootings.

It is paralyzing to think of these tragic shootings as accidents—like assigning car crash deaths to "driver error." Just as Haddon saved tens of thousands of lives by mandating a few simple changes in the design of cars, every one of the children in these stories would be alive today if we mandated a few simple changes in the design of guns. These simple and cheap design features have been around for decades, but you won't find them on most guns in America. "Magazine safeties" cause the gun to lock up if the clip isn't in the handle. "Grip safeties" make it harder for weak hands of small children to pull the trigger. Trigger locks and gun locks prevent anyone other than the owner from using a gun. One safety feature that *isn't* for sale now—but that would not be hard to develop—is a personalized "smart gun" that refuses to fire unless it is in the hands of the owner. It would be easy for the U.S. Congress, or for that matter any state legislature, to require existing safety features like these on guns, or even to require that gun makers produce smart guns by some date in the near future. You would think they would want to save the thirteen thousand people a year injured from these gun "accidents," especially because the devices wouldn't prevent a single hunter from hunting, or a single person worried about his personal safety from owning a working gun and shooting it whenever he felt like it.

Even if we accept that our everyday world will be littered with guns, there are obvious things we can do right now to reduce the destruction they cause. But why should we accept that? Where is it written that our six-year-olds must play with loaded guns? Guns are consumer products like any others, and the principles of accessibility that we discussed in chapter 5 apply to them, too. A Harvard study found that in the five states with the highest levels of gun ownership, children were sixteen times more likely to die from unintentional shootings, seven times more likely to die from gun suicide, and three times more likely to die from gun homicides that children in the states with the lowest gun ownership.[33] Anything that reduces the number of guns sold or owned—like tighter regulations on gun dealers—will mean fewer guns are in fewer houses, and even if it is only 10 percent fewer, it still means fewer children will find them under their father's pillow and kill their siblings.

Deliberate acts?

It may seem that the 5 percent of gun deaths that are unintentional aren't enough to build gun policy around (unless one of those killed is your child). But the same safety features that prevent these "accidental" deaths may lower the deaths from intentional shootings too. Anything that makes it more difficult for anyone to fire a gun will save lives from the bigger killers of suicide and homicide.

As much as we fear being shot by strangers on the street, we are more likely to kill ourselves than to be killed by others. Each year about seventeen thousand Americans, including a thousand children, end their lives by deliberately firing bullets into themselves.[34] The act of suicide is so horrifying that it is tempting to assume that these people had great determination in doing it—that if they didn't have guns, they would have found some other way to do it. But in fact the mere presence of a gun makes a big difference.

Every one of us—including people suffering from depression—has swings in mood from day to day, hour to hour, and even minute to minute. Probably most of us at one time or another have had moments in which we've wondered whether life is really worth living. Would you want a loaded gun in your hands during these moments? But because the worst moments do pass, some (perhaps many) suicide victims might very well *not* have killed themselves if the only gun they'd had around had been locked or unloaded—or better yet, if there hadn't been a gun around at all. That is not just theory. A study published in the *New England Journal of Medicine* showed that a person is nearly five times as likely to kill himself if he or she has a gun at home, even after taking into account depression, alcohol and drug use, and other factors known to be linked to suicide.[35] According to the CDC, the United States—with the most guns per capita in the developed world—has non-gun suicide rates in children about equal to those of other industrialized countries, but its gun-caused suicide rates are eleven times higher.[36] And in 1976, after the District of Columbia adopted a virtual ban on handgun sales, even though people could drive a few short miles to Virginia or Maryland to buy guns, gun suicides dropped by 23 percent, and suicides by other means did *not* rise to take their place.[37]

What about the safety features? Even if a distraught person were to find a relative's gun, he wouldn't be able to shoot himself if it was locked with a trigger lock or a combination lock. If it wasn't loaded, by the time he found the bullets his agony might have passed. And if it was "personalized" to someone else, of course he couldn't kill himself with it.

For homicides in which we have information, about 70 percent of victims were killed by someone who knew them—relatives, lovers, friends, acquaintances—and the most common circumstances around the killings were arguments.[38] Most killers aren't homicidal maniacs; they are fairly ordinary people who go off the deep end in a quarrel with someone they otherwise care for. Just how easy it is for them to grab and shoot a loaded gun is roughly proportional to how often these fairly ordinary people manage to end the fight by killing their (ex-) friends. In fact, people who have guns at home are nearly three times as likely to die from homicide as people who don't, even after adjusting for other things that might make a person more likely to be killed by another, such as past violent behavior, drinking, or drug use.[39] The risk is higher if a gun is not locked away or is kept loaded. Individually, that study means that you shouldn't buy a gun for "protection," because it is far more likely to kill you than to protect you. For all of us it means that any step that cuts back on the number of guns in houses, or the number easily accessible, unlocked, or loaded, would save many lives. That is to say, the same steps to reduce the flood of guns in the United States, and the same safety features that might protect a three-year-old from shooting herself, might also save the lives of the rest of us.

The crime of guns

Not all homicides happen among friends and relatives, and the fact that most do isn't very comforting if you happen to be one of the Americans that *is* threatened by a stranger with a gun. But why should we accept the idea that every seventeen-year-old drug addict in need of a fix should have a gun?

How do gangbangers get their guns? They buy them, legally.

Under federal law, gun dealers have to be licensed and can't sell handguns to minors.[40] But the law doesn't stop dealers from selling guns to individuals by the truckload, and it doesn't stop those individuals from then reselling them to anyone else. So street gun dealers just buy piles of guns from licensed dealers and resell them to gang members. In a 1998 sting operation, the Chicago police department showed that licensed dealers knew full well that the guns they sold were being passed along to street criminals.[41] In fact, many of them showed the undercover cops exactly how to get around the law.

Tightening the very loose restrictions on gun sales will cut down on the guns available to criminals. Requiring that all gun sales be made by federally licensed and regulated gun dealers, and requiring background checks on all gun purchasers, will greatly cut down on the number of criminals that get guns. Restrictions like these have a real impact on deaths from guns, even if they don't completely stop the flow of guns. The same Washington, DC, law that restricted handgun sales and ownership cut gun homicides in the city by 25 percent, even though people could simply drive to Maryland or Virginia to buy guns (and even though in these states gun homicides *increased* 23 percent during the same time period).[42]

Our elected leaders who shield gun manufacturers are not listening to the people they represent. About three quarters of Americans want the government to regulate guns to make them safer.[43] But then, it isn't the American people that the elected leaders are listening to, it's the big-spending National Rifle Association and its friends in the gun industry. Just as the car industry for years blocked requirements for safe cars by arguing that it was drivers, not cars, that "caused" accidents, it is the gun industry that is blocking requirements for safe guns by arguing that "guns don't kill people, people do."

It's not just the guns

Thinking people will point out that gun availability alone can't explain the much higher rates of homicide in some populations (such as young black men) than in others. There is a lot more to homicide than gun availability. Two items in particular matter a lot: alcohol and media violence.

In chapter 11 we discussed the connection between alcohol and car crashes and mentioned the tight link between alcohol and both homicides and suicides. Given what alcohol does to their brains, people are much more likely to drive into a cement embankment, shoot their relatives, or fire a bullet into their own head if they are drunk. Looking at the statistics, it is a fair bet that if people didn't drink alcohol at all, injury deaths as a whole would drop by close to 40 percent. We'll never end drinking, but cutting it back could make a huge dent in the problem.

As would ending the orgy of violence in the media. In chapter 8 we talked about the constant barrage we see on television and in movies of fights, rapes, assaults, and murders, mostly with guns. And when so much of the violence is shown as good clean fun, why then should we expect our teens, who spend many more hours a week watching television than talking to their parents, to *not* view killing as sport?

Think of it this way: if you wanted to groom a child to become a cold-blooded killer, how would you do it? You'd keep him away from other humans, so he never learns how to care for others, maybe by wiring him to the TV. On the TV you'd show him how killing is done, and you'd use the Pavlovian approach to making him enjoy it by consistently combining killing with pleasure. Then you'd help him practice his killing skills by hooking him up to a virtual-reality video game that rewards him when he stalks and pumps bullets into other humans. You might give him plenty of reasons to prove himself by sending him every morning to a too-crowded, decrepit school in which the adults tell him regularly that he'll never amount to anything in life. You'd lower any inhibitions he might still have left by offering him a few beers to drink. And then you'd hand him a loaded gun. Why are we surprised, then, that teenage killers terrorize city streets or occasionally mow down their classmates in high schools?

And all the rest

We can save more years of life lost in America by preventing injuries than by any other single act. And the changes in our world that can prevent this health problem are perhaps clearer than they are for any other health problem. The ranking of injuries by mechanism—cars, guns, poisonings, falls, suffocation, drownings—gives us the priority list. The steps we can take for cars and guns are clear. There are also simple, effective things we can do to address the other mechanisms. The prevention steps in these areas parallel the steps for cars and guns, particularly making physical changes (such as safer bottles of prescription medicines) and lowering alcohol consumption. The principles are the same, and they are the principles laid out by William Haddon: redesign the object that is hurting people or redesign the physical space that allows it to hurt people. As Haddon said, "We use insulation on lamp cords rather than trying to get everyone to put on gloves each time they must handle the cords."[44]

CHAPTER 14

UNEQUAL AFFLICTIONS

Arlette King doesn't think life has been unfair to her, even though she grew up poor and black. She was raised in a small Southern town a short drive from a major city. Her mother used to work in a glass factory and now cleans houses, and her father does maintenance for a local public housing agency. Arlette is the only one in her family to attend college, and not only did she finish, she now holds a solid staff position at a university, is married to a building engineer, and lives in a middle-class neighborhood with neat houses and ample, manicured lawns. She has a matter-of-fact way of speaking about her life, sounding at the same time proud of how far she's come and disdainful of others she grew up with who haven't done as well.

And when it comes to health, Arlette's relatives haven't done well at all. Her oldest sister, Enjoli, at age forty-one weighs 285 pounds and has both diabetes and hypertension; she doesn't take medicines for these conditions, and Arlette thinks she should. Another sister, Janelle, is only thirty-six but is just as obese. She also has diabetes and a heart problem for which she has been treated with nitroglycerin. Her older brother Raymond isn't obese, but he smokes crack and shoots heroin, and Arlette wonders if he has caught HIV from his shooting partners yet. Her sister Lynette, at forty, still has to live with her mom, because although no doctor has ever given her problem a name, she has the mind of a child. At age sixty-two, Arlette's father is obese, a smoker, and an alcoholic with cirrhosis, kidney problems, and prostate cancer.

The problems continue in the extended family. Of Arlette's four grandparents, two died in their sixties and one survived until age seventy-five only thanks to a decade of dialysis. Of her seven aunts and uncles, one died at age thirty-two of a gunshot wound; one has diabetes, heart disease, and breast cancer at age fifty-three; one is a drug user who has been diagnosed with hepatitis and tuberculosis; and one who is gay she suspects has AIDS. Adding them up, only a third of Arlette's eighteen close relatives are not chronically ill.

That sounds bad, but from what Arlette knows about her husband's family, they fare even worse. Of his "twelve or so" siblings, eight have diabetes. Both of his parents had diabetes also, his mother having both of her legs amputated before she died of complications at age sixty-three. "I think diabetes is one of those things that everybody has," Arlette says, and hearing about her relatives, you can understand why she believes that.

Poverty kills

It isn't just bad luck that has convinced Arlette that chronic diseases and early death are normal. Across the board, poor blacks in America suffer from many more diseases at younger ages and die sooner than people who are white or better off. These effects are separate but pile up on each other —that is, when it comes to health, it hurts to be poor and of any race, it hurts to be black no matter how much money you make, and it hurts doubly to be poor and black. The excessive mortality rates among the poor and in African Americans show up in just about every major category of disease, including diabetes, heart disease, stroke, cancer, chronic lung and liver disease, and injuries.[1] The differences are not small, either. In a national study done in the 1980s of a half million people, blacks between the ages of twenty-five and forty-four were more than twice as likely as whites to die over the ten-year study period, and young adults of any race who made less than $5,000 a year were about three times as likely to die as those making over $50,000.[2] Black men in Harlem have twice the mortality rates of whites—in fact, they are less likely to reach sixty-five years of age than men in Bangladesh.[3] Dark skin and poverty even hit children hard. Black children under fourteen years of age are about 50 percent more likely to die each year than white children—about the same number of excess deaths as the poor suffer when compared to the rich.[4] The effects on children are long-lasting also. Even if they become solidly middle-class as adults, children who grow up poor just don't live as long as children who grow up better off.[5]

The reasons why being on the bottom of the social heap makes people drop dead too soon are not at all obvious; in fact, the more you look into the statistics, the harder they are to explain. People living in poverty have less money to buy things, but it certainly can't be poverty in the absolute sense that causes poor health in the United States. It isn't hard to imagine why the poor would be more likely to die young than the rich when they lived in the infectious squalor of the nineteenth century or the near famine of the Great Depression, but now the leading causes of death in the United States are diseases of *excess*. They arise from eating too many calories and resting too much (obesity and its complications, including diabetes), taking in too much salt (hypertension, heart disease, and stroke), smoking (heart disease, chronic lung diseases, cancer), and drinking alcohol (liver disease, motor vehicle accidents, injuries caused by firearms). And as our nation as a whole has gotten richer and healthier in the last few decades and the mortality rates in all income groups have fallen, the gaps in mortality rates by race and income are actually increasing.[6]

This effect goes way beyond poverty's extremes to include the middle class. Maybe it is understandable that a homeless person sleeping on the streets and eating scraps from the garbage can would be more likely to succumb to everything from tuberculosis to gunshot wounds. But there is a straight downward trend across all income groups—that is, even small differences in income do damage. In the 1980s mortality study, people making $15,000–20,000 a year were about 20 percent more likely to die than those making only $5,000 a year more.[7] In some of the most perplexing studies ever done, a group of British researchers followed more than seventeen thousand British civil servants for ten years, whom they first categorized according to their employment grade as "administrative" (meaning the top level managers), "professional/executive," "clerical," and "other" (mainly messengers and unskilled manual workers). Over the next decade, the lowest-level workers were about three times as likely as the top managers to die. Maybe that's not too surprising. But then the "clerical" workers died at about 2.5 times the rate of the top-level managers, and the "professional/executives" were about 60 percent more likely to die than these same managers.[8] Compared to other important risks to our health that we know about, these differences are huge. For example, smoking is probably the single unhealthiest habit there is, but the "administrators" who smoked were far less likely to die than the manual laborers who didn't.[9] British civil servants who are labeled as professionals or executives may not feel rich, but it would be laughable to call them poor, and they certainly aren't foraging for food in others' trash. Why shouldn't they be as healthy as their bosses?

These "Whitehall studies" of British civil servants touched off a national blue-ribbon review of the effect of social class on health in the United Kingdom along with an international investigation of the relationship between income and mortality. This investigation shows that this strange effect is not just peculiar to the British. In nearly every developed country, with each step down in social class statistics there is a step up in death rates.[10] Studies from the United States, Europe, and Scandinavia consistently show that the excess death rates are linked to *relative*, not absolute, poverty. The poor in these industrialized countries have much more money than even the middle class in poorer countries—in fact, on a global scale the poor in these countries are pretty rich—but their health statistics are often worse. And the death rates for developed countries as a whole are statistically correlated not with the average income, but with how much *inequality* there is in the country. So Sweden, Norway, and the Netherlands, in which the rich are not much richer than the poor, have the lowest overall mortality rates, and the United States, where the rich are many times richer than the poor, has among the highest.[11] This strange pattern holds even within the United States; the bigger the gap between a state's rich and poor, the quicker people die.[12] Louisiana and Mississippi, with plenty of poor people and more very rich people than you might guess, have the biggest income gaps and the highest mortality rates, while New Hampshire, Utah, and Wisconsin, with the fewest people at either end, have the lowest mortality rates.

What do race, poverty, and income inequality have to do with health —even when people have plenty to eat?

Most people's first instinct is to blame it on lack of medical care. Unlike the rich, poor people can't afford to go to doctors. Arlette King's relatives with chronic diseases don't see doctors or take medicines nearly as often as doctors (or Arlette) would hope. But one conclusion that everyone who has studied these health inequalities agrees on is that access to health care has nothing to do with them. First, as we argued in the first chapter, we shouldn't expect health care to have much effect on how long we live no matter how much money we have to spend on it. Most killer diseases (for example, lung cancer) simply aren't curable with drugs or surgery, and mortality gaps between the rich and the poor show up especially strongly in these incurable diseases.[13] And second, these health inequalities are especially big in some countries where everyone has equal access to doctors and hospitals. The Whitehall clerks are enrolled in the United Kingdom's system of social medicine, so they can see a doctor just as easily as their bosses who live longer. You can only conclude from this that all of the clamoring for health insurance coverage for the poor in this country won't do anything to help them live as long as the rich.

If our individual behavior has such a powerful impact on our health, can differences in how people live their lives explain the excess deaths in the poor? This gets a little closer. The poor in the United States have much unhealthier habits than the well-off. For example, 31 percent of people making $15,000 a year smoke, compared to only 17 percent of those making over $50,000.[14] The poor are also more likely to drink excessively and less likely to wear seat belts and get regular exercise. They eat just as much meat and poultry as the rich but eat more French fries and far fewer fruits and vegetables.[15] And they show the biologic markers of their behavior, with higher rates of obesity and high blood pressure.[16] Arlette King's family story is rife not just with disease but with the causes: smoking, drinking, drug use, and other risky behavior.

At least part of the reason the poor have these unhealthier habits is because of where and how they live. Everything about the everyday world of poorer people encourages them to behave in ways that hurt them. Poor minority neighborhoods have fewer supermarkets but more liquor stores, in part because residents are in a weaker position to demand otherwise.[17] Arlette's town didn't have a supermarket, and her neighborhood had only two corner stores; since people in her neighborhood often didn't have cars or time to drive, they had little choice but to buy their food from these stores, which meant meals at home featured "chips, PB&J, bologna, and if we were lucky, tuna." The stores sold plenty of alcohol and tobacco, though, including single cigarettes for kids and poor folks who only had a few cents in their pockets.

The unhealthy neighborhood stores in poor neighborhoods can't explain it all, though. First, they are not *that* much different from the stores in richer neighborhoods. And second, when epidemiologists delving into the mortality statistics take into account the unhealthy behaviors like smoking and nutrition, the death gaps get smaller but don't go away. Best estimates are that all of the unhealthy behaviors together account for less than half of the social class differences in mortality.[18]

There is something else afoot here, something mysterious. How could having more or less money change your likelihood of living or dying? The mystery really boils down to two questions. First, why do people who are lower on the social ladder take up unhealthy habits more often than people higher up—is it only from the availability of unhealthy products, or is there something else at play? And second, what else unrelated to habits like smoking, drinking, diets, and exercise could cause people lower on the social ladder to die early?

Plenty of researchers are studying this now. So far, we have clues, but no definite answers.

Stressed baboons

The studies of British civil servants uncovered some strange patterns that may be the best clues. Compared to their supervisors, lower-ranking civil servants not only died earlier, but they also were literally shaped differently. They were shorter—about an inch shorter on average, when you compared the lowest grade to the highest grade—and they had bigger waist sizes even though they were not fatter overall.[19] Like the death rates, these strange differences weren't just between the highest and the lowest grades but grew stepwise across all work classes. The short, big-bellied body type is more than a curiosity. It is the classic type seen in people who get a chronic overdose of stress steroids, especially one called cortisol.

When animals (including humans) sense a threat—a predator or other assailant nearby—they shift into a heightened state of readiness to defend themselves or escape. Certain brain cells start firing, sending messages to the adrenal glands to pump out two types of hormones: epinephrine (or "adrenalin") and cortisol. The epinephrine causes the symptoms we recognize as signs of panic: a racing heart, sweaty palms, goose bumps, and a hyper-alertness. The cortisol works a little slower, but among other effects it raises blood sugar and mobilizes stored fatty acids for energy that the animal might need for a battle or to flee. These responses may be lifesaving for monkeys who are only one step ahead of a lion ready to pounce, but they don't help those animals if the body's alarm bells ring repeatedly over months or years. In effect, mobilizing a body's resources to defend itself in the immediate term depletes those resources over the long term.

People with chronic overdoses of cortisol—such as those taking high doses of steroids to treat asthma or some cancers—become obese, with their body fat settling especially in their abdomens; if their chronic overdoses began when they were children, they grow less tall than they would otherwise. More important, they get high blood pressure, a tendency for their blood to clot quicker, a higher risk of diabetes, and weakened immune systems. All this leads to a greater chance of dying of heart disease, stroke, and infections, just for a start.

We humans, after all, are animals—specifically primates—and British civil servants aren't the only primates who pull rank on each other. When monkeys and apes live in social groups, they quickly sort themselves into dominant and subordinate roles. The dominant ones tend to get the best choices of food, first dibs on sex partners, and the honor of being "groomed" by the subordinates. Like schoolyard bullies, they keep the subordinates in their place rarely by fighting with them, but more often by threats and harassment. Subordinate primates look anxious, spending time vigilantly scanning the others in the troop to avoid confrontation with the dominants, are more often alone, and frequently adopt a "collapsed posture" which is taken as a sign of depression.[20] A primate biologist from Stanford named Robert Sapolsky, who has spent years watching a troop of baboons in Kenya, found that the lower-ranking baboons, the butt of harassment by the higher-ranking ones, have chronically higher levels of cortisol in their blood.[21] The cortisol levels in all the animals in the troop surge when a lower-ranking one challenges a high-ranking one to be the alpha male and the entire pecking order is being reshuffled. In primates that are less competitive than baboons, the stress hormones aren't always higher in the subordinates, but they are consistently higher if the subordinates are harassed by higher-ranked animals or if they don't have many friends and allies.[22]

Besides high levels of cortisol, Sapolsky's low-ranking baboons have other changes in their blood familiar to internists, particularly lower counts of HDL ("good") cholesterol and higher levels of factors that might make blood clots form more easily in small arteries.[23] These changes might not hurt free-living baboons, but they do damage to captive British civil servants, who show the same patterns and in whom these blood levels heighten the risk of heart disease and stroke.[24] On top of that, Sapolsky's picked-on baboons have lower counts of immune cells in their blood; a parallel to this hasn't been reported in humans, but if it is, it might explain why lower ranking humans would be more susceptible to infections and cancer.

The links among social rank, stress, and health problems is a hot research area right now, so more definite conclusions aren't available yet, but here is one tempting explanation: people lower on a society's totem pole are faced down, humiliated, "dissed," more often than people higher up. This triggers their bodies' stress hormones to jump into high gear—not once, but repeatedly over years—causing chronically higher levels of cortisol and other metabolic changes. The constant pulses of cortisol make people deposit fat in their abdomen and, if the low rank began in childhood, limit how tall they grow. The lifelong stress response makes them more susceptible to nearly all of the major killers, including heart disease, cancer, stroke, diabetes, and infections. If the social stress also causes them to be anxious and depressed, like other subordinate primates, it might even make them more likely to descend into mental illness (and suicide) and more tempted to take anxiety-relieving drugs (like alcohol or nicotine). This mechanism could explain a lot of what we see in humans, particularly how both unhealthy behaviors and mortality rates increase not with how much money people have in an absolute sense, but with how much they have compared to others, money being the best barometer of social rank in the United States. And this might explain a connection that epidemiologists have seen for a long time between employment and health. Not only do unemployed people have more symptoms of illness, they die sooner than people who have jobs.[25] Being unemployed immediately drops you in social rank, and it can be incredibly stressful. Even the *threat* of becoming unemployed makes people seriously ill. During corporate downsizing people who aren't laid off but who are considered for possible layoffs have higher mortality rates.[26] And it could explain why African Americans of any income are less healthy, because their skin color makes them the victim of harassment (rarely overt these days, but often subtle) even when they have money.

There goes the neighborhood

In your city or town, where do the poorest people live? And the richest?

It probably wouldn't take you long to answer these questions. America is a segregated society, not just by race but also by income. Just ask a real estate agent what the "good neighborhoods" are, or what neighborhoods you should avoid. Poverty in America means not only having less money than others but also living in a neighborhood surrounded by those struggling just as much. Maybe the unhealthy effects of these two things are separate—and cumulative.

A whole group of studies published in the late 1990s supports that idea. People living in poor neighborhoods have higher mortality rates than people in more affluent ones, even after taking into account their individual income and race.[27] They also are more likely to smoke, have higher blood pressure and cholesterol, be shorter, and tell people on surveys that they are less healthy.[28]

What is it about a poor neighborhood that makes living in it unhealthy no matter who you are? There isn't a lot of hard evidence on this, but we can speculate.

First, there is the physical nature of rundown neighborhoods. Think about what a slum looks like in a city near you. It's a good bet it is strewn with decrepit buildings, abandoned cars, and the smaller trash of modern America: empty liquor and soda pop bottles, candy wrappers, and plastic bags. The schools are decaying and the schoolyards—if there are any—are guarded by chainlink fences and barbed wire. The few neighborhood parks are overgrown, littered, and inhabited by men who look drunk or menacing. The stores that are not boarded up are donut shops, hamburger joints, check-cashing outlets, snack-food convenience stores, and liquor stores. In case anyone forgets what these stores are selling, there are plenty of billboards pushing liquor, beer, snacks, and violent movies.

It is hard to measure this kind of neighborhood physical decay, but one simple index of it seems to makes a difference. In studies that we conducted, neighborhoods and cities that have more abandoned houses have higher mortality rates due to a whole range of causes, even after taking into account race, income, and social class.[29]

How could merely living in this kind of neighborhood damage people's health? Not only do the stores fill their world with unhealthy products, but also the neighborhood conditions themselves tells residents that they are unimportant—that no one cares about them. And if no one cares about them, why should they care about themselves? Living in a neighborhood like this is a constant reminder that they are at the bottom of the heap. It's a daily humiliation. If being notches below others on the social power scale causes human primates to boost production of stress hormones, it isn't much of a leap to see why living in a poor neighborhood, no matter how much money a person has in his pocket, might do the same.

Then there are the social patterns of the poorest neighborhoods, in part related to the physical nature. When the world outside looks ugly and threatening, and the anarchy of the neighborhood attracts homeless people, drug addicts, and robbers looking for victims, sensible people retreat indoors. The daily courtesies and willingness of neighbors to help each other fall apart. Parents, afraid of their children becoming victims or being drawn into dangerous street life, barricade them inside until they are too old to be controlled anymore. The age-old practice of parents watching over or disciplining neighbors' children disappears. Teenage males—the ones most desperate to break free from parental control—by default take over the streets; they tend to form gangs and experiment with vandalism and petty crime, which completes the vicious circle by making the neighborhood uglier and more threatening.

The health effects of this vicious circle spin off at several points. Fearful people are more stressed, with all that that means to their health. People hunkering in their homes are also more isolated, without the health protection of social support that we discussed in chapter 7. The quality of the air indoors is often worse than the air outdoors, which may exacerbate asthma and chronic lung disease. People indoors tend to commune with their television sets—with less reality-checking from conversations with friends and neighbors—so they are more vulnerable to the media messages that tell them to smoke, drink, overeat, and use violence to solve problems. Teenage boys left to fend for themselves outside are especially more likely to use the fists and guns they see on television.

The idea that differences in the mere physical appearance of a neighborhood could trigger a cascade of effects so profound that it could double people's mortality rates may seem a little far-fetched, and maybe it is. But these effects are compounded by our habit in America of clustering poor people together. As we've argued all along, behavior is contagious. No matter how an individual person might have felt without these influences, living around a lot of other people who feel threatened, depressed, fearful, and isolated would tend to make her feel the same way. Living around others who smoke, drink in binges, and snack constantly on junk food, will tend to make him act likewise. If a teenager is surrounded by teens who are uncontrollable and who are themselves experimenting with alcohol and sex, he or she will be more likely to do the same. Studying the poor in Chicago, sociologist William Julius Wilson has called these factors "concentration effects"—the amplification of unhealthy and antisocial behaviors when they reverberate through poor and marginalized people packed together in slums. This echoing pattern might just have the ability to turn the small influences of an ugly neighborhood into a major social pathology.

Arlette King doesn't feel that she has ever been personally discriminated against because she is black, and there is no reason to doubt her. But she doesn't have to have been discriminated against personally to have suffered at the hands of the neighborhood in which she grew up.

Action amid the confusion

We can't expect to eliminate poverty in America (especially because *relative* poverty seems so important), and we're a long way off from eliminating racial discrimination, so it's hard to be optimistic that we can eliminate the inequalities of health associated with income or race any time soon. But it is worth trying to narrow these inequalities.

Our understanding of how poverty and racial discrimination affect health is murky at best. "Social epidemiologists" are still making their careers studying how poverty kills. The National Institutes of Health has recently opened a new center just to study the causes of racial and health "disparities." But we don't have to fully understand *how* our environment makes people sick in order to change it to improve our health, any more than John Snow and Edwin Chadwick needed to understand bacteriology to recognize that we needed better sewers and water systems. It really isn't very hard to identify the types of situations, the relationships, and the designs of neighborhoods and communities in which people are the healthiest. If we do that, then we can work to shape our neighborhoods and towns in these ways.

The most obvious step is to revive a once-popular idea that seems to have died a quiet death in America: integration. We still have plenty of racial segregation in the United States—not only in where people live but especially in where their children go to school—and on top of that we have burgeoning economic segregation, not just among whites but also among blacks and Hispanics.[30] Assigning people to different neighborhoods and different towns based on their skin color or how much money they have, as we've seen, seems catastrophic for the poor and minorities. Because we all influence each other in some ways, those effects spill over into other groups, so it probably isn't healthy for the middle class or the rich either. Building economically integrated neighborhoods means disrupting the monoculture mindset of suburbia in which all houses in the same neighborhood have to be in the same price range, and allowing apartment buildings, duplexes, small houses, and large houses to mingle.

One major project is testing the theory that moving poor people to less-poor neighborhoods might help them socially and physically. In the mid 1990s the Department of Housing and Urban Development went to public housing projects, randomly chose some families (all poor and almost all black or Hispanic), and gave them vouchers to pay for housing in middle-class neighborhoods. They are now following these families and those left behind for ten years to see the effects of the move on employment, income, education, and health. At the midpoint (four to seven years after moving), the adults leaving the slums said they saw less crime, were less stressed, had healthier diets, got more exercise, and were less overweight.[31] They weren't healthier by such other measures as their frequency of asthma attacks or likelihood of having high blood pressure, but it might have been too early to see these longer-term changes.

Economic integration—even if everyone were enthusiastic about it, which many aren't—would take some time to achieve. In the meantime, there are concrete things to be done in poor neighborhoods that ought to help make them healthier. Because fear is so much a part of the lives of people living in these neighborhoods, and because it has such a powerful ripple effect on how people live each day, making these neighborhoods safer should have health benefits ranging from reductions in heart disease to lower levels of asthma. Improving neighborhood safety isn't a new idea, and it isn't necessarily easy, of course, but it isn't impossible either, through programs like community policing (which focus on preventing crime rather than on the traditional police orientation toward catching criminals) as well as through the Crime Prevention Through Environmental Design techniques discussed in chapter 6. Part of making neighborhoods safer is fixing up or knocking down the abandoned buildings that proliferate in older cities. Besides drying up the number of tempting sites for drug dealers or prostitutes, this would make the neighborhoods look less ugly and threatening, which might be just as important. Cities with shrinking populations have been trying to dig out from the avalanche of blighted houses for decades, and many are just as buried as they ever were, but seeing a connection between boarded-up housing and health might help this problem get the political attention it needs. Beyond removing these toxic structures, local governments should work harder to maintain the physical condition of poor neighborhoods than they do in wealthy ones, which is just the opposite of how political pressures usually direct them.

Then there are all those products for sale that inflict damage. Alcohol, cigarettes, and high-calorie junk food are bountiful in poor neighborhoods. It's not healthy for any of us to find these at arm's length at the cash register, but they are likely to hit the poor especially hard because of their isolation and focus on getting by one day at a time. Any steps we might want to take to restrict the availability of the products that kill us or enhance the availability of those that protect us are particularly important in poor neighborhoods—where otherwise they would tend the get the least attention.

If part of the reason the poor die early is because they are disconnected—jobless, alone, fearful, disaffected—then deliberately building social structures to reconnect them to each other and to people outside their neighborhoods should help their health. As a nation, we responded to the social devastation of the Great Depression with government jobs programs and to the needs of disconnected returning GIs after World War II with scores of neighborhood clubs and organizations. These ideas fell out of favor with the Great Society programs, which disdained jobs and clubs in favor of welfare payments and social workers, but maybe it's time to bring them back. Government jobs programs for the poor incense some conservatives, but aren't they preferable to welfare payments, social workers, crime, and prison costs, especially when you count the added benefits in health? We can also set up social structures that have direct and indirect benefits, like community recreation programs that not only get people exercising but also reestablish social networks. In rich suburbs, the opportunities for teenagers to join clubs, dance classes, and sports leagues are so overwhelming that their schedules become tighter than those of their parents, but in poor neighborhoods teens often have nothing to do but hang out and play video games. Getting teens into well-organized recreation programs might not only reduce crime, it also could cut drug use, along with all of the social problems that flow from that. But it shouldn't stop with teens; adults need to meet each other too, so organized community recreation programs for adults could cut mortality rates.

Of all the ideas we have proposed in this book, maybe these social structures seem the most utopian, or at least the most expensive, so it's worth saying why we should care. Most of the readers of this book, we expect, will not be poor or disaffected. It is tempting to see the problems of those on the lowest rung as so distant or intractable that they are not worth wasting our time, energy, or money on. The reasons why we should care are both social and personal. First, America was founded on ideas of freedom and opportunity, but it also was built by groups who believed they were creating not just a free society but also a morally better one, one in which words like "serf" and "peasant" would never be used. Forget the statistics for the moment. In the America that we (the authors) want to live in, it just strikes us as fundamentally the right thing to do to care about the health of people like Arlette King's family, whose main mistake in life is that they were born with a different skin color or on the wrong side of the railroad tracks. And second, the poor are not disconnected from us. The influences of one human on another and the contagiousness of behavior reach far. If any people are violent, we still live in fear. When others smoke, drink, and eat too much, we still watch and learn from them and become less healthy. And when we all, like Sapolsky's baboons, feel threatened and stressed about the risk of falling down one rung on the social ladder, we all grind our bodies down unnecessarily. Like it or not, what happens to the poor and the cast-asides matters to all of us. If we can take basic steps to prevent them from dying young, we should.

CHAPTER 15

HEALTH, POLICIES, *and* POLITICS

One of the more dramatic moments of Louisiana's 1999 legislative session came in a rerun of a show from seventeen years earlier. Nancy Camel, the director of the Baton Rouge Safety Council, who while near retirement was by her description "pretty athletic," approached the hearing table in the House Transportation Committee room dressed in a white linen jacket, dark slacks, and heels and carrying a cabbage, a motorcycle helmet, and her grandson's baseball bat. As the ordinarily distracted legislators stopped gossiping and stood for a better view, she calmly placed the cabbage on the witness table next to the microphone and covered it with the helmet. "Now this is a brain," she said in a sweet Southern accent, "with a helmet"— whereupon she gave the helmet a solid whack with the bat. All she got was a loud bang. Then she took off the helmet, said "And this is a brain without a helmet"—and swung again. The cabbage exploded, as did the spectators.[1] The case against repealing the state's mandatory motorcycle helmet law was made.

But the representatives voted to repeal the law anyway. Republican governor Mike Foster, an eccentric millionaire who rode a Harley, wanted it done away with, and shredded cabbage wasn't about to change his mind. Throughout the entire legislative session, he leaned hard on the legislators—harder, in fact, than he did for any other single issue during his eight-year term. The governor's exultation in his victory for the freedom of his biker friends was not dampened in the slightest three years later when James Champagne, the executive director of the Louisiana Highway Safety Commission, came back to the legislature to report that helmet use had dropped from 99 percent to 42 percent and that the number of motorcycle riders killed in crashes had nearly doubled from 102 to 196.[2] Rather than grieving over the deaths of an extra 94 bikers, the governor seemed to feel that it was Champagne who had a problem. "Jim Champagne can't help himself," he commented, adding that he would veto any bill to reinstate the mandate.[3]

Fixing our everyday world to improve our health will not necessarily be easy. When important decisions are made, data on body counts rarely carry the day. The decisions arise instead from a messy world of competing ideas and agendas, power and politics.

Radical ideas and risks

Today, people who push the idea that we should deliberately build a healthier world are sometimes branded as radical. But there is nothing radical about designing our environment to improve our health, or for that matter, nothing even new about it. As we wrote in chapter 2, the solution to much of the human misery spawned by the industrial revolution was changing the environment—mainly installing water and sewage lines. While the Lords in the British Parliament at the time thought these ideas were radical, today it is unthinkable that the government would *not* do them. In our time we now have a massive infrastructure of government environmental protection agencies to limit discharges of toxic chemicals in our air, water, and soil. These agencies and citizen environmentalists battle with industry and politicians over what kind of environment we will accept and what we won't. While the battles can be bloody and the specific rules set by these agencies controversial, the *idea* of environmental protection isn't. With the exception of a few extremists, everyone in America thinks our government should make sure that the air we breathe and the water we drink don't make us sick.

Toxins terrify people. We can't see them, feel them, smell them, taste them, or touch them, but if they are in our water or in our house, twenty years from now they can strike us with cancer. If we think about it, we all will concede that life is full of risks that we can't control, but people living in neighborhoods where they believe they are exposed to toxins often demand *complete* removal of them. They refuse to accept any level of risk. Government agencies consider a neighborhood too dangerous for human habitation if as few as one out of ten thousand residents would get cancer from exposure to a toxin in the air, water or soil for a seventy-year lifetime;[4] most environmentalists want the threshold set at one in a million.[5] But we accept without fear features of our environment that we can see and touch, even if they are far riskier. How many of us worry about being killed in a crash during that ten-mile drive to the mall once a week, the lifetime fatality risk of which is about one in two thousand (five times the government's highest acceptable cancer risk)?[6] How many of us worry that the gun stored in our bedroom drawer might be turned on us—when it poses a lifetime risk more than ten times the government carcinogen threshold?[7] How many of us worry about passing a snack counter piled high with high-calorie junk foods every day, which, if it tempts us to eat just one extra doughnut per week, would on average cause us to gain enough weight to hit the one in ten thousand mortality risk limit?[8]

But those are *voluntary* risks, people have told us. Everyone has to breathe and drink water, but not everyone has to drive recklessly or gobble doughnuts. After a little thought, though, this distinction looks fuzzier. First, if we are truly dedicated, we actually can avoid the toxic wastes of our modern economy, for example, by moving to a rural area far from other humans and drinking only spring water. Second, avoiding the "voluntary" risks can be pretty hard or impossible. Even if we drive carefully ourselves, we can still be broadsided by a drunk driver. Even if we undergo gun safety classes, an intruder or angry relative can shoot us with our own gun. And even if we believe snack foods are bad for us (and even if we believe we have uncommonly strong self-control), the plain fact is that we are more likely to indulge if we pass that snack counter every day than if we don't. Environmental risks come in many types and affect us in many ways. If we care enough about our health to try to fix them, it shouldn't matter whether they are chemical toxins that we can't touch or physical structures that we can.

The designers and the market

The world we inhabit is constructed increasingly by humans. Most of us spend precious little time communing with nature; we live our lives in buildings or cars designed by humans, consuming food concocted by humans, following rules written by humans, and absorbing media messages written, drawn, or filmed by humans. But it is not these individuals who really shape the landscape of our modern world. It is humans working in organizations—particularly large ones. Corporations and governments, working sometimes independently, sometimes together, sometimes in opposition, ultimately decide whether our neighborhoods have sidewalks, what food is on grocery store shelves, whether billboards we pass advertise beer, how much we pay for cigarettes, and how many people are murdered on prime time. Individually we have very little to say about their decisions —about as much influence as one vote in an election or one grocery purchase in a manager's calculation of what to put on shelves. But collectively —if we want to—we can have plenty of influence in the decisions of these major organizations. There is no reason that we cannot require the designers of the world we live in to act responsibly about our health if we want them to.

Some might gripe that this is interfering with free enterprise. To many economists, and to plenty of the rest of us who hear their arguments through the media, "the market" is always the best arbiter of what people need. If people need something, they will want to pay for it, and if they want to pay for it, in a free economy some business will start selling it. Often this works. But sometimes it just doesn't. For example, Bobby Jindal, a neoconservative prodigy who nearly won the Louisiana governorship at age thirty-two, argued in a debate against smoking restrictions in restaurants, saying, "I think we should let the marketplace work."[9] But "the marketplace" does a terrible job of protecting us from the ravages of tobacco. Because tobacco is an addictive drug, there is and always will be plenty of money to be made selling it. Addicted smokers suffer its consequences, and to a lesser degree so do the rest of us, and the laws of economics don't help one bit. For decades, even though everyone knew cigarettes were killers, nonsmokers, waiters, and waitresses had to accept breathing second-hand smoke in restaurants because they had no alternative. Individual restaurant owners weren't about to be the first to go smoke-free, fearing that they'd lose their smoking customers to the restaurant down the street. When no restaurants were smoke-free, nonsmokers who wanted a meal out never had a choice to spend their money in one. In most of the United States it is still like this. To get any completely smoke-free restaurants in the few areas that have them, it took state and local governments (like California and New York City) structuring the market—passing laws, that is.

And in those areas, does that change feel so terrible? Did it ruin their economy? Because every restaurant has to follow the laws, none gets any advantage. Careful studies show that smoking bans in restaurants and bars haven't cut sales one bit.[10]

When it comes to health, there is no reason to expect that the market will do what is best for our health—not 150 years ago, and not now. Classical economics defines a market failure when, left to itself, the market does not allocate resources efficiently. The most common reason is a "negative externality"—a cost to the whole society that neither a seller nor a buyer pays for. Pollution is an externality that a completely free market encourages, because polluters save money by not treating their toxic discharges, shifting the economic losses of polluted water and air to everybody who shares these resources. This is "the tragedy of the commons" that biologist Garrett Hardin explained in the 1960s.[11] In a small world filled with humans, everything we share—such as our air, water, and land—eventually is devastated by individuals acting rationally under market forces. That is why we ask government to protect these common resources from us all. That is one of the main reasons we have government in the first place.

In health, a free market creates its own "negative externalities." The food and drugs on display in our stores, the layout of our neighborhoods and towns, and the images that flicker across our media landscape affect us all, for better or worse. Companies sell products like tobacco and alcohol that make us sick. When we get sick, they don't pay for it; with our public and private health insurance system, we all do. So a free market will always encourage these companies to sell more, no matter how sick we all get. And the market will also never produce a shared resource that protects our health, like a public park in which we can exercise. Health is not an individual item we can buy at Wal-Mart. Health is a common good that unfettered market forces will never preserve.

Who's responsible?

The most common complaint we hear when we talk about making a healthier world is that we are trampling on the great American value of personal responsibility.

A typical argument is this: We all know that eating at Burger King every day is bad for us. People who do it, then, are just irresponsible. They suffer the consequences of their irresponsibility by getting fat or dying of heart disease. It is not our society's responsibility to protect them from those consequences. The fear of consequences might just make them more responsible. In fact, if we pamper people—if we as a society take responsibility by removing the Burger King or forcing it to change to a healthier menu—it *relieves* people of needing to take personal responsibility. Which, the argument concludes, only rewards their irresponsibility, which hurts their character in the long run. It is easy to make the same argument against motorcycle helmet bans, cigarette taxes, and restrictions on violence on television.

But the more you think about this argument, the less sense it makes. First of all, why should we ask individuals to "be responsible" when the far more knowledgeable and more powerful forces are not? When school food services led by nutritionists offer kids food that they know are not good for them, is it fair to ask the kids to practice self-control and not eat it? Second, our taking social responsibility just flat out doesn't make people more reckless or negligent. When the water company filters our water to keep us disease-free, does it destroy our moral strength? Would we be stronger humans if we had to take the personal responsibility of boiling it before drinking? And third and most important, the argument assumes that responsibility only resides in one place—either an individual or society as a whole—and if society takes some social responsibility, individuals will have none. The truth is that the only way we can be much healthier in America is if individuals *and* society as a whole share responsibility for our largest health problems. No matter how much we regulate Burger King, we will still be swimming in a sea of junk food. No matter how much we regulate alcohol, there will be plenty of booze around with which individuals can drink themselves to death. No matter how strictly we enforce helmet bans, reckless motorcycle riders will still find it very easy to careen into trucks. Nothing about taking collective responsibility will hurt any single person's ability (or need) to take individual responsibility for his health.

In fact, it seems to us that the effect is more likely just the opposite. Does surrounding people with cigarettes teach them how to *avoid* smoking? Or is it the opposite, that when we as a society treat cigarettes as fundamentally dangerous—by banning billboards or sales to kids—we encourage people to take the personally responsible step of not smoking?

For many decades Americas saw alcoholism as a sign of personal failure. People who drank too much were morally, spiritually, or intellectually weak. They were just drunks who ought to be ashamed of themselves. In the last thirty years or so, thanks to the medicalization of American culture, an amazing transformation has happened. Based on evidence that alcoholism runs in families, doctors and alcoholics themselves have lifted responsibility from individuals and deposited it in their DNA. Drunks are not drunks—they are alcoholics. They are not lazy, stupid, or irresponsible—they have a disease. In fact, they are valiant humans battling a genetic curse. But this reframing is as much an oversimplification as the earlier picture. Yes, people born of alcoholics are at greater risk, but for this health problem, genes are not destiny. Responsibility for the problem is shared, not just between a person's genes and his willpower, but among his genes, his individual self-control, and the world in which he lives. It would be just as accurate to reassign full responsibility for alcoholism from an individual to her neighborhood as it would be to reassign it to her genes. Diseases of all kinds arise in any individual from the interplay among three influences: genes, personal choices, and society. Prevention rests on changing the parts of that triad that are most changeable—which are both personal choices *and* the influences of society.

Choices and control

Any time reformers try to make a healthier world, a gang of critics labels it "nanny government." The image they are conjuring is of a stern woman slapping our hands for having any fun, telling us she knows what is best for us—an image that makes any red-blooded American want to rebel.

We Americans cherish our individual freedom. There is no amendment in the Bill of Rights listing freedom to eat junk food, but most of us feel we have that right, even when we know it's bad for us—a right that is irrevocable by government. Since the founding of the nation, Americans have had deep suspicions about government interference, even (or especially) when the government is trying to help them.

But there is much we can do through laws that do *not* limit personal freedom. Do we Americans feel that our civil rights have been violated by the ban on cigarette advertising on television? What kind of loss of freedom would occur if city ordinances removed liquor billboards from our neighborhoods? Would a ban on beer commercials be a trampling of the Bill of Rights? Would subsidies of fresh fruits and vegetables really feel like Big Brother?

And nothing we have proposed in this book, or would propose, bans Twinkies. In any future we might imagine, plenty of junk food, alcohol, tobacco, and any number of other unhealthy products will be around for anyone to buy and consume. Taxing these products, reducing their availability, or removing them from schools will mean that people might consume less, but they will always be there for people who want them.

And then we may not really be as free now as we think we are. Sure, we are free to eat junk food, but how free are we to *not* eat junk food when we are, say, in a hurry, hungry, and away from home? How free are we to walk in our neighborhoods when walking across the street means risking death from a car barreling by at forty miles an hour? Often our everyday world doesn't give us choices, it limits them. The choices we have today are frequently the small ones that don't matter—pseudochoices—like the option of six different brands of lager beer made in the same factory. Too often, the big choices, such as whether our children find beer everywhere they go, are made for us. So some of our proposals, like building sidewalks and crosswalks so we can walk places if we want to, actually give us more real choices than we have now.

We do favor some restrictions on what can be done. But we mostly argue for regulation not of individuals, but of big organizations. People can choose to walk or not, but developers should not build streets without sidewalks. People can drink if they want, but gas stations should not sell beer on ice. People can eat what they want, but fast-food joints should offer food in reasonable portions. It is particularly important to reign in big organizations that can hurt the health of our kids, who are the most vulnerable. School districts shouldn't sell unhealthy food in schools. Beer companies shouldn't advertise to children. Developers of subdivisions should build in parks and playgrounds. The bigger the organization and the more influence it has on the health of our whole society, the more we should collectively have a say in how it operates.

There are a few situations in which we support laws and regulations that *do* restrict what individual people can do. Workplace smoking bans, for example, and bans on open containers of alcohol in cars. And mandatory seat belt laws. And yes, motorcycle helmet laws.

In most of these situations, like the smoking bans and the open container bans, the laws protect not only the people affected, but also the people around them (such as coworkers who might have to breathe secondhand smoke and other drivers who might be killed by drinking drivers). Some might argue that if the only people put at risk are the people taking those risks, we have gone too far—that is, there is nothing wrong for a motorcycle rider who is fully aware of the risk he takes to ride helmetless. Of course, many helmetless riders *aren't* fully aware of the risks. Even Governor Foster, who argued that "government ought not to tell us what we can do to protect ourselves. We should have enough sense to protect ourselves," repeatedly cited his bedrock faith—against all evidence—that wearing a helmet made a motorcyclist *less* safe.[12] "If I get on the open road, I am better off without it," he said.[13] Should we expect much more from average citizens than from our elected leaders?

Even if we ignore the problem of riders' ignorance, these rules about our behavior still make sense to us, for two reasons. First, no human is an island; any fatal motorcycle crash will have more victims than the rider, such as his parents, children, or friends, or even the guilt-ridden driver of the car that hit him, and any nonfatal motorcycle crash will stick the government, a hospital, an insurance company, or a bunch of relatives with the cost and pain of putting the rider back together again. Second, a society where humans *are* all islands, in which no one cares for anyone else, is a pretty nightmarish one that we (the authors) don't particularly want to live in. How many of us, coming across an unhelmeted motorcyclist on the roadside who is bloody and mangled but alive after a crash, would refuse to call 911? We feel responsible for each other, even for strangers, and we should. If we take responsibility for each other after a crash, why not be smarter and take responsibility for each other beforehand, when it is so much more effective? That doesn't mean we should turn every health behavior into a mandatory law. But it does mean where the risks are high (such as riding a motorcycle) and the prevention steps effective and not intrusive (such as wearing a helmet), we have the right—maybe even the obligation—to help each other out by spelling out the preventive steps in common rules.

Even more poisonous than the phrase "nanny government" is the charge that we are proposing "social engineering." The image that terrorizes us is Stalin's U.S.S.R., or at least a "Brave New World" society in which people are not exactly unhappy, but are oblivious to the government's technological totalitarianism. But in a democracy, what is social engineering anyway? Anything designed by government, in the name of its citizens, to try to make a better society? In that case, public schools are social engineering. And Social Security. And for that matter, water and sewer lines. "Social engineering" is everywhere. Since the first time humans got together to form city-states, they have tried collectively to engineer the social structure. Sometimes they've done it well, sometimes abysmally. We humans long ago accepted the idea of social engineering; what we have been fighting about since is *what kind* of social engineering we want. We cherish freedom, and we want health. If we do it right—thinking along the way of the tradeoffs—we can keep both. People who cry about "social engineering" should worry about the health of our democracy, not about a democratic approach to protecting our health.

Not all opponents of curve-shifting solutions to health problems are libertarians or from the political right. An argument that we often hear from liberals is that "the solutions to our problems can't come from the top down, they must come from the bottom up." Translation: it is a mistake for powerful people or organizations to decide what must be done to help the afflicted or the statistically likely to soon be afflicted, who are often poor and powerless. By this logic, the only people who ought to make policy on HIV/AIDS are people who are infected, having unprotected sex, or shooting drugs, and the only people who can decide how to address the racial and socioeconomic disparities in health in America are poor African Americans. By extension, maybe only smokers can prevent smoking, only obese persons should solve our nation's obesity epidemic, and only alcoholics can teach our children not to drink and drive. Besides *sounding* ridiculous, this approach just doesn't work well. When the *problems* come from the 800-pound gorillas in our society—the industries that stock food on grocery store shelves, advertise beer on football games, and build the streets and cars that shape our world—how can we turn to the poor and powerless for the *solutions?* They are the ones *least* capable of taking on the powerful.

That is not to say that we shouldn't listen to the people who get the heaviest dose of our modern toxic environment. We should listen—listen hard, in fact. And it is also not to say that the people who are most heavily hit by diseases shouldn't wield whatever political power they do have to change things for the better. It is just that the final act in any play that changes our world for the better will involve one center of power— usually a government or some public body responsive to people's wishes— wrestling with another. Nearly all of us are uncomfortable with the idea of some people and organizations wielding power over others. Political battles are ugly and can get dirty. But they are the only mechanism by which we can make our world a healthier place.

What do people think?

For all of these arguments that we hear against creating more rules and regulations to change our world to make ourselves healthier, Americans as a group actually *like* the idea. The hottest, most exclusive, and most expensive neighborhoods these days are gated communities, which are so heavily regulated that people can't even choose what color to paint their own houses. Even beyond subdivision rules, when it comes to things that harm them, citizens generally want *more* regulation. Majorities of Americans favor complete bans on drinking on streets, in parks, on beaches, and on college campuses; by roughly 2:1 margins, citizens support bans on alcohol billboards and television ads.[14] In national polls, a majority of Americans want the federal government to do more to regulate violence on television, 77 percent of Americans think violence in movies is "very" or "somewhat" responsible for the violence among teens, and 64 percent think we need stronger laws to protect teens from violent and sexually explicit images.[15]

Increasingly, Americans are also seeing obesity as a public problem that the government needs to help solve. Nearly 60 percent of Americans want to ban junk food vending machines in schools.[16] Roughly the same percent want to restrict junk food ads aimed at kids on TV.[17] To fight obesity, 81 percent of Americans think we should create more public spaces for people to exercise, and 77 percent support government-funded campaigns promoting eating right and exercising.[18]

And in this society that supposedly hates government, citizens even have a soft spot for taxes on products that hurt us, as long as the money goes to something worthwhile. In virtually every state that has polled on this, including tobacco-growing states like Virginia, large majorities of citizens favor higher cigarette taxes.[19] The support generally varies with how the tax revenues are to be used, but healthy majorities support these taxes even if the money is only used to help balance state budgets.[20] In a national poll commissioned by the Robert Wood Johnson Foundation, 82 percent of Americans favored an increase in the tax on alcohol to pay for programs to prevent teen drinking, and 70 percent supported an increase in alcohol taxes just to lower other taxes.[21] Even if the money were used "for any government purpose," which to most Americans sounds like throwing it away, 37 percent of Americans want higher alcohol taxes.[22] And for all that it is ridiculed, 41 percent of Americans support a tax on junk food, even when the tax money is not specified to prevent obesity.[23]

Then who is against it?

There are plenty of people resisting the idea of changing our environment to improve our health. But the main opponents are *not* people passionate about their individual freedoms or those haunted by the specter of nanny government, social engineering, or heavy-handed government.

In 1842, when Edwin Chadwick went to the House of Lords to argue that the government should take responsibility for the health of the poor by paving the streets and building sanitary sewer lines, he was a lonely man. His fellow Poor Law Commissioners had publicly severed ties with him and with the "radical ideas" in his *Report on the Sanitary Conditions of the Labouring Population of Great Britain*. They weren't willing to expend their political capital asking the Lords to find money to build sewers for the poor, and judging from the reception that Chadwick's recommendations first received, they had reason to be skeptical. The Lords resisted the idea strongly, and only after Chadwick and a cadre of other persistent reformers agitated publicly for six years did they pass the watered-down Public Health Act of 1848. The resistance of the wealthy Lords to getting involved in keeping poor people healthy was, to say the least, shortsighted, but it has a familiar ring to it. Chadwick had another source of opposition, though. With no sewer lines and no municipal trash pickup, citizens threw all types of refuse in the streets. Food scraps, dead animals, and feces of pigs, horses, chickens, and humans formed small, fetid hills in nearly every neighborhood. People in the wealthier neighborhoods hired cart-haulers to periodically sweep the streets, pick up the rotting piles of stench and disease, and wheel them away. It wasn't exactly an honored profession, but for the cart-haulers, it was a living. These same cart-haulers, who themselves were often stricken by the latest epidemics because of the diseases they shoveled up every day, were part of Chadwick's roadblock. As he explained it, "The parish officers frequently oppose improved modes of paving and efficient cleansing [of streets] . . . for the avowed reason that it is expedient to keep the streets in their present state of filth in order to keep up the means of employing indigent persons as street-sweepers."[24] The lesson? No matter how miserable human conditions are, and no matter how obvious the solution is, there will always be plenty of people who fight it because they make their living from those conditions.

The opposition to Chadwick's recommendations of course included people who were more powerful than the poor street-sweepers. Many employers, landowners, and local officials of various kinds had something to lose if streets were cleaned, manure disposed of efficiently, and housing conditions improved. If the advantages they got from filth have long been forgotten, the arguments against Chadwick's "radical" reforms have lasted. As an editor of Chadwick's work put it, "Those whose interests were threatened [by Chadwick's proposed changes] opposed them, and if, in doing so, they involved the 'principle of *laissez-faire*,' they were only grasping at a perfectly legitimate straw in the circumstances. Thus the campaign for sanitary reform was not opposed by an immutable and unchallengeable principle; it was faced instead with a powerful opposition whose economic and political interests might be threatened by measures likely to reduce some incomes or diminish local autonomy."[25]

It isn't much different today. The resistance to environmental solutions to our health problems comes of course from the organizations that profit from our unhealthy habits. Big tobacco still makes huge profits selling an addictive drug, as do the alcohol companies. When obesity is vying with smoking as America's biggest killer, and Americans are snacking more than ever before, the snack food and soft drink industries have a lot to lose by our making our environments healthier.

These corporations are not sitting on the sidelines while thoughtful people debate what we should do to be healthier; they are protecting their profits. For decades the automobile industry fought building safety features into cars.[26] By now the tobacco industry's political bullying is old news. The alcohol industry is far more sophisticated and subtle in the way it protects its business. During repeated state budget crises, the alcohol lobbyists in Louisiana were proud that they had blocked an alcohol tax increase every year since 1948—tax increases that plenty of people recognized would make a healthier state.[27] Even Governor Foster—the unhelmeted Harley rider—was clear where the power lay. "Lobbyists control a lot of what happens in the Legislature," he said to explain the death of his proposed beer tax increase; the liquor industry, he mused, was "just about bulletproof."[28] Their political strength doesn't come from popular appeal— it comes from strategic use of cash. For example, the beer industry gave $200,000 to Louisiana legislators over three years, including $2,000 to Representative Rob Marionneaux the very day that he voted to kill a bill to lower the allowable blood-alcohol level for drivers.[29] Not long thereafter, in case anyone wondered what the alcohol industry thinks about drunk driving, their lobbyists openly and gleefully killed a bill that would have prevented people from driving with an open container of alcohol in the car.[30]

Louisiana is only one state, but the alcohol industry blankets all fifty of them. Anheuser-Busch alone has a lobby in every state capital.[31] They do not neglect the federal government, either. According to an article in the *New York Times Magazine*, Anheuser-Busch donated more than $400,000 to the Democratic Party in the 1996 election cycle, enough to earn a spot for the Clydesdales in Bill Clinton's inaugural parade and kindly treatment from his administration for years afterward.[32]

The snack food industry, watching as the obesity epidemic produces more calls for government response, is starting to operate the same way. In 1992 Maryland levied a tax on snack foods. Frito-Lay, the producer of chips and other snacks, later let Maryland politicians know in no uncertain terms that it wouldn't expand its factory in Aberdeen if the tax stood. People complained about the blackmail, but the legislators rolled over and repealed the tax anyway.[33]

But what about all the conservative citizen groups that are fighting against government interference in our daily lives? Claiming this mantle in health is the Center for Consumer Freedom, which says it exists to "promote personal responsibility and protect consumer choices."[34] Among other things, the nonprofit CCF has put up money for print and radio ad campaigns against taxes on snack foods and against lawsuits targeting fast-food companies for responsibility for obesity. The ads, which attack "food cops" who use "junk science" and are seeking "government control of everything you eat," ran in Washington, DC, getting plenty of press in a town packed with powerful people.[35]

The Center for Consumer Freedom, though, is not even close to what it appears. It is run by lobbyist Rick Berman out of an office a couple of blocks away from the White House. The name outside of CCF's door announces that it is the "Intergalactic Headquarters" of Berman and Company. In this single office, Berman runs a whole network of organizations with puffed-up names that fight to prevent regulation or taxation of cigarettes, alcohol, and food. Under the name of the "American Beverage Institute" he blocks alcohol taxes and regulation, and with the "Employment Policies Institute" he fights to keep the minimum wage low. In 1995, with $600,000 from tobacco-and-food giant Philip Morris, he started the "Guest Choice Network" to (in his words) "unite the restaurant and hospitality industries in a campaign to defend their consumers and marketing programs against attacks from anti-smoking, anti-drinking, anti-meat, etc. activists."[36] The Guest Choice Network has morphed since then into the Center for Consumer Freedom, but its mission hasn't changed. Its director of research told us that the Center for Consumer Freedom was funded by donations from "thousands" of individuals, but on the forms it files with the government, its income comes from only a handful of unnamed donors.[37] The Web site www.disinfopedia.org, which has tracked Berman's organizations, reported that its major contributors in 2001 were Coca-Cola, Monsanto, Tyson Foods, Wendy's International, and Outback Steakhouse.[38] "Our work is restricted to and focused on issues that affect shareholder value," Berman said in an interview in 1999.[39]

So the Center for Consumer Freedom is not a center, is not interested in consumers, and doesn't have anything to do with freedom. This front organization is entirely about protecting the profits of restaurant owners, the food industry, the alcohol companies, and the tobacco corporations.

There are no grass-roots movements to prevent laws from banning beer commercials or taxes on junk food. The major opposition to initiatives to stop the major killers of our era doesn't come from individuals guarding their freedom. It comes from corporations guarding their profits. Of course there is nothing wrong with corporations going after profits. But that doesn't mean we should listen to them when our health is at stake.

The real health advocates

Health is intensely political in America today. Unfortunately, the main political battles around health are not over the issues that matter the most.

The biggest fights, gargantuan even by Washington standards, are about health insurance. Fifteen percent of the economy is up for grabs, and the titans of the medical care industry regularly brawl over their shares. Health insurers, hospitals, doctors, and drug manufacturers all want more money and they pressure representatives for it both directly and through surrogates holding up banners like jobs. When they are not doing the bidding of industry, elected representatives usually fall back on the party canon, with Democrats, who believe that more services are always better, pushing to expand access to medical care and Republicans, who don't like government, pushing back to hold down spending. These fights make great theater for the evening news, but when you consider how little medical care contributes to keeping us healthy, they really are mostly a sideshow.

Because our nation's leading killers are behaviors like smoking, high-calorie diets, sedentary behaviors, and drinking, the fights that really matter are the ones over the design of our world as it shapes these behaviors. There are a few health advocacy organizations pushing for healthy laws in these areas. Because they fight not about money and services but about policy, they are mostly ignored not just by politicians but also by the media and therefore by the rest of us. They deserve some recognition for the good work they do, so here are the names of a few of them: the National Campaign for Tobacco-Free Kids, the Center for Science in the Public Interest (which fights mainly for healthier foods), the National Coalition for Bicycling and Walking, and the Marin Institute (which advocates for better regulation of alcohol). In general, their knowledge is encyclopedic, their analyses are insightful, and their recommendations dead on target.

How much is too much?

Is it possible to take these ideas too far? It is hard to imagine that our political system could ever become *too* protective of citizens' health, but it's a fair question. The rules we support do have an impact on businesses, which we need for jobs—jobs that help people be healthy—and the economy that we all rely on. All businesses have to put up with plenty of government regulations now; some of the changes we propose would add to these regulations and further limit what businesses could do. Those businesses are likely to scream about any new restrictions—of course, they already do. In our opinion, it would not be a great loss to the republic if we had fewer fast-food hamburger joints, but there may be some restrictions that effectively shut down worthwhile businesses. Our economy is so vibrant, fast-moving, and unpredictable that some other businesses (maybe ones that promote health rather than hinder it) might soon take their place, but still, there may be situations in which we (the authors) would think the health-promotion steps are just too restrictive. We would not support, to take a fairly ridiculous example, a ban on potato chips, even though you could make a strong case that such a ban would do a lot for our health. Nor would we support a complete ban on advertising food, even though that single step might put a real dent in the obesity epidemic.

Other steps to promote health would interfere with our freedom too much. For example, even though motorcycles kill 3,200 people per year, we would not be in favor of a complete ban on them. (They are so dangerous, though, that requiring helmets is the least we can do.) And we would not favor mandatory exercise programs at work, even though obesity is soon to be the major killer in America and though we are told these have helped prevent obesity in the military. But we do favor mandatory exercise *breaks* in which employees can exercise if they want to. There *is* a balance between our freedom and our health that we should strike.

And we never know everything we want to know about the effects of policies that affect our health. One proposal to reduce alcohol consumption is to lower the alcohol content of beer. But would this make people just drink more to get the buzz they want? And would their habit of guzzling low-alcohol beer then carry over to other drinks, backfiring and causing them to drink *more* in the long run? We just don't know yet. If we regulate our world for health's sake, we need to be sure that the targets of our regulation are influencing people's behavior and health, and we need to have pretty good evidence that the change would have a net benefit. Right now, though, there are many steps we could make that meet this standard. And when we don't know, we need to pilot-test changes and study them carefully before we make broad policy.

While we are at it, we ought to study the health effects of policies that we are putting in place for reasons other than health. We don't know much about the effects of lots of changes that are occurring in our society daily. We know little about the health effects of new housing developments, sprawl, or the paving over of our natural environment, gated communities, and parks. We don't know whether people are healthier with longer or shorter work hours, or more vacations, or whether government employment programs would prevent violence. We spend billions of tax dollars on medical research on drugs and the human genome, but we spend almost nothing learning how the structures of our everyday world or the rules we put in place to shape it affect our health.

What we should fight about

When people agree about how the world around us affects our health, it will still be difficult, complicated, and at times confusing to decide exactly how to fix it. The best policies are those where the health benefits are large, the evidence that the changes will work is strong, and any restrictions on our choices are minimal. Not all policy options will be this clear, though. Some people who read this book will disagree with us about whether we should mandate some changes to our world. More important, in our chaotic democracy, it will not be easy to have an intelligent debate about the benefits or risks of any change in our environment.

But when we talk about health, this is the debate we ought to have. We should be talking about (and if necessary, fighting over) whether to require workplace exercise breaks, or ban junk food vending machines from schools and offices, or require side-impact air bags. The headlines, the editorials, the rallying cries at political conventions should swirl around the shape of the environment that affects us all, not about who has health insurance. The number of policies we could enact, with all their variations, is enormous; it is for us working jointly as citizens to decide which ones we *should* enact. And the debate should be driven by citizens, not by corporations that profit by selling products that make us sick.

Healthy government

In our time people are deeply cynical about government. It goes beyond exasperation with specific government actions or inactions. People are questioning the very idea of government, as if anarchy can provide us with security, safe streets, clean water, and decent jobs. But what other institutions can keep billion-dollar companies from trampling ordinary people? The laws of a free marketplace may lead to low prices, but left unchecked they can be very cruel to humans.

Of course we already have plenty of government agencies chartered to promote health. But they are just not organized in a way to solve the environmental problems that are the root of the major diseases of our time. Like the five blind men and the elephant, they each sense a piece of the problem, but none can picture it fully. The Medicare program sees the rising costs of caring for people with diabetes. The National Institutes of Health understands the genetic risks of breast cancer. The Centers for Disease Control and Prevention counts the deaths from stroke and colon cancer and sends money to state health departments to prevent them. The state health departments are partitioned into pigeonholes to prevent diabetes, heart disease, infant health, AIDS, or injuries. The overwhelmed local health departments try to juggle this clutter of disease-specific programs while keeping up with their traditional inspections of water and sewer systems and restaurants. But none of these agencies studies or regulates the features of our everyday world that cause the leading killers of our time.

Which is why we need citizens to act. Although the crucial actions to make a healthier everyday world will be decisions made by formal councils, these bodies have to be prodded by the rest of us. We would never have had the victories of the past thirty years in the tobacco wars if it weren't for a few agitators in California who demanded indoor smoking bans from their town and city councils. Our cars and highways would be much more dangerous and many people alive now would have been buried long ago if it weren't for outsiders saying that car crashes didn't have to kill people.

Government agencies by nature are reactive, only stepping into new areas when they are dragged or shamed there. We need citizens—not consumers, but citizens—who will think about how our buildings are designed, whether our children can walk safely to school, what kind of food we want in our school and worksite cafeterias, where people should be allowed to smoke and drink, and what kind of images we should see on our movie screens. Those citizens need to goad our democratic leaders to use their powers to make the world a healthier place. That is why we wrote this book.

This means that health is political. We will get it by fighting the good fight. It will take fighting in Congress to get the booze ads off television, arguing in the town council to build sidewalks or fix the recreation equipment in the park, or calling state legislators to ban smoking in all restaurants. Unlike the partisan politics that seem to seesaw over the decades, achieving nothing, the politics of health can be measured in concrete progress in building healthier environments that we see every day.

Does this sound unrealistic? Maybe only because we haven't tried it. We may find it is much easier to achieve than it sounds. We spend a trillion dollars a year on sick care. If we had our priorities straight, don't you think we could come up with the money to build enough parks for our children to play in? If we cared enough about it, couldn't we find the money for a tough antismoking or antidrinking media campaign? In the end, the school boards, town councils, state legislatures, and U.S. Congress answer to us. Right now they feel the pressure from citizens to spend money for sick care, and as we found with the recent federal prescription drug plan, even though the money isn't really there, they spend it. If they feel the pressure from citizens to make our world a healthier one, they will respond to that also. If they don't, we can elect replacements who will.

Of course, we don't have to do any of this. If we think politics is just dirty, if we are squeamish about offending companies that make us sick, or if we think health—like religious conviction—is strictly a private matter, we can just carry on as we do now. If we do that, though, don't expect doctors to have a magical cure for the ailments most likely to strike you, and don't expect our national health statistics to surpass those of Slovenia.

The future

Our greatest obstacle to building a healthier world is not that we don't care about our health, and it is not political opposition, either. Our greatest obstacle is our imagination. We have trouble envisioning a world in which most people walk to a neighborhood grocery store filled with fresh produce, or where Hollywood stars don't smoke on-screen. But ten years ago few people imagined offices where people couldn't light up cigarettes (let alone restaurants or nightclubs that didn't reek of tobacco smoke), and now it is hard to imagine otherwise. A healthier world really isn't that far away. We only have to start by drawing a picture of it in our minds.

The world we want is one in which people will be healthy because they live in healthy communities. In a future healthy America, neighborhood groups will work to replace vacant lots with parks and convenience store shelves of cheap liquor with racks of fresh fruits and vegetables. Children in these neighborhoods will be less likely to hunker down in their houses, tended by TV sets hawking junk food, and more likely to ride bicycles to neighborhood stores to pick up fresh bread for dinner. Adults will spend less time fuming behind the wheel in traffic jams or pounding on treadmills to fight their weight, and more time strolling through neighborhoods chatting with friends. Politicians will spend less time arguing about how many sigmoidoscopies Medicare will pay for, and more time arguing about the best ways to keep tobacco away from our children. All of us will spend less time reading obituaries of teenagers killed in car crashes or friends wasted by AIDS, and more time reading the scores of the local recreational sports league. This—not pills, doctors, or hospitals—is health.

We will be healthiest in America when the environment that keeps us healthy is something we barely notice—when we stay healthy just by waking up, taking care of our homes and families, going to work, spending time with friends, and enjoying our communities. We know how to create a healthscape in America like this. We just have to do it.

ACKNOWLEDGMENTS

Many of the ideas in this book are not new, but originated with our heroes in public health, especially Edwin Chadwick, Geoffrey Rose, and William Haddon. We are also indebted to the people who gave us their personal stories to illustrate the book's ideas; we have changed their names, but they know who they are. We thank our colleague Richard Scribner, who introduced us to Hygeia and Panacea and whose ideas are included in chapter 11. Shelley Roth, Amy Caldwell, and the staff at Beacon Press were willing to take a chance on our ideas, and the *Washington Monthly* was kind enough to print an earlier version of what is now chapter 10 as *Fixing a Fat Nation*. Bob Gunn and Jim Hadler read early drafts of chapters and made helpful comments. Lindsay Mitchell helped track down facts. And Alice Farley deserves thanks for listening far too much for far too long about this project.

Chapter 1. The Wrong Remedy

1. Susan Brink, "Living on the Edge," *U.S. News and World Report*, October 14, 2002, 58.
2. Mariko Thompson, "Bitter Pill: Soaring Prescription Costs Put Seniors in a Financial and Medical Bind," *Daily News (Los Angeles)*, September 9, 2002, Section U.
3. John M. Broder, "Problem of Lost Health Benefits is Reaching into the Middle Class," *New York Times*, November 25, 2002, Section A.
4. National Center for Health Statistics, *Health, United States, 2003* (Hyattsville, MD: 2003), 140.
5. Richard H. Cales and Donald D. Trunkey, "Preventable Trauma Deaths: A Review of Trauma Systems Development," *JAMA* 254 (1985): 1059–1063.
6. Avery B. Nathens et al., "The Effect of Organized Systems of Trauma Care on Motor Vehicle Crash Mortality," *JAMA* 283 (2000): 1990–1994.
7. NCHS, *Health, United States, 2003*, 136; and Pamela A. Sytkowski, William B. Kannel, and Ralph B. D'Agostino, "Changes in Risk Factors and the Decline in Mortality from Cardiovascular Disease: The Framingham Study," *New England Journal of Medicine* 322 (1990): 1635–1641.
8. NCHS, *Health, United States, 2003*, 204.
9. NCHS, *Health, United States, 2003*, 136.
10. John P. Bunker et al., "Improving Health: Measuring Effects of Medical Care," *Milbank Quarterly* 72 (1994): 225–258.
11. U.S. Preventive Services Task Force, "Guide to Clinical Preventive Services," 3rd ed. (Agency for Health Care Research and Quality, U.S. Department of Health and Human Services, 2004) (available at http://www.ahrq.gov/clinic/uspstfix.htm).
12. United Kingdom Prospective Diabetes Study (UKPDS) Group, "Intensive Blood-Glucose Control with Sulphonylureas or Insulin Compared with Conventional Treatment and Risk of Complications in Patients with Type 2 Diabetes," *Lancet* 352 (1998): 837–853; and Genell L. Knatterud et al., "Effects of Hypoglycemic Agents on Vascular Complications in Patients with Adult-Onset Diabetes: VII. Mortality and Selected Nonfatal Events with Insulin Treatment," *JAMA* 240 (1978): 37–42.
13. University Group Diabetes Program, "A Study of the Effects of Hypoglycemic Agents on Vascular Complications in Patients with Adult-Onset Diabetes," *Diabetes* 19, suppl. 2 (1970): 747–830.
14. USPSTF, "Guide to Clinical Preventive Services," 3rd ed.
15. J. Fuller et al., "Antihypertensive Therapy for Preventing Cardiovascular Complications in People with Diabetes Mellitus," *Cochrane Database of Systematic Reviews*, 1st Quarter (2003). Online database accessed at http://gateway1.ma.ovid.com/ovidweb.cgi

16. Nancy Houston Miller, "Compliance with Treatment Regimens in Chronic Asymptomatic Diseases," *American Journal of Medicine* 102 (1997): 43–49.

17. Ihab Hajjar and Theodore A. Kotchen, "Trends in Prevalence, Awareness, Treatment, and Control of Hypertension in the United States, 1988–2000," *JAMA* 290 (2003): 199–206.

18. John R. H. Charlton and Ramon Velez, "Some International Comparisons of Mortality Amenable to Medical Intervention," *British Medical Journal* 292 (1986): 295–301.

19. Douglas B. Manual and Yang Mao, "Avoidable Mortality in the United States and Canada, 1980–1996," *American Journal of Public Health* 92 (2002): 1481–1484.

20. J. P. Mackenbach et al., "'Avoidable' Mortality and Health Services: A Review of Aggregate Data Studies," *Journal of Epidemiology and Community Health* 44 (1990): 106–111.

21. Mackenbach et al., "'Avoidable' Mortality," 106–111.

22. John P. Bunker, "Medicine Matters After All," *Journal of the Royal College of Physicians of London* 29 (1995): 105–112.

23. Elliot S. Fisher et al., "The Implications of Regional Variations in Medicare Spending. Part 1: The Content, Quality, and Accessibility of Care," *Annals of Internal Medicine* 138 (2003): 273–287.

24. Elliot S. Fisher and John E. Wennberg, "Health Care Quality, Geographic Variations, and the Challenge of Supply-Sensitive Care," *Perspectives in Biology and Medicine* 46 (2003): 69–79.

25. Elliot S. Fisher et al., "The Implications of Regional Variations in Medicare Spending, Part 2: Health Outcomes and Satisfaction with Care," *Annals of Internal Medicine* 138 (2003): 288–298.

26. Institute of Medicine, *To Err Is Human: Building a Safer Health System* (Washington, DC: National Academy of Sciences, 1999).

27. Barbara Starfield, "Is US Health Really the Best in the World?" *JAMA* 284 (2000): 483–485.

28. James J. James, "Impacts of the Medical Malpractice Slowdown in Los Angeles County: January 1976," *American Journal of Public Health* 69 (1979): 437–443.

29. Milton J. Roemer, "More Data on Post-Surgical Deaths Related to the 1976 Los Angeles Doctor Slowdown," *Social Sciences and Medicine* 15C (1981): 161–163.

30. "The Trials of Gene Therapy," *Nature*, 420 (2002): 107; and Erika Check, "Cancer Risk Prompts US to Curb Gene Therapy," *Nature* 422 (2003): 7.

31. J. Michael McGinnis and William H. Foege, "Actual Causes of Death in the United States," *JAMA* 270 (1993): 2207–2212.

32. Ali S. Mokdad et al., "Actual Causes of Death in the United States, 2000," *JAMA* 291 (2004): 1238–1245.

33. Christopher J. L. Murray and Alan D. Lopez, "Quantifying the Burden of Disease and Injury Attributable to Ten Major Risk Factors," in *The Global Burden of Disease* (Boston: Harvard University Press, 1996), Tables 6.3–6.12.

34. The CDC's budget in FY 2003 was $4.2 billion. National health expenditures for 2001 were $1,424 billion, according to the *Health, United States, 2003*.

35. NCHS, *Health, United States, 2003*, 306.

36. Centers for Disease Control and Prevention, "Cigarette Smoking among Adults— United States, 2002," *Morbidity and Mortality Weekly Report* 53 (2004): 427–431.

37. Fruit and vegetable consumption data from Centers for Disease Control and Prevention (available at www.cdc.gov/nccdphp/aag/aag_dnpa.htm); fat consumption data from the *Healthy People 2010 Review* (available at www.healthypeople.gov).

38. Centers for Disease Control and Prevention, "Physical Activity Trends—United States, 1990–1998," *Morbidity and Mortality Weekly Report* 50 (2001): 166–168.

39. John E. Anderson, "Condom Use and HIV Risk Among U.S. Adults," *American Journal of Public Health* 93 (2003): 912–914.

40. Louise B. Russell, *Is Prevention Better than Cure?* (Washington, DC: Brookings Institution, 1986).

CHAPTER 2. GREEK GODS AND AMERICAN MYTHS

1. Wade Hampton Frost, *Snow on Cholera* (New York: The Commonwealth Fund, 1936), 60–65.

2. Ibid., xxxv.

3. Ibid., xxxvi.

4. Ibid., 39.

5. Macÿk Porcher Ravenel, ed., *A Half Century of Public Health* (1921; reprint, New York: Arno Press, 1970), 100–102.

6. John Duffy, *The Sanitarians: A History of American Public Health* (Urbana and Chicago: University of Illinois Press, 1990), 99.

7. Dr. Baron Howard, quoted in Edwin Chadwick, *Report on the Sanitary Conditions of the Labouring Population of Great Britain*, ed. M. W. Flinn (Edinburgh: Edinburgh University Press, 1965), 111–112.

8. Duffy, *The Sanitarians,* 102.

9. Ibid., 128–129.

10. Ibid., 129; and Elizabeth Fee, "The Origins and Development of Public Health in the United States," in *Oxford Textbook of Public Health,* 3rd edition, ed. Roger Detels et al. (New York: Oxford University Press, 1997), 38–39.

11. Ravenel, ed., *A Half Century of Public Health,* 102.

12. Duffy, *The Sanitarians,* 128.

13. Paul Starr, *The Social Transformation of American Medicine* (New York: Basic Books, 1982), 190.

14. "William T. G. Morton," in Wikipedia (available at www.wikipedia.org).

15. Albert S. Lyons and R. Joseph Petrucelli II, *Medicine: An Illustrated History* (New York: Abradale Press, 1978), 553.

16. Ibid., 553–554.

17. Information available from the Jenner Museum at www.jennermuseum.com

18. Edward W. Brink et al., "Diphtheria," in John M. Last, ed., *Public Health and Preventive Medicine* (Norwalk, CT: Appleton-Century-Crofts, 1986), 206.

19. Centers for Disease Control and Prevention, "Summary of Notifiable Diseases, United States, 1993," *Morbidity and Mortality Weekly Report* 42 (1993): Tables 1–5.
20. Ibid.
21. James Le Fanu, *The Rise and Fall of Modern Medicine* (New York: Carol and Graf, 2000), 5–15.
22. Thomas McKeown, *The Role of Medicine: Dream, Mirage, or Nemesis?* (Princeton, NJ: Princeton University Press, 1979), 51.
23. Ibid.

CHAPTER 3. HUMANS BEHAVING BADLY

1. James H. Capshew, "Engineering Behavior: Project Pigeon, World War II, and the Conditioning of B. F. Skinner," *Technology and Culture* 34 (1993): 835–857.
2. Howard Kirschenbaum and Valerie Lane Henderson, eds., *The Carl Rogers Reader* (Boston: Houghton Mifflin, 1989).
3. Howard Kirschenbaum and Valerie Lane Henderson, eds., *Carl Rogers—Dialogues: Conversations with Martin Buber, Paul Tillich, B. F. Skinner, Gregory Bateson, Michael Polanyi, Rollo May, and Others* (Boston: Houghton Mifflin, 1989), 83.
4. Ibid., 83.
5. B. F. Skinner, "Why I Am Not a Cognitive Psychologist," in *Reflections on Behaviorism and Society* (Englewood Cliffs, NJ: Prentice-Hall, 1978), 97.
6. Irwin M. Rosenstock, "Historical Origins of the Health Belief Model," *Health Education Monographs* 2 (1974): 328–335; and Irwin M. Rosenstock, "The Health Belief Model: Explaining Health Behavior through Expectancies," in *Health Behavior and Health Education: Theory, Research and Practice* (San Francisco: Jossey-Bass, 1990).
7. Icek Ajzen and Martin Fishbein, *Belief, Attitude, Intention, and Behavior: An Introduction to Theory and Research* (Reading, MA: Addison-Wesley, 1975).
8. Mary Monk et al., "Evaluation of an Antismoking Program among High School Students," *American Journal of Public Health* 55 (1965): 994–1004.
9. Eva Lynn Thompson, "Smoking Education Programs 1960–1976," *American Journal of Public Health* 68 (1978): 250–257.
10. Shelli Avenevoli and Kathleen Ries Merikangas, "Familial Influences on Adolescent Smoking," *Addiction* 98, suppl. 1 (2003): 1–20; and Patrick West, Helen Sweeting, and Russell Ecob, "Family and Friends' Influences on the Uptake of Regular Smoking from Mid-adolescence to Early Adulthood," *Addiction* 94 (1999): 1397–1412.
11. Albert Bandura, "Social Learning through Imitation," in M. R. Jones, ed., *Nebraska Symposium on Motivation*, vol. 10 (Lincoln, NE: University of Nebraska Press, 1962), 211–274.
12. Leonore Loeb Adler and Helmut E. Adler, "Ontogeny of Observational Learning in the Dog (*Canis Familiaris*)," *Developmental Psychobiology* 10 (1977): 267–271.
13. Albert Bandura, *Social Foundations of Thought and Action* (Englewood Cliffs, NJ: Prentice-Hall, 1986), 99.

14. Ibid.

15. Bandura, "Social Learning through Imitation," 211–274.

16. David P. Phillips, "The Influence of Suggestion on Suicide: Substantive and Theoretical Implications of the Werther Effect," *American Sociological Review* 39 (1974): 340–354.

17. Ibid.

18. David P. Phillips and Lundie L. Carstensen, "The Effect of Suicide Stories on Various Demographic Groups 1968–1985," *Suicide and Life-Threatening Behavior* 18 (1988): 100–114.

19. Marion Howard and J. B. McCabe, "Helping Teenagers Postpone Sexual Involvement," *Family Planning Perspectives* 22 (1990): 21–26.

20. Douglas Kirby et al., "The Impact of the Postponing Sexual Involvement Curriculum among Youths in California," *Family Planning Perspectives* 29 (1997): 100–108.

21. William Dejong, "A Short-Term Evaluation of Project DARE (Drug Abuse Resistance Education): Preliminary Indications of Effectiveness," *Journal of Drug Education* 17 (1985): 279–294.

22. Susan T. Ennett et al., "How Effective Is Drug Abuse Resistance Education? A Meta-Analysis of Project DARE Outcome Evaluations," *American Journal of Public Health* 84 (1994): 1394–1401.

23. Ibid.; and Richard R. Clayton et al., "The Effectiveness of Drug Abuse Resistance Education (Project DARE): 5-Year Follow-Up Results," *Preventive Medicine* 25 (1996): 307–318.

24. Arthur V. Peterson et al., "Hutchinson Smoking Prevention Project: Long-Term Randomized Trial in School-Based Tobacco Use Prevention—Results on Smoking," *Journal of the National Cancer Institute* 92 (2000): 1979–1991.

25. Stephen P. Fortmann et al., "Community Intervention Trials: Reflections on the Stanford Five-City Project Experience," *American Journal of Epidemiology* 142 (1995): 576–586; Russell V. Luepker et al., "Community Education for Cardiovascular Disease Prevention: Risk Factor Changes in the Minnesota Heart Health Program," *American Journal of Public Health* 84 (1994): 1383–1393; and Richard A. Carleton et al., "The Pawtucket Heart Health Program: Community Changes in Cardiovascular Risk Factors and Projected Disease Risk," *American Journal of Public Health* 85 (1995): 777–785.

CHAPTER 4. BELL CURVES AND BAD APPLES

1. Geoffrey Rose, *The Strategy of Preventive Medicine* (New York: Oxford University Press, 1992), 62.

2. Ibid., chs. 4–5.

3. Ole-Jorgen Skog, "The Collectivity of Drinking Cultures: A Theory of the Distribution of Alcohol Consumption," *British Journal of Addiction* 80 (1985): 83–89.

4. James D. Neaton et al., "Serum Cholesterol, Blood Pressure, Cigarette Smoking, and Death from Coronary Heart Disease: Overall Findings and Differences by Age for 316,099 White Men," *Archives of Internal Medicine* 152 (1992): 56–64.

5. Jiang He and Paul K. Whelton, "Epidemiology and Prevention of Hypertension," *Medical Clinics of North America* 81 (1997): 1077–1096.

6. Cheryl J. Cherpitel et al., "Alcohol and Non-Fatal Injury in the U.S. General Population: A Risk Function Analysis," *Accident Analysis and Prevention* 27 (1995): 651–661.

7. S. Leonard Syme, "To Prevent Disease: The Need for a New Approach," in *Health and Social Organization: Towards a Health Policy for the Twenty-First Century,* ed. David Blane et al. (London: Routledge, 1996), 22.

8. Malcolm R. Law et al., "By How Much Does Dietary Salt Reduction Lower Blood Pressure: III-Analysis of Data from Trials of Salt Reduction," *British Medical Journal* 302 (1991): 819–824.

9. Rose, *The Strategy of Preventive Medicine,* 103.

10. Data compiled by Stanton Glanz and available at www.smokefreemovies.ucsf.edu

Chapter 5. More Is More: Accessibility

1. "Slotting Fees, Consolidation in Food Industry Examined," *Food and Drink Weekly,* October 25, 1999.

2. Angela Hausman, "A Multi-Method Investigation of Consumer Motivations in Impulse Buying Behavior," *Journal of Consumer Marketing* 17 (2000): 403–419.

3. J. Jeffrey Inman and Russell S. Winer, *Where the Rubber Meets the Road: A Model of In-Store Consumer Decision-Making,* Marketing Science Institute Working Paper No. 98–122 (available at www.msi.org).

4. J. B. Wilkinson, J. Barry Mason, and Christine H. Paksoy, "Assessing the Impact of Short-Term Supermarket Strategy Variables," *Journal of Marketing Research* 19 (1982): 72–86; and Ronald C. Curhan, "The Relationship between Shelf Space and Unit Sales in Supermarkets," *Journal of Marketing Research* 9 (1972): 406–12.

5. Ronald E. Frank and William F. Massey, "Shelf Position and Space Effects on Sales," *Journal of Marketing Research* 7 (1970): 59–66.

6. Ibid.

7. Wilkinson, Mason, and Paksoy, "Assessing the Impact," 72–86.; and Michel Chevalier, "Increase in Sales Due to In-Store Display," *Journal of Marketing Research* 12 (1975): 426–431.

8. Inman and Winer, *Where the Rubber Meets the Road.*

9. Barbara J. Rolls, Erin L. Morris, and Liane S. Roe, "Portion Size of Food Affects Energy Intake in Normal-Weight and Overweight Men and Women," *American Journal of Clinical Nutrition* 76 (2002): 1207–1213.

10. Data collected by the authors.

11. Ronald C. Curhan, "The Effects of Merchandising and Temporary Promotional Activities on the Sales of Fresh Fruits and Vegetables in Supermarkets," *Journal of Marketing Research* 11 (1974): 286–294.

12. Richard A. Scribner. David P. MacKinnon, and James H. Dwyer, "Alcohol Outlet Density and Motor Vehicle Crashes in Los Angeles County Cities," *Journal of Studies*

on Alcohol (1994): 447–453; Richard A. Scribner, David P. MacKinnon, and James H. Dwyer, "The Risk of Assaultive Violence and Alcohol Availability in Los Angeles County," *American Journal of Public Health* 85 (1995): 335–340; and Richard A. Scribner, Deborah A. Cohen, and Thomas A. Farley, "A Geographic Relation between Alcohol Availability and Gonorrhea Rates," *Sexually Transmitted Diseases* 25 (1998): 544–548.

13. Scribner, MacKinnon, and Dwyer, "The Risk of Assaultive Violence," 335–340; Scribner, Cohen, and Farley, "A Geographic Relation," 544–548.

14. Harold D. Holder et al., "Effect of Community-Based Interventions on High-Risk Drinking and Alcohol-Related Injuries," *JAMA* 284 (2000): 2341–2347.

15. Thomas L. Robertson et al., "Epidemiologic Studies of Coronary Heart Disease and Stroke in Japanese Men Living in Japan, Hawaii, and California: Incidence of Myocardial Infarction and Death from Coronary Heart Disease," *American Journal of Cardiology,* 39 (1977): 239–43.

16. Alexander C. Wagenaar and Traci L. Toomey, "Effect of Minimum Age Drinking Laws: Review and Analyses from the Literature, 1960 to 2000," *Journal of Studies on Alcohol,* suppl. 14 (2002): 206–225.

17. Deborah A. Cohen et al., "Implementation of Condom Social Marketing in Louisiana, 1993 to 1996," *American Journal of Public Health* 89 (1999): 204–208.

18. Hana Ross and Frank J. Chaloupka, "The Effect of Cigarette Prices on Youth Smoking," *Health Economics* 12 (2003): 217–230.

19. Ibid.

20. Robert L. Flewelling et al., "First-Year Impact of the 1989 California Cigarette Tax Increase on Cigarette Consumption," *American Journal of Public Health* 82 (1992): 867–869.

21. Caroline M. Fichtenberg and Stanton A. Glantz, "Association of the California Tobacco Control Program with Declines in Cigarette Consumption and Mortality from Heart Disease," *New England Journal of Medicine* 343 (2000): 1772–1777; and Dorothy Griffith, "State Sees Sizable Drop in Tobacco-Related Cancers," *Sacramento Bee,* November 15, 2003, A1.

22. Siu Fai Leung and Charles E. Phelps, " 'My Kingdom for a Drink...?' A Review of Estimates of the Price Sensitivity of Demand for Alcoholic Beverages," in Michael E. Hilton and Gregory Bloss, eds., *Economics and the Prevention of Alcohol-Related Health Problems,* NIAAA Research Monograph No. 25, NIH Pub. No. 93-3513 (Bethesda, MD: National Institute on Alcohol Abuse and Alcoholism, 1993), 1–32.

23. Frank J. Chaloupka, Michael Grossman, and Henry Saffer, "The Effects of Price on Alcohol Consumption and Alcohol-Related Problems," *Alcohol Research and Health,* 26 (2002): 22–34.

24. Michael F. Jacobson and Kelly D. Brownell, "Small Taxes on Soft Drinks and Snack Foods to Promote Health," *American Journal of Public Health* 90 (2000): 854–857.

25. Curhan, "The Effects of Merchandising," 286–294.

26. Simone A. French et al., "Pricing and Promotion Effects on Low-Fat Vending Snack Purchases: The CHIPS Study," *American Journal of Public Health* 91 (2001): 112–117.

27. Katherine B. Horgen and Kelly D. Brownell, "Comparison of Price Change and

Health Message Interventions in Promoting Healthy Food Choices," *Health Psychology* 21 (2002): 505–512.

28. Deborah A. Cohen et al., "Cost As a Barrier to Condom Use: The Evidence for Condom Subsidies in the United States," *American Journal of Public Health* 89 (1999): 567–568.

CHAPTER 6. SIDEWALKS AND FALLING CHILDREN: PHYSICAL STRUCTURES

1. Charlotte N. Spiegel and Francis C. Lindaman, "Children Can't Fly: A Program to Prevent Childhood Morbidity and Mortality from Window Falls," *American Journal of Public Health* 67 (1977): 1143–1147.

2. Lawrence Bergner et al., "Falls from Heights: A Childhood Epidemic in an Urban Area," *American Journal of Public Health* 61 (1971): 90–96.

3. Ibid.

4. Spiegel and Lindaman, "Children Can't Fly," 1143–1147.

5. Ibid.

6. Barbara Barlow et al., "Ten Years of Experience with Falls from a Height in Children," *Journal of Pediatric Surgery* 18 (1983): 509–511.

7. Ibid.

8. Gregory B. Rodgers, "The Effectiveness of Child-Resistant Packaging for Aspirin," *Archives of Pediatric and Adolescent Medicine* 156 (2002): 929–933.

9. Ibid.

10. Ibid.

11. William W. Walton, "An Evaluation of the Poison Prevention Packaging Act," *Pediatrics* 69 (1982): 363–370.

12. David B. Scott, "The Dawn of a New Era," *Journal of Public Health Dentistry* 56 (1996; 5 Spec No): 235–238.

13. Ibid.

14. Clive G. Harper et al., "Prevalence of Wernicke-Korsakoff Syndrome in Australia: Has Thiamine Fortification Made a Difference?" *Medical Journal of Australia* 168 (1998): 542–545.

15. Brian E. Saelens et al., "Neighborhood-Based Differences in Physical Activity: An Environment Scale Evaluation," *American Journal of Public Health* 93 (2003): 1552–1558.

16. Reid Ewing et al., "Relationship between Urban Sprawl and Physical Activity, Obesity, and Morbidity," *American Journal of Health Promotion* 18 (2003): 47–57.

17. Reid Ewing et al., "Urban Sprawl as a Risk Factor in Motor Vehicle Occupant and Pedestrian Fatalities," *American Journal of Public Health* 23 (2003): 1541–1545.

18. William H. Lucy, "Mortality Risk Associated with Leaving Home: Recognizing the Relevance of the Built Environment," *American Journal of Public Health* 93 (2003): 1564–1569.

19. Lisa D'Innocenzo, "On-the-Go Snacks Are Where It's At," *Strategy*, September 9, 2002, 1.

20. Ibid.

21. "Raising the Bar," *Confectioner* 88 (September 2003): 53.

22. David M. Cutler et al., "Why Have Americans Become More Obese?" *NBER Working Paper No. W9446,* January 2003 (available at http://ssrn.com/abstract=370430).

23. Ibid.

24. Deborah A. Cohen et al., "Neighborhood Physical Conditions and Health," *American Journal of Public Health* 93 (2003): 467–471.

25. Paul V. Gump, "A Short History of the Midwest Psychological Field Station," *Environment and Behavior* 22 (1990): 436–457.

26. Francis T. McAndrew, *Environmental Psychology* (Pacific Grove, CA: Brooks/Cole Publishing, 1993), 152.

27. Michael Bakos et al., "Effects of Environmental Changes on Elderly Residents' Behavior," *Hospital and Community Psychiatry* 31 (1980): 677–682.

28. Kenneth J. Gergen, Mary M. Gergen, and William H. Barton, "Deviance in the Dark," *Psychology Today*, October 1973, 129–130.

29. Oscar Newman, *Creating Defensible Space* (Washington, DC: U.S. Department of Housing and Urban Development, Office of Policy Development and Research, April 1996) (available at www.huduser.org/publications/pubasst/defensib.html).

30. Ibid., 55.

31. Sherry Plaster Carter et al., "Zoning Out Crime and Improving Community Health in Sarasota, Florida: 'Crime Prevention through Environmental Design,'" *American Journal of Public Health* 93 (2003): 1442–1445.

32. Raymond Fleming, Andrew Baum, and Jerome E. Singer, "Social Support and the Physical Environment," in Sheldon Cohen and S. Leonard Syme, eds., *Social Support and Health* (Orlando, FL: Academic Press, 1985), 327–346.

33. Yeates Conwell, Paul R. Duberstein, and Eric D. Caine, "Risk Factors for Suicide in Later Life," *Biological Psychiatry* 52 (2002): 193–204.

34. Catherine Schaefer, Charles P. Quesenbery Jr., and Soora Wi, "Mortality Following Conjugal Bereavement and the Effects of a Shared Environment," *American Journal of Epidemiology* 141 (1995): 1142–1152.

35. Lisa F. Berkman, "Assessing the Physical Health Effects of Social Networks and Social Support," *Annual Reviews of Public Health* 5 (1984): 413–432; and James S. House, Karl R. Landis, and Debra Umberson, "Social Relationships and Health," *Science* 24 (1988): 540–545.

36. James Q. Wilson and George L. Kelling, "Broken Windows: The Police and Neighborhood Safety," *Atlantic,* March 1982, 29–38.

37. Philip G. Zimbardo, "The Human Choice: Individuation, Reason, and Order versus Deindividuation, Impulse, and Chaos," *Nebraska Symposium on Motivation* 17 (1969): 237–307.

CHAPTER 7. PLAYING BY THE RULES: SOCIAL STRUCTURES

1. Benjamin W. Pace, Richard Thailer, and Thomas G. Kwiatkowski, "New York Mandatory Seatbelt Use Law: Patterns of Seatbelt Use Before and After Legislation," *Journal of Trauma* 26 (1986): 1031–1033.

2. Ibid.

3. Daniel R Longo, Ross C. Brownson, Jane C. Johnson, et al., "Hospital Smoking Bans and Employee Smoking Behavior: Results of a National Survey," *JAMA* 275 (1996): 1252–1257.

4. For example, Lois Biener, David B. Abrams, Michael J. Follick, and Larry Dean, "A Comparative Evaluation of a Restrictive Smoking Policy in a General Hospital," *American Journal of Public Health* 79 (1989): 192–195; Lyle R. Petersen et al., "Employee Smoking Behavior Changes and Attitudes Following a Restrictive Policy on Worksite Smoking in a Large Company," *Public Health Reports* 103 (1988): 115–120; and Glorian Sorenson, Nancy A. Rigotti, Amy Rosen, John Pinney, and Ray Prible, "Employee Knowledge and Attitudes about a Work-Site Nonsmoking Policy: Rationale for Further Smoking Restrictions," *Journal of Occupational Medicine* 33 (1991): 1125–1130.

5. Luis G. Escobedo, Terence L. Chorba, Patrick L. Remington, et al., "The Influence of Safety Belt Laws on Self-Reported Safety Belt Use in the United States," *Accident Analysis and Prevention* 24 (1992): 643–653.

6. Donna Glassbrenner, "Safety Belt Use in 2002—Use Rates in the States and Territories," Research Note DOT HS 809587, May 2003 (available at www-nrd.nhtsa.dot.gov/pdf/nrd-30/NCSA/RNotes/2003/809-587.pdf).

7. Donna Glassbrenner, "Safety Belt Use in 2003", Technical Report DOT HS 809646, September 2003 (available at www.nhtsa.gov/people/injury/airbags/seatbelts.htm).

8. National Academy of Sciences, *55: A Decade of Experience* (Washington, DC: National Research Council, 1984).

9. Steven Garber and John D. Grahman, "The Effects of the 65 Mile-Per-Hour Speed Limit on Rural Highway Fatalities: A State-by-State Analysis," *Accident Analysis and Prevention* 22 (1990): 137–149.

10. Charles M. Farmer, Richard A. Retting, and Adrian K. Lund, "Changes in Motor Vehicle Occupant Fatalities after Repeal of the National Speed Limit," *Accident Analysis and Prevention* 31 (1999): 537–543.

11. Eric M. Ossiander and Peter Cummings, "Freeway Speed Limits and Traffic Fatalities in Washington State," *Accident Analysis and Prevention* 34 (2002): 13–18.

12. Stanislav V. Kasl and Beth A. Jones, "The Impact of Job Loss and Retirement on Health," in *Social Epidemiology*, ed. L. F. Berkman and I. Kawachi (New York: Oxford University Press, 2000); and Robert L. Jin, Chandrakant P. Shah, and Tomislav J. Svoboda, "The Impact of Unemployment on Health: A Review of the Evidence," *Canadian Medical Association Journal* 153 (1995): 529–540.

13. M. Osler, U. Christensen, R. Lund, et al., "High Local Unemployment and Increased Mortality in Danish Adults: Results from a Prospective Multilevel Study," *Occupa-

tional and Environmental Medicine (2003), 60:e16 (available at http://oem.bmjjournals
.com/cgi/content/full/60/11/e16).

14. Michael D. Resnick, Peter S. Bearman, Robert W. Blum, et al., "Protecting Adolescents from Harm," *JAMA* 278 (1997): 823–832.

15. Lisa F. Berkman and S. Leonard Syme, "Social Networks, Host Resistance, and Mortality: Nine-Year Follow-Up Study of Alameda County Residents," *American Journal of Epidemiology* 109 (1979): 186–204.

16. Ichiro Kawachi, Bruce P. Kennedy, Kimberly Lochner, and Deborah Prothrow-Stith, "Social Capital, Income Inequality, and Mortality," *American Journal of Public Health* 87 (1997): 1491–1498.

17. Sheldon Cohen, William J. Doyle, David P. Skoner, et al., "Social Ties and Susceptibility to the Common Cold," *JAMA* 277 (1997): 1940-1944.

18. Robert D. Putnam, "Health and Happiness," in *Bowling Alone: The Collapse and Revival of the American Community* (New York: Simon and Schuster, 2000), 326.

Chapter 8. It's the Real Thing: Media

1. Helen Peterson and Dick Sheriden, "Two Killed, Two Injured Copying Film Stunt," *New York Daily News*, October 19, 1993, A1; and Michael deCourcy Hinds, "Not Like the Movie: A Dare Leads to Death," *New York Times*, October 19, 1993, A1.

2. Description of *The Program* at www.amazon.com (in DVD store, select VHS under the Search DVD menu).

3. Hinds, "Not Like the Movie," A1.

4. Ibid.

5. Ibid.

6. www.fradical.com/Canadian_copycat_incidents.htm

7. Christophe Boesch and Michael Tomasello, "Chimpanzee and Human Cultures," *Current Anthropology* 39 (1998): 591–614.

8. Robert D. Putnam, *Bowling Alone: The Collapse and Revival of American Community* (New York: Simon and Schuster, 2000), 222.

9. Ibid.

10. Ibid., 222, 224, 227.

11. Ibid.

12. Ibid., 225, graph.

13. Donald F. Roberts, Ulla G. Foehr, Victoria J. Rideout, and Mollyann Brodie, "Kids & Media @ the New Millennium," Kaiser Family Foundation, November 1999, 15 (available at www.kff.org/entmedia/1535-index.cfm).

14. Todd Gitlin, *Inside Prime Time* (Berkeley: University of California Press, 2000), 31.

15. Data compiled by *Advertising Age* and available at www.adage.com

16. Gitlin, *Inside Prime Time,* 72.

17. Stephen Fox, *The Mirror Makers: A History of American Advertising and Its Creators* (New York: William Morrow and Company, 1984), 183.

18. A brief biography is available at www.marketers-hall-of-fame.com/1-john-watson-marketing.html

19. Jon Steele, *Truth, Lies, and Advertising: The Art of Account Planning* (New York: John Wiley and Sons, 1998), xiii.

20. James B. Twitchell, *Twenty Ads That Shook the World: The Century's Most Ground-breaking Advertising and How It Changed Us All* (New York: Crown Publishers, 2000), 126.

21. Putnam, *Bowling Alone,* 241.

22. Robert D. McIlwraith, "'I'm Addicted to Television': The Personality, Imagination, and TV Watching Patterns of Self-Identified TV Addicts," *Journal of Broadcasting and Electronic Media* 42 (Summer 1998): 371–386.

23. Robert William Kubey and Mihaly Csikszentmihalyi, *Television and the Quality of Life: How Viewing Shapes Everyday Experience* (Hillsdale, NJ: L. Erlbaum Associates, 1990), 139–141.

24. Gabriel Weimann, *Communicating Unreality* (Thousand Oaks, CA: Sage Publications, 2000), 8.

25. Robert C. Klesges, Mary L. Shelton, and Lisa M. Klesges, "Effects of Television on Metabolic Rate: Potential Implications for Childhood Obesity," *Pediatrics* 91 (1993): 281–286.

26. Twitchell, *Twenty Ads,* 70–73; and Erik Barnouw, *Tube of Plenty: The Evolution of American Television* (New York: Oxford University Press, 1975), 45.

27. Fox, *The Mirror Makers,* 152–155.

28. Cy Schneider, *Children's Television: The Art, the Business, and How It Works* (Chicago: Lincolnwood, NTC Business Books, 1987), 15–29.

29. Mary Story and Patricia Faulkner, "The Prime Time Diet: A Content Analysis of Eating Behavior and Food Messages in Television Program Content and Commercials," *American Journal of Public Health* 80 (1990): 738–740.

30. Ibid.

31. Elizabeth M. Perse, *Media Effects and Society* (Mahwah, NJ: L. Erlbaum Associates, 2001), 182.

32. Alan Mathios et al., "Alcohol Portrayal on Prime-Time Television: Manifest and Latent Messages," *Journal of Studies on Alcohol* 59 (1998): 305–310.

33. Joel W. Grube, "Alcohol Portrayals and Alcohol Advertising on Television: Content and Effects on Children and Adolescents," *Alcohol Health and Research World* 17 (1993): 61–66; and Patricia A. Madden and Joel W. Grube, "The Frequency and Nature of Alcohol and Tobacco Advertising in Televised Sports, 1990 through 1992," *American Journal of Public Health* 84 (1994): 297–299.

34. Grube, "Alcohol Portrayals," 61–66.

35. Joel W. Grube and Lawrence Wallack, "Television Beer Advertising and Drinking Knowledge, Beliefs, and Intentions among Schoolchildren," *American Journal of Public Health* 84 (1994): 254–259.

36. Grube, "Alcohol Portrayals," 61–66.

37. Perse, *Media Effects and Society,* 184–185.

38. Barnouw, *Tube of Plenty,* 132.

39. Karen M. Emmons, Ichiro Kawachi, and Gillian Barclay, "Tobacco Control: A Brief Review of its History and Prospects for the Future," *Hematology/Oncology Clinics of North America* 11 (1997): 177–195.

40. Adam O. Goldstein, Rachel A. Sobel, and Glen R. Newman, "Tobacco and Alcohol Use in G-Rated Children's Animated Films," *JAMA* 281 (1999): 1131–1136; data on smoking by movie characters compared to real people collected by Stanton Glanz (available at www.smokefreemovies.ucsf.edu).

41. Joel Federman, ed., *National Television Violence Study,* vol. 3, Executive Summary (University of California, Santa Barbara, 1998), 27 (available at www.ccsp.ucsb.edu/execsum.pdf).

42. Weimann, *Communicating Unreality,* 86–89.

43. Ibid., 94.

44. Federman, ed., *National Television Violence Study,* 27.

45. Nick Browne et al., "American Film Violence: An Analytic Portrait," *Journal of Interpersonal Violence* 17 (2002): 351–370.

46. George Gerbner, "TV Violence and the Art of Asking the Wrong Question," Center for Media Literacy (available at www.medialit.org).

47. Weimann, *Communicating Unreality,* 91.

48. Committee on Public Education, American Academy of Pediatrics, "Media Violence," *Pediatrics* 108 (2001): 1222–1226.

49. Weimann, *Communicating Unreality,* 95–97; and L. Rowell Huesmann et al., "Longitudinal Relations between Children's Exposure to TV Violence and Their Aggressive and Violent Behavior in Young Adulthood: 1977–1992," *Developmental Psychology* 39 (2003): 201–221.

50. Tannis MacBeth Williams, ed., *The Impact of Television: A Natural Experiment in Three Communities* (Orlando, FL: Academic Press, 1986), 341.

51. Weimann, *Communicating Unreality,* 95–97.

52. Joint Statement on the Impact of Entertainment Violence on Children, July 26, 2000 (available at www.aap.org/advocacy/releases/jstmtevc.htm).

53. Dale Kunkel et al., *Sex on TV 3: A Biennial Report to the Kaiser Family Foundation,* 17 (available at www.kff.org).

54. Ibid., 36.

55. Jane D. Brown and Susan F. Newcomer, "Television Viewing and Adolescents' Sexual Behavior," *Journal of Homosexuality* 21 (1991): 77–91.

56. Jim Balloch, "Clues Sought in I-40 Shooting; Cocke Authorities Search for Suspects, Motive in Fatal Attack," *Knoxville News-Sentinel,* June 27, 2003, A1; and Laura Ayo, "Victim of Shooting Loved the Outdoors; Death on I-40 Came at End of Day in Mountains," *Knoxville News-Sentinel,* July 1, 2003, A1.

57. "Boys Charged in I-40 Shootings," *Associated Press State and Local Wire,* June 27, 2003; and Jim Balloch, "Teens Plead Guilty to I-40 Shootings; Stepbrothers to Serve Indeterminate Term in State Custody," *Knoxville News-Sentinel,* August 29, 2003, A1.

58. See www.rockstargames.com

59. Roberts et al., *Kids & Media @ the New Millennium,* 42.

60. Chris Cuomo, "A Delinquent's Dream: The Video Game *Grand Theft Auto* Has Riled Up the Critics," *ABCNews.com* (Good Morning America), October 31, 2002.

61. Bryan Mitchell, "Arrests of Two Teens Puzzle, Stun Newport," *Knoxville News-Sentinel*, June 29, 2003, A1.

62. "Boys Charged in I-40 Shootings."

63. Hank Seiden, *Advertising Pure and Simple: The New Edition* (New York: Amacom, 1990), 16.

64. Ibid.

65. David Ogilvy, *Ogilvy on Advertising* (New York: Crown Publishers, 1983), 110.

66. J. C. Louis and Harvey Z. Yazijian, *The Cola Wars*, (New York: Everest House, 1980).

67. Ibid., 352–353.

68. Michael Medved, "Hollywood's Three Big Lies about Media and Society," Ricks College Forum, October 20, 1994 (available at http://emp.byui.edu/DavidR/202/Medved.htm).

69. Ibid.

70. Haejung Paik, "Prosocial Television Programs and Altruistic Behavior: A Meta-analysis," *Mass Communication Review* 22 (1995): 147–165.

71. Susan Hearold, "A Synthesis of 1043 Effects of Television on Social Behavior," in George Comstock, ed., *Public Communication and Behavior*, vol. 1 (New York: Academic Press, 1986), 66–135.

72. Paik, "Prosocial Television Programs," 147–165.

73. Reed Hundt, "Television, Kids, Indecency, Violence, and the Public Interest," speech given February 9, 1996, at the Duke Law Journals 27th Administrative Law Conference (available at www.benton.org/publibrary/policy/tv/rhundt_tvkids.html).

74. Lawrence O. Gostin, "Corporate Speech and the Constitution: The Deregulation of Tobacco Advertising," *American Journal of Public Health* 92 (2002): 352–355.

75. Teh-wei Hu, Hai-Yen Sung, and Theodore E. Keeler, "Reducing Cigarette Consumption in California: Tobacco Taxes vs. an Anti-Smoking Media Campaign," *American Journal of Public Health* 85 (1995): 1218–1222; and Jeff Niederdeppe, Matthew C. Farrelly, and M. Lyndon Haviland, "Confirming 'Truth': More Evidence of a Successful Countermarketing Campaign in Florida," *American Journal of Public Health* 94 (2004): 225–257.

76. Keating Holland, "Poll: Violence in the Media Should Be Regulated," *CNN.com*, May 3, 1999.

CHAPTER 9. THE KILLER LEAF

1. W. A. Penn, *The Soverane Herb: A History of Tobacco* (London: Grant Richards, 1901).

2. Martin R. Jarvis, "Why People Smoke," *British Medical Journal* 328 (2004): 277–279.

3. Department of Health and Human Services, *The Health Consequences of Smoking: Nicotine Addiction: A Report of the Surgeon General*, DHHS Pub. No. (CDC) 88-8406 (Rockville, MD: Center for Health Promotion and Education, Office on Smoking and Health, 1988), 189.

4. Ibid., 314.
5. Department of Health and Human Services, *The Health Consequences of Smoking: A Report of the Surgeon General* (2004), 44 (available at www.surgeongeneral.gov/library/smokingconsequences/).
6. Ibid.
7. Estimates from the Centers for Disease Control and Prevention (available at www.cdc.gov/nccdphp/bb_tobacco/index.htm).
8. Ronald M. Davis, "Exposure to Environmental Tobacco Smoke: Identifying and Protecting Those at Risk," *JAMA* 280 (1998): 1947–1949.
9. Eva Lynn Thompson, "Smoking Education Programs, 1960–1976," *American Journal of Public Health* 68 (1978): 250–257.
10. The COMMIT Research Group, "Community Intervention Trial for Smoking Cessation (COMMIT): I. Cohort Results from a Four-Year Intervention," *American Journal of Public Health* 85 (1995): 183–192.
11. Arthur V. Peterson, Kathleen A. Kealey, Sue L. Mann, et al., "Hutchinson Smoking Prevention Project: Long-Term Randomized Trial in School-Based Tobacco Use Prevention—Results on Smoking," *Journal of the National Cancer Institute* 92 (2000): 1979–1991.
12. Data from Monitoring the Future Study at the University of Michigan (available at www.monitoringthefuture.org).
13. Stanton A. Glantz and Edith D. Balbach, *Tobacco War: Inside the California Battles* (Berkeley: University of California Press, 2000), 8.
14. Ibid., 14.
15. Michael S. Givel and Stanton A. Glantz, "Tobacco Lobby Political Influence on US State Legislatures in the 1990s," Tobacco Control 10 (2001): 124–134.
16. Jenny White and Lisa A. Bero, "Public Health Under Attack: The American Stop Smoking Intervention Study (ASSIST) and the Tobacco Industry," *American Journal of Public Health* 94 (2004): 240–250.
17. Ibid.
18. Ibid.
19. Michael F. Bierer and Nancy A. Rigotti, "Public Policy for the Control of Tobacco-Related Disease," *Medical Clinics of North America* 76 (1992): 515–539.
20. Jean L. Forster and Mark Wolfson, "Youth Access to Tobacco: Policies and Politics," *Annual Review of Public Health* 19 (1998): 203–235.
21. Department of Health and Human Services, *Reducing Tobacco Use: A Report of the Surgeon General* (Washington, DC: Public Health Service, Centers for Disease Control, Center for Chronic Disease Prevention and Health Promotion, Office on Smoking and Health, 1989), 184–185.
22. Ibid., 113–118.
23. Ross C. Brownson, David P. Hopkins, and Melanie A. Wakefield, "Effects of Smoking Restrictions in the Workplace," *Annual Review of Public Health* 23 (2002): 333–348.
24. DHHS, *Reducing Tobacco Use*, 45.
25. Ibid.

26. Ibid., 33, 45.

27. Ursula E. Bauer, Tammie M. Johnson, Richard S. Hopkins, and Robert G. Brooks, "Changes in Youth Cigarette Use and Intentions Following Implementation of a Tobacco Control Program: Findings from the Florida Youth Tobacco Survey, 1998–2000," *JAMA* 284 (2000): 723–728.

28. Teh-wei Hu, Hai-Yen Sung, and Theodore E. Keeler, "Reducing Cigarette Consumption in California: Tobacco Taxes vs. an Anti-Smoking Media Campaign," *American Journal of Public Health* 85 (1995): 1218–1222; and Lois Biener, Jeffrey E. Harris, and William Hamilton, "Impact of the Massachusetts Tobacco Control Programme: Population Based Trend Analysis," *British Medical Journal* 321 (2000): 351–354.

29. Michael S. Givel and Stanton A. Glantz, "Failure to Defend a Successful State Tobacco Control Program: Policy Lessons from Florida," *American Journal of Public Health* 90 (2000): 762–767; and Glantz and Balbach, *Tobacco War.*

30. DHHS, *Reducing Tobacco Use,* 33.

31. John M. Broder, "Cigarette Makers in a $368 Billion Accord to Curb Lawsuits and Curtail Marketing," *New York Times,* June 21, 1997, A1.

32. Peter Passell, "Economic Scene: Tobacco Might Thrive with a $1.50-a-Pack Rise for Cigarettes," *New York Times,* September 25, 1997, D2.

33. John M. Broder, "Tobacco Profits May Soar under Deal, Government Study Shows," New York Times, September 22, 1997, A21.

34. David E. Rosenbaum, "Senate Committee Makes Fast Work of Cigarette Bill," *New York Times,* April 2, 1998, A1.

35. David E. Rosenbaum, "Cigarette Makers Quit Negotiations on Tobacco Bill," *New York Times,* April 9, 1998, A1.

36. David E. Rosenbaum, "The Tobacco Bill: The Overview; Senate Drops Tobacco Bill with '98 Revival Unlikely; Clinton Lashes Out at G.O.P.," *New York Times,* June 18, 1998, A1.

37. Barry Meier, "Remaining States Approve the Pact on Tobacco Suits," *New York Times,* November 21, 1998, A1.

38. Cary P. Gross, Benny Soffer, Peter B. Bach, et al., "State Expenditures for Tobacco-Control Programs and the Tobacco Settlement," *New England Journal of Medicine* 347 (2002): 1080–1086.

39. *Federal Trade Commission Cigarette Report for 1999* (Washington, DC: Federal Trade Commission, 2001), 2–3 (available at www.ftc.gov).

40. Stanton A. Glantz, Karen W. Kacirk, and Charles McCulloch, "Back to the Future: Smoking in Movies in 2002 Compared with 1950 Levels," *American Journal of Public Health* 94 (2004): 261–263.

41. J. Michael McGinnis and William H. Foege, "Mortality and Morbidity Attributable to Use of Addictive Substances in the United States," *Proceedings of the Association of American Physicians* 111 (1999): 109–118.

CHAPTER 10. HABITS OF THE HEART

1. National Center for Health Statistics, *Health, United States, 2003*. (Hyattsville, MD: 2003), 234.

2. Ibid., 230–231.

3. Ibid., 136.

4. Norman M. Kaplan, "The Deadly Quartet: Upper Body Obesity, Glucose Intolerance, Hypertriglyceridemia, and Hypertension," *Archives of Internal Medicine* 149 (1989): 1514–1520.

5. Vicki L. Burt et al., "Prevalence of Hypertension in the U.S. Adult Population," *Hypertension* 25 (195): 305–313; and James D. Neaton et al., "Serum Cholesterol, Blood Pressure, Cigarette Smoking, and Death from Coronary Heart Disease," *Archives of Internal Medicine* 152 (1992): 56–64.

6. Michael J. Martin et al., "Serum Cholesterol, Blood Pressure, and Mortality: Implications from a Cohort of 361,662 Men," *Lancet* 2 (1986): 933–936; and Neaton et al., "Serum Cholesterol," 56–64.

7. Centers for Disease Control and Prevention, "Prevalence of Diabetes and Impaired Fasting Glucose in Adults—United States, 1999–2000," *Morbidity and Mortality Weekly Report* 52 (2003): 833–837.

8. NCHS, *Health, United States, 2003*, 136, 144.

9. Centers for Disease Control and Prevention, "Trends in Intake of Energy and Macronutrients—United States, 1971–2000," *Morbidity and Mortality Weekly Report* 53 (2004): 80–82.

10. Ibid., 80–82.

11. Malcolm R. Law et al., "By How Much Does Dietary Salt Reduction Lower Blood Pressure?" *British Medical Journal* 302 (1991): 811–815.

12. Aram V. Chobanian and Martha Hill, "National Heart, Lung, and Blood Institute Workshop on Sodium and Blood Pressure: A Critical Review of Current Scientific Evidence," *Hypertension* 35 (2000): 858–863.

13. Authors' calculations, based on a 70-kilogram person expending 110 calories per hour driving and 330 calories per hour walking. The relationship between caloric balance and weight gained is not precisely established; this is based on a conservative estimate of 1 pound gained for 5,000 calories consumed in excess of expenditure.

14. Authors' calculations, based on 150 calories for a 12-ounce can of Coca-Cola and 5,000 calories per pound of weight gained.

15. Simone E. French et al., "Environmental Influences on Eating and Physical Activity," *Annual Review of Public Health* 22 (2001): 309–335.

16. CDC, "Trends in Intake," 80–82.

17. Claire Zizza et al., "Significant Increase in Young Adults' Snacking between 1977–1978 and 1994–1996 Represents a Cause for Concern!" *Preventive Medicine* 32 (2001): 303–310.

18. Samara J. Nielsen et al., "Trends in Energy Intake in U.S. Between 1977 and 1996: Similar Shifts Seen across Age Groups,." *Obesity Research* 10 (2002): 370–378.

19. Zizza et al., "Significant Increase," 303–310.

20. Department of Health and Human Services, *Physical Activity and Health: A Report of the Surgeon General* (Atlanta: Centers for Disease Control and Prevention, National Center for Chronic Disease Prevention and Health Promotion, 1996).

21. Michael Pratt et al., "Levels of Physical Activity and Inactivity in Children and Adults in the United States: Current Evidence and Research Issues," *Medicine and Science in Sports and Exercise* 31 (1999): S526–S533; and Centers for Disease Control and Prevention, "Physical Activity Trends—United States, 1990–1998," *Morbidity and Mortality Weekly Report* 50 (2001): 166–169.

22. bhblog.jhsph.edu

23. Data collected by the authors in twenty-five convenience stores in New Orleans, August 2001.

24. Data collected by the authors in three supermarkets in New Orleans, August 2001.

25. National Restaurant Association, *2004 Restaurant Industry Forecast* (available at www.restaurant.org).

26. Simone A. French et al., "Environmental Influences on Eating and Physical Activity," *Annual Review of Public Health* 22 (2001): 309–335.

27. "2004 Vending Market Report," *Vending Times* (available at www.vendingtimes.com).

28. "Domestic Advertising Spending by Category and Medium," *Advertising Age* (available at www.adage.com).

29. "100 Leading National Advertisers," *Advertising Age* (available at www.adage.com).

30. Department of Health and Human Services, National Institutes of Health, *FY 2001 Appropriation* (available at www.nci.nih.gov/aboutnci).

31. Patricia S. Hu and Jennifer R. Young, "Summary of Travel Trends: 1995 Nationwide Personal Transportation Survey" (available at http://npts.ornl.gov/npts/1995/doc/index.shtml).

32. Department of Transportation, "NHTS 2001 Highlights Report, BTS03-05 (Washington, DC: Bureau of Transportation Statistics, 2003); and Hu and Young, "Summary of Travel Trends."

33. Robert C. Klesges et al., "Effects of Television on Metabolic Rate: Potential Implications for Childhood Obesity," *Pediatrics* 91 (1993): 281–286.

34. Barbara E. Ainsworth et al., "Compendium of Physical Activities: Classification of Energy Costs of Human Physical Activities," *Medicine and Science in Sports and Exercise* 25 (1993): 71–80.

35. Pratt et al., "Levels of Physical Activity and Inactivity in Children and Adults in the United States," S526–S533; and Penny Gordon-Larsen et al., "Determinants of Adolescent Physical Activity and Inactivity Patterns," *Pediatrics* 105 (2000): 1–8.

36. Eric A. Finkelstein, Ian C. Fiebelkorn, and Guijing Wang, "State-Level Estimates of Annual Medial Expenditures Attributable to Obesity," *Obesity Research* 12 (2004): 18–24; American Diabetes Association, "Economic Costs of Diabetes in the U.S. in 2002," *Diabetes Care* 26 (2003): 917–932; and Thomas A. Hodgson and Liming Cai, "Medical Care Expenditures for Hypertension, Its Complications, and Its Comorbidities," *Medical Care* 39 (2001): 599–615.

37. Allen R. Nissenson and Richard A. Rettig, "Medicare's End-Stage Renal Disease Program: Current Status and Future Prospects," *Health Affairs* (Jan/Feb 1999): 161–179;

and David W. Ploth et al., "Prospective Analysis of Global Costs for Maintenance of Patients with ESRD," *American Journal of Kidney Diseases* 42 (2003): 12–21.

38. NCHS, *Health, United States, 2003,* 311.

39. Aram V. Chobanian et al., "Seventh Report of the Joint National Committee on Prevention, Detection, Evaluation, and Treatment of High Blood Pressure," *Hypertension* 42 (2003): 1206–1252.

40. National Institutes of Health, *Third Report on the National Cholesterol Education Program (NCEP) Expert Panel on Detection, Evaluation, and Treatment of High Blood Cholesterol in Adults (Adult Treatment Panel III): Final Report* (Bethesda, MD: National Heart, Lung, and Blood Institute, 2002).

41. UK Prospective Diabetes Study (UKPDS) Group, "Intensive Blood-Glucose Control with Sulphonylureas or Insulin Compared with Conventional Treatment and Risk of Complications in Patients with Type 2 Diabetes," *Lancet* 352 (1998): 837–853; and Genell L. Knatterud et al., "Effects of Hypoglycemic Agents on Vascular Complications in Patients with Adult-Onset Diabetes: VII. Mortality and Selected Nonfatal Events with Insulin Treatment," *JAMA* 240 (1978): 37–42.

42. National Institutes of Health, *Clinical Guidelines on the Identification, Evaluation, and Treatment of Overweight and Obesity in Adults: The Evidence Report* (Rockville, MD: National Heart, Lung and Blood Institute, 1998), 53–54.

43. Ibid., 42.

44. CDC, "Physical Activity Trends," 166–169.

45. Kelly D. Brownell and Katherine B. Horgen, *Food Fight: The Inside Story of the Food Industry, America's Obesity Crisis, and What We Can Do about It* (New York: McGraw Hill Contemporary Books, 2004), 217–233.

46. Michael F. Jacobson and Kelly D. Brownell, "Small Taxes on Soft Drinks and Snack Foods to Promote Health," *American Journal of Public Health* 90 (2000): 854–857.

47. Brownell and Horgen, *Food Fight,* 217–233.

48. Jacobson and Brownell, "Small Taxes," 854–857.

49. Marion Nestle, *Food Politics: How the Food Industry Influences Nutrition and Health* (Berkeley: University of California Press, 2002), 191–195, 197–218.

50. Ibid., 197–218.

51. U.S. Department of Transportation, Federal Highway Administration, "Summary of Federal Highway Administration Pedestrian and Bicycle Research and Program Activities—Prepared for the 2004 Annual TRB Meeting" (available at www.fhwa.dot.gov/environment/bikeped/pedbiketrb2004.htm).

52. Kelly D. Brownell et al., "Evaluation and Modification of Exercise Patterns in the Natural Environment," *American Journal of Psychiatry* 137 (1980): 1540–1545.

CHAPTER 11. TO OUR HEALTH?

1. Marilyn Robinson and Percy Ednalino, "Second Teen Dies after Weekend Crash: Half-Empty Keg Ejected from Car Trunk," *Denver Post*, June 5, 2001, A01; and "Police Say Teenage Driver Was Drunk," *Associated Press*, June 11, 2001.

2. Gary Massaro and Lobat Asadi, "Teen Asks for Prayers for Driver, Two Who Died in Crash," *(Denver) Rocky Mountain News*, June 13, 2001, 28A.

3. Marilyn Robinson, "Three Teens in Fatal Crash Drunk: Freshman Victim Sober; Charges Sought for Driver," *Denver Post*, June 12, 2001, B01.

4. Robert Sanchez, "Teen Facing 18 Years in Fatal Crash," *(Denver) Rocky Mountain News*, April 13, 2002, 8B.

5. Robinson and Ednalino, "Second Teen Dies," A01.

6. Ryan Morgan, "Parents of Littleton Teen Killed in Crash Create Football Scholarship," *Denver Post*, July 9, 2001, B03.

7. "Teenager May Face Vehicular Homicide Charge," *(Denver) Rocky Mountain News*, September 7, 2001, 33A.

8. "Metro Digest: Drunk-Driving Deaths Spur DUI Crackdown," *Denver Post*, December 6, 2001, B02; data from the Fatal Accident Reporting System compiled by the National Highway Traffic Safety Administration (available at www.nhtsa.gov).

9. Jason E. Gallate et al., "The Consequences of Beer Consumption in Rats: Acute Anxiolytic and Ataxic Effects and Withdrawal-Induced Anxiety," *Psychopharmacology* 166 (2003): 51–60.

10. Herbert Moskowitz and Dary Fiorentino, "A Review of the Literature on the Effects of Low Doses of Alcohol on Driving-Related Skills," prepared for the Department of Transportation, National Highway Traffic Safety Administration, April 2000 (available at www.nhtsa.gov); and Michael J. Eckardt, Sandra E. File, Gian Luigi Gessa et al., "Effects of Moderate Alcohol Consumption on the Central Nervous System," in *Alcoholism: Clinical and Experimental Research* 22 (1998): 998–1040.

11. Peter S. Hoaken and R. O. Pihl, "The Effects of Alcohol Intoxication on Aggressive Responses in Men and Women," *Alcohol and Alcoholism* 356 (2000): 471–477.

12. Alyson Bond and Malcolm Lader, "The Relationship between Induced Behavioral Aggression and Mood after the Consumption of Two Doses of Alcohol," *British Journal of Addiction* 81 (1986): 65–75.

13. J. Michael McGinnis and William H. Foege, "Mortality and Morbidity Attributable to Use of Addictive Substances in the United States," *Proceedings of the Association of American Physicians* 111 (1999): 109–118.

14. National Highway Traffic Safety Administration, "Traffic Safety Facts 2002" (available at www.nhtsa.gov).

15. McGinnis and Foege, "Mortality and Morbidity," 109–118.

16. Department of Health and Human Services, National Institutes of Health, National Institute on Alcohol Abuse and Alcoholism, *10th Special Report to the U.S. Congress on Alcohol and Health*, June 2000 (available at www.niaaa.nih.gov); and Michael J. Thun et al., "Alcohol Consumption and Mortality among Middle-Aged and Elderly U.S. Adults," *New England Journal of Medicine* 337 (1997): 1705–1714.

17. DHHS, *10th Special Report*.

18. A. V. Nemtsov, "Alcohol-Related Harm and Alcohol Consumption in Moscow Before, During, and After a Major Anti-Alcohol Campaign," *Addiction* 93 (1998): 1501–1510.

19. Arva Chui and Pedro E. Perez, "The Effect of an Alcohol Ban on the Number of

Alcohol-Related Hospital Visits in Barrow, Alaska," *International Journal of Circumpolar Health* 57, suppl. 1 (1998): 439–442; and Arva Chiu, Pedro E. Perez, and Robert Nash Parker, "Impact of Banning Alcohol on Outpatient Visits in Barrow, Alaska," *JAMA* 278 (1997): 1775–1777.

20. Norman Kreitman, "Alcohol Consumption and the Prevention Paradox," *British Journal of Addiction* 81(1986): 353–363.

21. Cheryl J. Cherpitel et al., "Alcohol and Non-Fatal Injury in the U.S. General Population: A Risk Function Analysis," *Accident Analysis and Prevention* 27 (1995): 651–661; and Ole-Jorgen Skog, "The Prevention Paradox Revisited," *Addiction* 94 (1999): 751–757.

22. Kreitman, "Alcohol Consumption," 353–363.

23. Brian M. Quigley and Lorraine R. Collins, "The Modeling of Alcohol Consumption: A Meta-Analytic Review," *Journal of Studies on Alcohol* 60 (1999): 90–98.

24. Helen Colhoun et al., "Ecological Analysis of Collectivity of Alcohol Consumption in England: Importance of the Average Drinker," *British Medical Journal* 314 (1997): 1164.

25. Joel W. Grube, "Alcohol Portrayals and Alcohol Advertising on Television: Content and Effects on Children and Adolescents," *Alcohol Health and Research World* 17 (1993): 61–66.

26. Substance Abuse and Mental Health Services Administration, *2002 National Survey on Drug Use and Health* (data available at www.oas.samhsa.gov/nhsda.htm).

27. Bridget F. Grant, "Prevalence and Correlates of Alcohol Use and DSM-IV Alcohol Dependence in the United States: Results of the National Longitudinal Alcohol Epidemiology Survey," *Journal of Studies on Alcohol* 58 (1997): 464–473.

28. Ernest Hurst Cherrington, *The Evolution of Prohibition in the United States of America* (Westerville, OH: American Issue Press, 1920), 18.

29. National Commission on Marihuana and Drug Abuse, "History of Alcohol Prohibition" (available at www.druglibrary.org).

30. Ian Tyrrell, "The US Prohibition Experiment: Myths, History, and Implications," *Addiction* 11 (1997): 1405–1409.

31. Rodger Doyle, "Deaths Caused by Alcohol," *Scientific American* 275 (1996): 30–31.

32. NCMDA, "History of Alcohol Prohibition."

33. Department of Justice, Bureau of Alcohol, Tobacco, and Firearms, "Alcohol Programs" (available at www.atf.gov/alcohol/index1.htm).

34. McGinnis and Foege, "Mortality and Morbidity," 109–118.

35. Johanna Birckmayer and David Hemenway, "Minimum-Age Drinking Laws and Youth Suicide, 1970–1990, *American Journal of Public Health* 89 (1999): 1365–1368; and NHTSA, "Traffic Safety Facts 2002."

36. Deborah A. Cohen, Karen Mason, and Richard A. Scribner, "The Population Consumption Model, Alcohol Control Practices, and Alcohol-Related Traffic Fatalities," *Preventive Medicine* 34 (2001): 187–197.

37. Frank J. Chaloupka, Michael Grossman, and Henry Saffer, "The Effects of Price on Alcohol Consumption and Alcohol-Related Problems," *Alcohol Research and Health*, 26 (2002): 22–34.

38. Ibid., 22–34.
39. Department of Transportation, National Highway Traffic Safety Administration, *Alcohol and Highway Safety 2001: A Review of the State of Knowledge* (available at www.nhtsa.dot.gov).
40. Ibid.
41. Ibid.
42. Alexander C. Wagenaar and Harold D. Holder, "Effect of Alcoholic Beverage Server Liability on Traffic Crash Injuries," *Alcoholism: Clinical and Experimental Research* 15 (1991): 942–947.
43. Gina Agostinelli and Joel W. Grube, "Alcohol Counter-Advertising and the Media," *Alcohol Research and Health* 26 (2002): 15–21.
44. Ibid.
45. Patricia A. Madden and Joel W. Grube, "The Frequency and Nature of Alcohol and Tobacco Advertising in Televised Sports, 1990 through 1992," *American Journal of Public Health* 84 (1994): 297–299.
46. See www.nbwa.org

Chapter 12. When Sex Is Lethal

1. Data available at www.cdc.gov/hiv/surveillance.htm
2. John M. Karon et al., "HIV in the United States at the Turn of the Century: An Epidemic in Transition," *American Journal of Public Health* 91 (2001): 1060–1068; data on the percent of HIV-infected persons who know their serostatus is in National Center for Health Statistics, *Healthy People 2000 Review, 1998–99* (Hyattsville, MD: Public Health Service, 1999), 181.
3. Karon et al., "HIV in the United States," 1060–1068.
4. Centers for Disease Control and Prevention, "Prevalence of Risk Behaviors for HIV Infection among Adults—United States, 1997," *Morbidity and Mortality Weekly Report* 50 (2001): 262–265.
5. Deborah A. Wendell et al., "Street Outreach for HIV Prevention: Effectiveness of a State-Wide Programme," *International Journal of STD and AIDS* 14 (2003): 334–340.
6. Centers for Disease Control and Prevention, "Youth Risk Behavior Surveillance— United States, 2003," in CDC Surveillance Summaries, May 21, 2004, *Morbidity and Mortality Weekly Report* 53 (2004) SS-5: 71–73.
7. Unpublished data from surveys conducted by the Louisiana Office of Public Health, 1995–1998.
8. Centers for Disease Control and Prevention, "Resurgent Bacterial Sexually Transmitted Diseases among Men Who Have Sex with Men—King County, Washington, 1997–1999," *Morbidity and Mortality Weekly Report* 48 (1999): 773–777; and Centers for Disease Control and Prevention, "Outbreak of Syphilis among Men Who Have Sex with Men—California, 2000," *Morbidity and Mortality Weekly Report* 50 (2001): 117–120.
9. CDC, "Youth Risk Behavior Surveillance," SS-2: 71–75; Centers for Disease Control

and Prevention, "HIV-Related Knowledge and Behaviors among High School Students—Selected U.S. Sites, 1989," *Morbidity and Mortality Weekly Report* 39 (1990): 385–391; and Charlotte A. Shoenborn et al., "AIDS Knowledge and Attitudes for 1992: Data from the National Health Interview Survey," *Advance Data*, no. 243 (Hyattsville, MD: National Center for Health Statistics, 1994), 1–16.

10. John E. Anderson et al., "HIV/AIDS Knowledge and Sexual Behavior among High School Students," *Family Planning Perspectives* 22 (1990): 252–255; and Harm J. Hospers and Gerjo Kok, "Determinants of Safe and Risk-Taking Sexual Behavior among Gay Men: A Review," *AIDS Education and Prevention* 7 (1995): 74–94.

11. Jeffrey A. Kelly et al., "Psychological Factors That Predict AIDS High-Risk versus AIDS Precautionary Behavior," *Journal of Consulting and Clinical Psychology* 58 (1990): 117–120.

12. Susan E. Mickler, "Perceptions of Vulnerability: Impact of AIDS-Preventive Behavior among College Adolescents," *AIDS Education and Prevention* 5 (1993): 43–53.

13. Edward O. Laumann et al., *The Social Organization of Sexuality: Sexual Practices in the United States* (Chicago: University of Chicago Press, 1994), 179.

14. Gary L. Oxman et al., "Mathematical Modeling of Epidemic Syphilis Transmission: Implications for Syphilis Control Programs," *Sexually Transmitted Diseases* 23 (1996): 30–39.

15. John J. Potterat et al., "Gonorrhea as a Social Disease," *Sexually Transmitted Diseases* 12 (1985): 25–32.

16. Lou Harris and Associates, *Sexual Material on American Network Television during the 1987–88 Season* (New York: Planned Parenthood Federation of America, 1988).

17. Dale Kunkel et al., *Sex on TV 3: A Biennial Report to the Kaiser Family Foundation*, 45 (available at www.kff.org).

18. Ibid., 28–29.

19. Dale Kunkel et al., *Sex on TV 2: A Biennial Report to the Kaiser Family Foundation*, 26 (available at www.kff.org).

20. Dick Thornburg and Herbert S. Lin, eds., *Youth, Pornography, and the Internet* (Washington, DC: National Academy of Sciences 2002), 72.

21. Ibid.

22. Christina Rogala and Tanja Tyden, "Does Pornography Influence Young Women's Sexual Behavior?" *Women's Health Issues* 13 (2003): 39–43.

23. Charles F. Turner et al., "Sexual Behavior in the United States 1930–1990: Trends and Methodological Problems," *Sexually Transmitted Diseases* 22 (1995): 173–190; and Jacqueline E. Darroch et al., "Differences in Teenage Pregnancy Rates among Five Developed Countries: The Roles of Sexual Activity and Contraceptive Use," *Family Planning Perspectives* 33 (2001): 244–250, 281.

24. Barbara C. Leigh et al., "The Sexual Behavior of U.S. Adults: Results from a National Survey," *American Journal of Public Health* 83 (1993): 1400–1408.

25. John E. Anderson and Linda L. Dahlberg, "High-Risk Sexual Behavior in the General Population: Results from a National Survey, 1988–1990," *Sexually Transmitted Diseases* 19 (1992): 320–325.

26. Francis Fukuyama, *The Great Disruption: Human Nature and the Reconstitution of the Social Order* (New York: Simon and Schuster, 2000), 40–42.

27. Gita Ramjee and Eleanor Gouws, "Prevalence of HIV among Truck Drivers Visiting Sex Workers in KwaZulu-Natal, South Africa," *Sexually Transmitted Diseases* 29 (2002): 44–49.

28. Substance Abuse and Mental Health Services Administration, *Summary of Findings from the 2000 National Household Survey on Drug Abuse*, NHSDA Series H-13, DHHS Publication No. (SMA) 013549 (Rockville, MD: Department of Health and Human Services, 2001), 135.

29. Barbara C. Leigh et al., "The Relationship of Alcohol Use to Sexual Activity in a U.S. National Sample," *Social Science and Medicine* 39 (1994): 1527–1535; and Anderson and Dahlberg, "High-Risk Sexual Behavior," 320–325.

30. Karen Paige Ericksen and Karen F. Trocki, "Sex, Alcohol, and Sexually Transmitted Diseases: A National Survey," *Family Planning Perspectives* 26 (1994): 257–263.

31. Centers for Disease Control and Prevention, *FY 2005 CDC Budget Request—Funding by Disease* (available at www.cdc.gov/fmo/fmofybudget.htm).

32. Willard Cates Jr. and Alan R. Hinman, "AIDS and Absolutism—the Demand for Perfection in Prevention," *New England Journal of Medicine* 327 (1992): 492–494.

33. Rochelle N. Shain et al., "A Randomized, Controlled Trial of a Behavioral Intervention to Prevent Sexually Transmitted Disease among Minority Women," *New England Journal of Medicine* 340 (1999): 93–100; Nancy S. Padian et al., "Prevention of Heterosexual Transmission of Human Immunodeficiency Virus through Couple Counseling," *Journal of Acquired Immune Deficiency Syndromes* 6 (1993): 1043–1048; Robert S. Hanenberg et al., "The Impact of Thailand's HIV Control Programme, As Indicated by the Decline of Sexually Transmitted Diseases," *Lancet* 344 (1994): 243–245; Susan Weller and K. Davis, "Condom Effectiveness in Reducing Heterosexual HIV Transmission," *Cochrane Database of Systematic Reviews* 2 (2004); and National Institutes of Health, National Institute of Allergy and Infectious Diseases, "Workshop Summary: Scientific Evidence on Condom Effectiveness for Sexually Transmitted (STD) Prevention" (available at www.niaid.nih.gov/dmid/stds/condom-report.pdf).

34. Douglas Kirby, "Sexuality and Sex Education at Home and School," *Adolescent Medicine* 10 (1999): 195–209.

35. Philippe Lehmann et al., "Campaign against AIDS in Switzerland: Evaluation of a Nationwide Educational Programme," *British Medical Journal* 295 (1987): 1118–1120; and Francoise Dubois-Arber et al., "Increased Condom Use without Other Major Changes in Sexual Behavior among the General Population of Switzerland," *American Journal of Public Health* 87 (1997): 558–566.

36. Kirby, "Sexuality and Sex Education," 195–209.

37. Ibid.; and John S. Santelli et al., "Sexually Transmitted Diseases, Unintended Pregnancy, and Adolescent Health Promotion," *Adolescent Medicine* 10 (1999): 87–108.

38. Douglas Kirby et al., "The Impact of the Postponing Sexual Involvement Curriculum among Youths in California," *Family Planning Perspectives* 29 (1997): 100–108.

39. Douglas T. Fleming and Judith N. Wasserheit, "From Epidemiology Synergy to Public Health Policy and Practice: The Contribution of Other Sexually Transmitted Diseases to Sexual Transmission of HIV Infection," *Sexually Transmitted Infections* 75 (1999): 3–17.

40. Heiner Grosskurth et al., "Impact of Improved Treatment of Sexually Transmitted Diseases on HIV Infection in Rural Tanzania: Randomised Controlled Trial," *Lancet* 346 (1995): 530–536.

41. Deborah A. Cohen et al., "Implementation of Condom Social Marketing in Louisiana 1993–1996," *American Journal of Public Health* 89 (1999): 204–208.

42. Douglas B. Kirby and Nancy L. Brown, "Condom Availability Programs in U.S. Schools," *Family Planning Perspectives* 28 (1996): 196–202.

43. Sally Guttmacher et al., "Condom Availability in New York City Public High Schools: Relationships to Condom Use and Sexual Behavior," *American Journal of Public Health* 87 (1997): 1427–1433; Frank F. Furstenberg Jr. and Lynne Maziarz Geitz, "Does Condom Availability Make a Difference? An Evaluation of Philadelphia's Health Resource Centers," *Family Planning Perspectives* 29 (1997): 123–127; and Susan M. Blake et al., "Condom Availability Programs in Massachusetts High Schools: Relationships with Condom Use and Sexual Behavior," *American Journal of Public Health* 93 (2003): 955–962.

44. Kirby and Brown, "Condom Availability Programs," 196–202.

45. Douglas Kirby, *Sex Education in Schools* (Menlo Park, NJ: Henry J. Kaiser Family Foundation, 1994), 30.

46. Richard A. Scribner et al., "A Geographic Relation between Alcohol Availability and Gonorrhea Rates," *Sexually Transmitted Diseases* 25 (1998): 544–548.

47. Centers for Disease Control and Prevention, "Alcohol Policy and Sexually Transmitted Disease Rates, United States, 1981–1995," *Morbidity and Mortality Weekly Report* 49 (2000): 345–349; and Harrell Chesson et al., "Sex Under the Influence: The Effect of Alcohol Policy on Sexually Transmitted Disease Rates in the United States," *Journal of Law and Economics* 43 (2000): 215–238.

48. Wiput Phoolcharoen, "HIV/AIDS Prevention in Thailand: Success and Challenges," *Science* 280 (1998): 1873–1874.

CHAPTER 13. INJURIES, NOT ACCIDENTS

1. Elizabeth Arias et al., "Deaths: Final Data for 2001," *National Vital Statistics Reports* 52 (2003): 71–72.

2. Centers for Disease Control and Prevention, National Center for Injury Prevention and Control, "Ten Leading Causes of Death by Age Group—2001" (available at www.cdc.gov/ncipc/osp/charts.htm).

3. Committee on Trauma Research, Commission on Life Sciences, National Research Council, "Injury in America: A Continuing Public Health Problem" (Washington, DC: National Academy Press, 1985), 1–3.

4. Arias et al., "Deaths: Final Data for 2001," 71–72.

5. Berthold Brenner and Alexander Monto, "Increase in Automobiles with Seat Belts during a Year of Promotion Efforts," in William Haddon Jr. et al., eds., *Accident Research: Methods and Approaches* (New York: Harper and Row, 1964), 716–720.

6. Joel W. Eastman, *Styling vs. Safety: The American Automobile Industry and the Development of Automotive Safety, 1900–1966* (Lanham, MD: University Press of America, 1984), 181.

7. Ibid., 135–167; and "Highway Casualties Soar—What to Do About It?" *U.S. News and World Report,* March 1, 1965, 56–61.

8. Eastman, *Styling vs. Safety,* 242–243.

9. Ibid., 243.

10. James R. McCarroll and William Haddon Jr., "A Controlled Study of Fatal Automobile Accidents in New York City," in Haddon et al., eds., *Accident Research,* 172–184.

11. Haddon et al., eds., *Accident Research.*

12. Ibid., 2.

13. "Danger on the Highways: Interview with the National Safety Director," *U.S. News and World Report,* October 16, 1967, 66–69.

14. Colman McCarthy, "Curing the Auto Plague," *Washington Post,* March 16, 1985, A21.

15. Hugh de Haven, "Accident Survival—Airplane and Passenger Automobile," in Haddon et al., eds., *Accident Research,* 563.

16. Daniel P. Moynihan, "Epidemic on the Highways," *The Reporter,* April 30, 1959, 16–23.

17. Ralph Nader, *Unsafe at Any Speed* (New York: Grossman, 1965).

18. Eastman, *Styling vs. Safety,* 243–246.

19. John D. Graham, "Injuries from Traffic Crashes: Meeting the Challenge," *Annual Reviews of Public Health* 14 (1993): 515–543.

20. McCarthy, "Curing the Auto Plague," A21.

21. National Highway Traffic Safety Administration, National Center for Statistics and Analysis, "Traffic Safety Facts 2002" (available at www-nrd.nhtsa.dot.gov/ departments/nrd-30/ncsa).

22. Graham, "Injuries from Traffic Crashes," 515–543.

23. Ibid.

24. Donna Glassbrenner, "Safety Belt Use in 2003," Technical Report DOT HS 809646, September 2003 (available at www.nhtsa.gov/people/injury/airbags/seatbelts.htm).

25. D. S. Morrison et al., "What Are the Most Effective Ways of Improving Population Health through Transport Interventions? Evidence from Systematic Reviews," *Journal of Epidemiology and Community Health* 57 (2003): 327–333.

26. Reid Ewing et al., "Urban Sprawl as a Risk Factor in Motor Vehicle Occupant and Pedestrian Fatalities," *American Journal of Public Health* 93 (2003): 1541–1545.

27. William H. Lucy, "Mortality Risk Associated with Leaving Home: Recognizing the Relevance of the Built Environment," *American Journal of Public Health* 93 (2003): 1564–1569.

28. Todd Litman, "Comprehensive Evaluation of Rail Transit Benefits," Victoria Transport Policy Institute, 2004 (available at www.vtpi.org/railben.htm).

29. Wendy Melillo, "P.G. Teen Playing with Gun with Best Friend is Shot Dead," *Washington Post,* August 30, 1994, B1.
30. "Gun Play," *Minneapolis Star Tribune,* November 29, 1994, 12A.
31. Edward Walsh, "Horror of Son's Slaying Hits Detroit Man Twice," *Washington Post,* May 17, 1992, A3.
32. Scott Bowles, "D.C. Officer's Child Killed," *Washington Post,* May 27, 1996, B1.
33. Mathew Miller et al., "Firearm Availability and Unintentional Firearm Deaths, Suicide, and Homicide among 5–14 Year Olds," *Journal of Trauma* 52 (2002): 267–274.
34. Robert N. Anderson et al., "Deaths: Injuries, 2001," *National Vital Statistics Reports* 52 (2004): 1–35.
35. Arthur L. Kellermann et al., "Suicide in the Home in Relation to Gun Ownership," *New England Journal of Medicine* 327 (1992): 467–72.
36. Centers for Disease Control and Prevention, "Rates of Homicide, Suicide, and Firearm-Related Death among Children—26 Industrialized Countries," *Morbidity and Mortality Weekly Report* 46 (1997): 101–105.
37. Colin Loftin et al., "Effects of Restrictive Licensing of Handguns on Homicide and Suicide in the District of Columbia," *New England Journal of Medicine* 325 (1991): 1615–1620.
38. Department of Justice, *Crime in the United States, 2001: Uniform Crime Reports* (Washington, DC: Federal Bureau of Investigation, 2002), 24.
39. Arthur L. Kellerman et al., "Gun Ownership as a Risk Factor for Homicide in the Home," *New England Journal of Medicine* 329 (1993): 1084–1091.
40. "Major Federal Firearm Laws (Still in Effect), 1934–1999," in Kathleen Reich, ed., *Future of Children* 12 (Summer/Fall 2002): 174–175.
41. Garen J. Wintemute, "Where the Guns Come From: The Gun Industry and Gun Commerce," *Future of Children* 12 (Summer/Fall 2002): 55–71.
42. Loftin et al., "Effects of Restrictive Licensing of Handguns," 1615–1620.
43. Tom W. Smith, "Public Opinion about Gun Policies," *Future of Children* 12 (Summer/Fall 2002): 155–163.
44. McCarthy, "Curing the Auto Plague," A21.

CHAPTER 14. UNEQUAL AFFLICTIONS

1. National Center for Health Statistics, *Health, United States, 2003* (Hyattsville, MD: 2003), 137.
2. Paul D. Sorlie, Eric Backlund, and Jacob B. Keller, "U.S. Mortality by Economic, Demographic, and Social Characteristics: The National Longitudinal Mortality Study," *American Journal of Public Health* 85 (1995): 949–956.
3. Colin McCord and Harold P. Freeman, "Excess Mortality in Harlem," *New England Journal of Medicine,* 322 (1990): 173–177.
4. Gopal K. Singh and Stella M. Yu, "U.S. Childhood Mortality, 1950 through 1993: Trends and Socioeconomic Differentials," *American Journal of Public Health* 86 (1996): 505–512.

5. George Davey Smith et al., "Adverse Socioeconomic Conditions in Childhood and Cause-Specific Adult Mortality: Prospective Observational Study," *British Medical Journal* 316 (1998): 1631–1635.

6. Constantine A. Yeracaris and Jay H. Kim, "Socioeconomic Differentials in Selected Causes of Death," *American Journal of Public Health* 68 (1978): 342–351; and Gregory Pappas et al., "The Increasing Disparity in Mortality between Socioeconomic Groups in the United States, 1960 and 1986," *New England Journal of Medicine* 329 (1993): 103–109.

7. Sorlie, Backlund, and Keller, "U.S. Mortality," 949–956.

8. M. G. Marmot, M. H. Shipley, and Geoffrey Rose, "Inequalities in Death—Specific Explanations of a General Pattern?" *Lancet* 1(8384) (1984), 1003–1006.

9. George Davey Smith and Martin J. Shipley, "Confounding of Occupation and Smoking: Its Magnitude and Consequences," *Social Science and Medicine* 32 (1991): 1297–1300.

10. Anton E. Kunst, Feikje Groenhof, Johan P. Mackenbach, et al., "Occupational Class and Cause Specific Mortality in Middle-Aged Men in Eleven European Countries: Comparison of Population Based Studies," *British Medical Journal* 316 (1998): 1636–1642; and Anton E. Kunst and Johan P. Mackenbach, "The Size of Mortality Differences Associated with Educational Level in Nine Industrialized Countries," *American Journal of Public Health* 84 (1994): 932–937.

11. Richard G. Wilkinson, *Unhealthy Societies: The Afflictions of Inequality* (London: Routledge, 1996), 76.

12. Bruce P. Kennedy, Ichiro Kawachi, and Deborah Prothrow-Stith, "Income Distribution and Mortality: Cross Sectional Ecologic Study of the Robin Hood Index in the United States," *British Medical Journal* 312 (1996): 1004–1007.

13. Michael Marmot, Martin Bobak, and George Davey Smith, "Explanations for Social Inequalities in Health," in Benjamin Amick et al., eds., *Society and Health* (New York: Oxford University Press, 1995).

14. Data from the Behavioral Risk Factor Surveillance System, National Center for Chronic Disease Prevention and Health Promotion, Centers for Disease Control (available at www.cdc.gov/nccdphp/tracking.htm).

15. Data from the USDA Continuing Survey of Food Intake in Individuals (available at www.barc.usda.gov/bhnrc/foodsurvey/pdf/income.pdf).

16. Data from the Behavioral Risk Factor Surveillance System.

17. Kimberly Morland et al., "Neighborhood Characteristics Associated with the Location of Food Stores and Food Service Places," *American Journal of Preventive Medicine* 22 (2002): 23–29; and Thomas A. LaVeist and John M. Wallace, "Health Risk and Inequitable Distribution of Liquor Stores in African American Neighborhood," *Social Science and Medicine* 51 (2000): 613–617.

18. Heiner C. Bucher and David R. Ragland, "Socioeconomic Indicators and Mortality from Coronary Heart Disease and Cancer: A 22-Year Follow-Up of Middle-Aged Men," *American Journal of Public Health* 85 (1995): 1231–1236; S. Goya Wannamethee and A. Gerald Shaper, "Socioeconomic Status within Social Class and Mortality: A Prospective Study of Middle-Aged British Men," *International Journal of Epide-*

miology 26 (1997): 532–541; and Marmot, Shipley, and Rose, "Inequalities in Death," 1003–1006.

19. E. J. Brunner et al., "Social Inequality in Coronary Risk: Central Obesity and the Metabolic Syndrome. Evidence from the Whitehall II Study," *Diabetologia* 40 (1997): 1341–1349.

20. Carol A. Shively, Kathy Laber-Laird, and Raymond F. Anton, "Behavior and Physiology of Social Stress and Depression in Female Cynomolgus Monkeys," *Biological Psychiatry* 41 (1997): 871–882.

21. Robert M. Sapolsky, "Endocrinology Alfresco: Psychoendocrine Studies of Wild Baboons," *Recent Progress in Hormone Research* 48 (1993): 437–468.

22. D. H. Abbott et al., "Are Subordinates Always Stressed? A Comparative Analysis of Rank Differences in Cortisol Levels among Primates," *Hormones and Behavior* 43 (2003): 67–82.

23. Sapolsky, "Endocrinology Alfresco," 437-468.

24. Brunner et al., "Social Inequality in Coronary Risk," 1341–1349.

25. Robert L. Jin, Chandrakant P. Shah, and Tomislav J. Svoboda, "The Impact of Unemployment on Health: A Review of the Literature," *Canadian Medical Association Journal* 153 (1995): 529–540.

26. Jussi Vahtera et al., "Organizational Downsizing, Sickness Absence, and Mortality: Ten-Town Prospective Cohort Study," *British Medical Journal Online,* doi:10.1136/bmj.37972.496262.OD, February 23, 2004 (available at www.bmj.com).

27. George Davey-Smith et al., "Individual Social Class, Area-Based Deprivation, Cardiovascular Disease Risk Factors, and Mortality: The Renfrew and Paisley Study," *Journal of Epidemiology and Community Health* 52 (1998): 399–405; Ana V. Diez-Roux et al., "Neighborhood Environments and Coronary Heart Disease: A Multilevel Analysis," *American Journal of Epidemiology* 146 (1997): 48–63.; and Stephanie A. Robert, "Neighborhood Socioeconomic Context and Health: The Mediating Role of Individual Health Behaviors and Psychosocial Factors," *Annals of the New York Academy of Sciences* 896 (1999): 465–468.

28. Diez-Roux et al., "Neighborhood Environments and Coronary Heart Disease," 48–63; Robert, "Neighborhood Socioeconomic Context and Health," 465–468.

29. Deborah A. Cohen et al., "Neighborhood Physical Conditions and Health," *American Journal of Public Health* 93 (2003): 467–471; and Deborah A. Cohen, Thomas A. Farley, and Karen Mason, "Why Is Poverty Unhealthy? Social and Physical Mediators," *Social Science and Medicine* 57 (2003): 1631–1641.

30. Paul A. Jargowsky, "Take the Money and Run: Economic Segregation in U.S. Metropolitan Areas," *American Sociological Review* 61 (1996): 984–998.

31. Office of Policy Development and Research, Department of Housing and Urban Development, "Moving to Opportunity: Interim Impacts Evaluation," September 2003 (available at www.huduser.org/publications/fairhsg/mtoFinal.html).

CHAPTER 15. HEALTH, POLICIES, AND POLITICS

1. Guy Coates, "Cabbage Head Doesn't Do the Trick This Time," *Associated Press State and Local Wire,* May 18, 1999; and authors' interview with Nancy Camel.

2. Ed Anderson, "Cycle Deaths Spiked after Helmet Law Loosened," *New Orleans Times-Picayune,* January 30, 2003, A2.

3. Ibid.

4. The Presidential/Congressional Commission on Risk Assessment and Risk Management, *Framework for Environmental Health Risk Management: Final Report,* vol. 1 (available through the Environmental Protection Agency at http://cfpub.epa.gov/ncea/cfm/recordisplay.cfm?deid=55006).

5. Ibid., 52.

6. Authors' calculations for a 70-year lifetime risk, assuming one 10-mile trip per week and a fatality rate of 1.5 per million vehicle-miles traveled.

7. Authors' calculations for a 70-year lifetime risk, based on a fatality rate for homicides in the home of 2 per 100,000 and a risk ratio associated with gun ownership of 2.7 (see Arthur L. Kellerman et al., "Gun Ownership as a Risk Factor for Homicide in the Home," *New England Journal of Medicine* 329 (1993): 1084–1091.)

8. Authors' calculations for a 70-year lifetime risk, assuming 250 calories per doughnut and an excess mortality risk of 25 per 100,000 for each unit of body mass index (BMI) gained.

9. John Hill, "Blanco, Jindal Show Subtle Differences on Health Care," *Alexandria (Louisiana) Town Talk,* October 30, 2003 (available at www.thetowntalk.com).

10. Centers for Disease Control and Prevention, "Impact of a Smoking Ban on Restaurant and Bar Revenues—El Paso, Texas, 2002," *Morbidity and Mortality Weekly Report* 53 (2004): 150–152.

11. Garrett Hardin, "The Tragedy of the Commons," *Science* 162 (1968): 1243–1248.

12. "Foster Unites with State Motorcyclists," *Associated Press State and Local Wire,* August 15, 1999.

13. Ibid.

14. Eileen M. Harwood, Alexander C. Waagenar, and Kay M. Zander, *Youth Access to Alcohol Survey: Summary Report,* prepared for the Robert Wood Johnson Foundation, September 1998 (available at www.rwjf.org/publications/publicationsPdfs/Youth_Access_to_Alcohol_Survey.pdf).

15. Keating Holland, "Poll: Violence in the Media Should Be Regulated," *CNN.com,* May 3, 1999; *CNN/Time* poll, conducted by Yankelovich Partners, June 9–10, 1999 (available at www.pollingreport.com/media.htm).

16. Lake, Snell, Perry, and Associates poll for the Harvard Forums on Health, May 28–June 1, 2003 (available at http://www.phsi.harvard.edu/health_reform/poll_results.pdf).

17. Ibid.

18. Ibid.

19. Campaign for Tobacco-Free Kids, *Voters across the Country Support Significant*

Increases in State Cigarette Taxes (available at http://www.tobaccofreekids.org/research/factsheets/pdf/0167.pdf).

20. Ibid.

21. Harwood, Waagenar, and Zander, *Youth Access to Alcohol Survey.*

22. Ibid.

23. Lake, Snell, Perry, and Associates poll.

24. Edwin Chadwick, *Report on the Sanitary Conditions of the Labouring Population of Great Britain*, ed. M. W. Flinn (Edinburgh: Edinburgh University Press, 1965), 165.

25. Ibid., 42.

26. Joel W. Eastman, *Styling vs. Safety: The American Automobile Industry and the Development of Automotive Safety, 1900–1966* (Lanham, MD: University Press of America, 1984).

27. Ed Anderson, "Foster Says Tax Code Impeding Louisiana's Economic Growth," *New Orleans Times-Picayune,* July 8, 2000, A12; James Gill, "There's a Draft; Beer Lobbyist Is Buying," *New Orleans Times-Picayune,* December 6, 2000, Metro section, 7.

28. Anderson, "Foster Says Tax Code," A12

29. Gill, "There's a Draft," Metro section, 7.

30. Ed Anderson, "Lobbyists Tip Over Open-Container Bill," *New Orleans Times-Picayune,* May 23, 2003, National section, 7.

31. Michael Massing, "Strong Stuff," *New York Times Magazine*, March 22, 1998.

32. Ibid.

33. Tom Johnson, "Frito-Lay to Expand Plant: Repeal of State's Snack Tax Influenced Decision to Add to Aberdeen Facility," *Baltimore Daily Record,* May 15, 1996, 1.

34. From www.consumerfreedom.com/main_faq.cfm

35. Information on ad campaigns available at www.consumerfreedom.com

36. Letter from Rick Berman to Ms. Barbara Trach, December 11, 1995, available at www.disinfopedia.org

37. Information obtained by the Center for Media and Democracy and available at www.disinfopedia.org

38. Ibid.

39. Charles Bernstein, "The Zealot," *Chain Leader*, December, 1999 (available at www.chainleader.com).